Praise for *The Services Shift*

"The global economy has changed immensely in the past decade, and the pace of change has recently accelerated. Leaders at multinational corporations have little time to stay on top of the opportunities and the challenges. *The Services Shift* provides a framework for understanding how globalization is affecting the services sector and a roadmap for firms that hope to sell and source abroad. The book also contains an explanation of the relevant policy challenges and pitfalls that arise in this new era. The book is essential reading for executives who look to capitalize on the continued promise of globalization."

—**Mike Johnston**, Chairman,
Visteon Corp.

"Today, understanding the global trade in services is central to any competitive strategy. Whether you are a small company in Michigan or a global bank, your cost base, capabilities, and competitive advantage will be influenced by how well you can tap into the global talent pool. Prof. Kennedy gives the most comprehensive and practical guide to finding value and managing risk. *The Services Shift* is must reading for anyone crafting a global competitive strategy."

—**Dr. John Sviokla**, Vice Chairman,
Diamond Management & Technology Consultants

"In *The Services Shift*, Kennedy connects a huge macro global trend to the micro-level decisions that managers make every day. A must read for organizations grappling with globalization, as well as for seasoned offshoring practitioners and providers like Genpact. The chapter on shifting skill sets is one of its kind!!"

—**V.N. "Tiger" Tyagarajan**, Executive Vice President,
Genpact

"*The Services Shift* offers business executives a practical, easy-to-understand framework for managing outsourcing and offshoring decisions. Kennedy does an outstanding job of weaving in the 'soft skills' essential for success: management commitment, change management skills, and an end-to-end process understanding of the business. Executives in any business looking to outsource will rapidly appreciate the need to attract leaders that manage remote teams with personal connection and cultural sensitivity."

—**Sharon M. Garavel**, VP Operations,
GE Capital Solutions

"*The Services Shift* provides unique insights into the strategic drivers behind the outsourcing and offshoring of services, and an invaluable set of tools to help manage the decision process. Business leaders of all types will benefit from understanding the potential value creation for their customers, employees, and shareholders."

—**David F. Dougherty**, President and CEO,
Convergys Corp.

"*The Services Shift* tackles one of the most important trends in the global economy today—the globalization of services, and in particular, of offshore outsourcing. Public discussion of the phenomenon has been dominated by myths and misunderstandings. Kennedy and Sharma demystify offshoring. They explain: why this is happening; how it affects countries, industries, firms, and individuals; and how to respond. This book is both an excellent description of current events and a roadmap that explains where it is going. A must read for both business executives and policymakers."

—**Alok Aggarwal**, CEO,
Evalueserve

The Services Shift

The Services Shift
Seizing the Ultimate Offshore Opportunity

ROBERT E. KENNEDY WITH AJAY SHARMA

Vice President, Publisher: Tim Moore
Associate Publisher and Director of Marketing: Amy Neidlinger
Acquisitions Editor: Martha Cooley
Editorial Assistant: Pamela Boland
Operations Manager: Gina Kanouse
Digital Marketing Manager: Julie Phifer
Publicity Manager: Laura Czaja
Assistant Marketing Manager: Megan Colvin
Cover Designer: Chuti Prasertsith
Managing Editor: Kristy Hart
Project Editor: Anne Goebel
Copy Editor: Bart Reed
Proofreader: Debbie Williams
Indexer: Angela Bess Martin
Senior Compositors: Gloria Schurick and Jake McFarland
Manufacturing Buyer: Dan Uhrig

© 2009 by Pearson Education, Inc.
Publishing as FT Press
Upper Saddle River, New Jersey 07458

FT Press offers excellent discounts on this book when ordered in quantity for bulk purchases or special sales. For more information, please contact U.S. Corporate and Government Sales, 1-800-382-3419, corpsales@pearsontechgroup.com. For sales outside the U.S., please contact International Sales at international@pearson.com.

Printed in the United States of America

First Printing January 2009

ISBN-10: 0-13-713350-2
ISBN-13: 978-0-13-713350-5

Pearson Education LTD.
Pearson Education Australia PTY, Limited.
Pearson Education Singapore, Pte. Ltd.
Pearson Education North Asia, Ltd.
Pearson Education Canada, Ltd.
Pearson Educación de Mexico, S.A. de C.V.
Pearson Education—Japan
Pearson Education Malaysia, Pte. Ltd.

Library of Congress Cataloging-in-Publication Data

Kennedy, Robert E. (Robert Emmett), 1962-

   The services shift : seizing the ultimate offshore opportunity / Robert E. Kennedy, Ajay Sharma.

      p. cm.

   ISBN 0-13-713350-2 (hardback : alk. paper) 1. Contracting out. 2. Offshore outsourcing. 3. Globalization. I. Sharma, Ajay, 1971- II. Title.

   HD2365.K465 2009

   658.4'058—dc22

                    2008040505

To Bill Davidson,
who had the vision to establish a truly extraordinary
Institute, and the patience and sense of humor to
allow me to run it.

Contents

Acknowledgments

This book pulls together several lines of work I have pursued over the past decade—on trends in the global economy, on business strategy in emerging economies, and on the transformative effects (both positive and negative) that outsourcing and offshoring have on firms, industries, and countries. It could not have been completed without support from many people who have played a part in my journey as a scholar.

Many people have contributed to this work in more ways than I can possibly recount. Starting a list is risky in that it is difficult to know where to stop, and there is always the risk of leaving someone off the list. So, I apologize for any oversights in advance.

I first became interested in services exports from developing countries nearly a decade ago. At that point, I was at the Harvard Business School focusing on business strategy issues in developing countries. Although most of the work focused on traditional industries—such as agribusiness, light manufacturing, and fast-moving consumer goods—I was struck by the anomaly of booming software exports from India. This high-tech industry, located in one of the world's poorest countries, had achieved compound growth of more than 40 percent for a decade, with operating margins exceeding 30 percent. More importantly for a business scholar, Indian firms were challenging the world's leading software firms and, in many cases, beating them in their core markets. This was almost unheard of—developing country firms prospering by marketing their know-how, not their physical labor or natural resources, and transforming a global industry.

But a funny thing happened when I traveled to Bombay (now Mumbai) to study India's leading software firms. Senior managers at TCS, Infosys, and Wipro all said roughly the same thing (paraphrasing):

> Software exports are interesting, but what we're *really* excited about is IT-enabled services (now known as BPO). The market is much larger, rivalry is lower, and India's advantage will be even bigger than it is in software.

If these executives were more excited about BPO than they were about software, I knew I was on to something important. Events since then have confirmed this insight. But the phenomenon did not fit neatly into existing academic categories—that is, business strategy, international business, economics, and so on.

Pursuing this line of inquiry required a novel, multidisciplinary approach, which was a risk for someone on the tenure track at a leading research university. I was, however, fortunate to have a group of mentors who encouraged this work. During my Harvard years, Richard Caves undertook the arduous task of transforming me from a clever consultant into a well-trained economist. John McArthur encouraged me to tackle issues "that mattered." Tom McCraw was an invaluable mentor on the crafts of both writing and teaching. And Pankaj Ghemawat was a mentor, co-author, and inspiration as someone who could successfully bridge the theory-practice gap.

After I moved to Michigan's Ross School of Business in 2003, I was grateful to find new mentors with this same theory-practice mindset. Bob Dolan, acting as Dean and President of the William Davidson Institute, provided consistent personal, financial, and administrative support. Ken Lieberthal was a supportive and encouraging presence. C.K. Prahalad has always been generous with his time and insights. Stuart Hart has been a friend, mentor, and colleague pursuing a like-minded path with his work on sustainability.

I have been fortunate to lead a truly extraordinary organization— the William Davidson Institute (WDI), which focuses on business and policy issues in emerging economies. Bill Davidson has been more supportive than I could possibly have imagined, and I am honored to dedicate this book to him. Ralph Gerson has taken a lead role on the board and is generous with both his time and insights.

WDI's board has also provided encouragement, guidance, contacts, and the resources to pursue a high-impact agenda. I am indebted to current and past board members Sue Ashford, Izak Duenyas, John Engler, Tom Lantos, George Siedel, Kathie Sutcliffe, and Bob Teeter.

We also have a great management team at WDI, without whom I would accomplish very little. Rosemary Harvey is a friend and colleague—tracking all the day-to-day details so I don't have to. Kendra Weasel provides outstanding support, runs interference with people I annoy or neglect, and keeps me grounded. Dan Shine, who handles external relations, pulls together the Institute's sometimes confusing storylines and is always there in a pinch.

Ted London (Base of the Pyramid Research Manager) is a fellow academic working to bridge the theory-practice gap and an excellent sounding board. Ajay Sharma (Globalization of Services Research Manager) has been an outstanding colleague on this research project and a reliable connection to leading organizations in the field. Kelly Janiga (Social Enterprise Research Manager) has created an outstanding network of practitioners and opportunities for our students.

Amy Gillett (Executive Education), John Branch (Educators Outreach), and Khalid Al-Naif (Development Consulting Services) all run their respective operations efficiently and effectively, creating practitioner connections, disseminating our research insights around the world, and generating the surpluses that fund much of what we do.

This book would not be possible without extensive and detailed input from leading offshoring and outsourcing firms. These firms opened their operations, shared data, and critiqued various pieces of the work—gently and constructively, pointing out errors and omissions. I thank Pramod Bhasin and Tiger Tyagarajan of Genpact; Mark Hodges and Mark Toon of EquaTerra; S. Ramadorai and N. Chandrasekaran of Tata Consultancy Services; Ashish Dhawan and Brahmal Vasudevan of ChrysCapital; Frank Cocuzza and his senior management team at Penske Truck Leasing; John Sviokla of Diamond Consulting; Vinay Gupta of Janeeva; and Anurag Jain of Perot Systems. We interviewed more than a dozen additional firms for the book who have chosen to remain anonymous.

I had an outstanding team of people working on book support. In the early days of the work, Barbara Feinberg helped me sort out many of my initial ideas. I have benefited from a series of outstanding research assistants, including Brian Irwin, Chris Dorle, Ben Cole, and Patricia Loh.

My agent, Helen Rees, helped bring the project into focus and found the right home for it. Jeff Cruickshank has been a wonderful development editor, sounding board, and friend. The support staff from Pearson—my editor, Martha Cooley, as well as Anne Goebel and her production team—have been a joy to work with.

Finally, I would like to close by thanking my various "families"—both the one I grew up in and my other sources of support. My parents, siblings, and in-laws have always been there. So thanks Bob and Mary, Erin and Peter, Chris and Michelle, Mary Shannon, and Mike and Amy.

Finally, Roger, Heidi, Laurie, Andrea, and Allison have all suffered through both the research and writing process—listening patiently to my incessant "noodling" on some new (mostly mundane) insight and my whining about the writing process, as well as sharing in the joy of small steps forward.

This book would not have happened without support from all the people listed here and, undoubtedly, many others. I only hope the next one will proceed more smoothly.

About the Authors

Robert E. Kennedy is Tom Lantos Professor of Business Administration, Director of the Global Initiative at University of Michigan's Ross School of Business, and Executive Director of the William Davidson Institute (WDI). He spent eight years at Harvard Business School, researching global strategy and teaching international business courses. He has consulted and invested venture capital throughout Europe and Asia.

Ajay Sharma is Research Manager for WDI's Globalization of Services Initiative. In 1992, he joined Infosys as it was ramping up its offshore software development business. Later, he joined PriceWaterhouse-Coopers as a technology consultant.

Introduction

If you're an active manager in the first decade of the twenty-first century, you already know about the phenomenon of globalization in the manufacturing sector—although perhaps you don't know the full scope of that phenomenon. But by any measure, it's enormous. In 2006, the U.S. trade-to-GDP ratio was 28.0 percent, compared with 11.1 percent in 1970 and 20.4 percent in 1990.[1] In 2006, U.S. companies committed $60 billion to new manufacturing foreign direct investment (FDI): a jump of 66 *percent* over the previous year.[2]

The reasons behind this phenomenon are well documented, and they are widely—often hotly—discussed. They include the low cost of labor overseas, fewer regulatory restrictions, proximity to emerging markets (facilitating sales in those markets), the ability to focus home country resources on product development and marketing, the commoditization of manufacturing technology, the rise of supplier clusters in different countries, and so on.

But there's a parallel phenomenon occurring today—another kind of offshoring—that may soon overtake its manufacturing-based cousin in scale and scope: *the globalization of services*.

We call it "the services shift."

This is a new and different phenomenon, and it's one whose implications are poorly understood by most corporate managers. True, most of us have heard stories about large corporations moving call centers and basic business processes (for example, software development, payroll, billing) offshore. And on a basic level, most of us understand the compelling logic that lies behind these developments. To the customer phoning in to argue about an entry on his or her monthly credit card statement, it doesn't matter much whether the contact center agent is sitting in Omaha, Nebraska, or Bangalore,

India. If it's cheaper to hire that agent in Bangalore than in Omaha, *and* if that offshore person is able to resolve the dispute successfully, then that service job is very likely to move offshore.

In fact, to a large extent, it already *has*.

But so far, it has been hard to get a clear picture of what's going on—and where and why. Where are the jobs going? Who's getting the benefits of the globalization of services? How big are those benefits? What companies benefit (or could benefit) from the offshoring of services? How, exactly, does it work? Who makes for a good partner in this realm? What are the public policy implications of this trend— and how can companies make long-term investments if the ground is shifting beneath their feet?

These are the questions we ask and answer in *The Services Shift*.

Outsourcing and Offshoring

First, some definitions, which we'll return to and flesh out in sub- sequent chapters. **Outsourcing** means moving a particular task out- side an organization's boundaries. When a company decides to eliminate its in-house food service department and hire an outside contractor to run its cafeteria, it is "outsourcing" that function. For lots of "non-core" practical activities—such as staffing the cafeteria and cleaning the headquarters building—outsourcing means buying the service fairly close to home.

But many other activities aren't necessarily rooted in geography. In theory, at least, you *could* outsource these tasks to a contractor anywhere in the world. When a task moves across a geographic boundary, we call this "offshoring."

For example, recent years have seen the emergence of a phe- nomenon called the "electronic ICU (intensive care unit)"—a vir- tual ICU that uses video conferencing, remote bedside terminals, and image-acquisition technology to monitor critically ill patients remotely. With eICU, a team of critical-care specialists sits at a remote location and continuously tracks patients' vital signs, and if something is amiss, the team contacts the onsite staff and recommends action.

One electronic ICU provider, VISICU, pitches its product as a way to cost-effectively improve medical care in hospitals that don't have enough critical-care physicians:

> ICU patients require around-the-clock specialized care, however most ICUs don't have the specially trained physicians available to provide this. With an eICU facility linked via telemedicine and computer monitors to their hospital ICU rooms, they now can.[3]

VISICU likens its eICU solution to the air traffic control function, in which a team of technical specialists relies on software and tracking technology to assist in airplane navigation without actually being in the cockpit. The company claims to have implemented some form of the eICU solution in 34 U.S. hospitals, and has recently inked a $25 million deal with Sutter Health, Northern California's leading non-profit provider of health-care services.

Currently, eICU is only outsourced—that is, turned over to domestic contractors—rather than offshored. But in this activity, *distance is irrelevant.* In fact, other than some truly formidable regulatory barriers, nothing stands in the way of moving the eICUs offshore, and thereby substituting foreign health-care technicians for domestic ones.

The white-coated doctor in your local hospital might seem forever immune to offshoring, but as the eICU example illustrates, that's not necessarily the case.

Offshoring, as the name implies, means moving a function and its associated jobs to another part of the world. Offshoring comprises a wide range of relationships between the "parent" company and remote service providers. Sometimes those providers stay within the corporate boundary, but operate at a geographic distance. Sometimes they are outside the corporate boundaries (they are "outsourced offshorers"). In this book, we focus mainly on the offshoring phenomenon, although certainly domestic outsourcing is another important kind of "services shift."

The word "offshoring," useful as it is, is something of a red herring. The globalization of services is not simply a story about jobs being moved offshore. It's about a *fundamental reorganization of work,* in which different tasks are being carried out by different individuals in different locations. As new global sourcing options become available, forward-looking managers are actively evaluating tasks, processes, and functions inside their firms—from back-office support to leading-edge research—to determine the most cost-effective *and* highest quality location to carry out these activities. In other words, it's not just about finding a low-cost location. It's about gaining access to the best combination of talent, resources, and local markets.

Why is it happening *now?* Again, we'll look into this question in greater depth in later chapters. But for now, we'll simply point to five compelling forces:

- **Technological innovations**—These innovations include the spread of computer literacy, broadband Internet access, inexpensive international telephony, widespread digital records, and so on.
- **Emerging market growth**—Today, developing countries are working to "grow" their service sectors at least as aggressively as their manufacturing sectors. Countries around the world have witnessed India's experience—with exports of software and IT-enabled services growing at a compounded annual growth rate of more than 43 percent, rising from $128 million in 1991 to $40.8 billion in 2007.[4] These exports can be achieved with relatively low capital investment and environmental impact. Finally, the sector is attractive because it involves using a country's brains, not its brawn.

- **Global macroeconomic liberalization** —Based on the standard measures of economic "openness," more countries are able to engage in international trade and investment than ever before.
- **The corporate imperative to both reduce costs and improve quality**—Most business practitioners understand the concept of lower cost through offshoring; fewer understand that offshoring can lead to major productivity and quality improvements.
- **A convergence of global business culture**—This includes the global dissemination of Western management principles, the emergence of English as the global language of business, and so on.

Even this brief review of the factors pushing for the globalization of services should suggest, *strongly,* that this powerful trend is not a fad, but a huge, fundamental, and irreversible shift. According to McKinsey/NASSCOM, offshore IT and business process outsourcing (BPO) have only reached *one-ninth* and *one-twelfth* of their respective market potentials![5]

What does this mean for your company? Business models and organizational structures will become more dynamic, more fluid, and more opportunistic. In fact, this transformation is already well underway.

What does this mean for *you?* Tomorrow's managers also will have to become more flexible, more versatile, and more broad-gauge. The old ways of providing services—both in the traditional "service sector" and in the services-oriented activities of manufacturing firms—just won't cut it in the face of the global services shift. You need to understand the offshoring options that are available to you, because—*without a doubt!*—your strongest competitors will certainly understand them, and exploit them.

Introducing the Authors

Who, exactly, is taking you on this global tour of offshoring? As much as possible in this book, we'll adopt the first-person plural voice: *we*. For the purposes of this part of the introduction, however, we'll switch briefly to the third person.

Author **Robert (Bob) Kennedy** is the Tom Lantos Professor of Business Administration and Director of the Global Initiative at the University of Michigan's Ross School of Business. He is also Executive Director of the William Davidson Institute (WDI): an independent, nonprofit research and educational institute located at the University of Michigan. Founded in 1992, the Institute focuses on business and policy issues in developing countries and operates in five broad areas: research, executive education, development consulting services, development and distribution of teaching materials, and supporting international activities at the University of Michigan.

Kennedy has been involved in research and advisory work directly related to offshoring for the better part of a decade. In 1999, he began working with Tata Consultancy Services, which is India's largest software firm, and one of the leading global drivers of services offshoring. Since then, Kennedy has published more than a dozen teaching cases on offshoring issues. Between 2002 and 2008, his international business and offshoring cases were assigned at every one of *BusinessWeek*'s top 25 business schools.

In addition to his academic credentials, Kennedy has extensive "real-world" experience. He has worked as a consultant in more than 20 countries, performing advisory work for many of the firms engaged in cutting-edge offshoring practices. Prior to his academic career, he worked as a venture-capital investor in central Europe and has maintained this real-world orientation ever since.

Coauthor **Ajay Sharma** is Research Manager for the "Globalization of Services" initiative at the William Davidson Institute, and is an expert in IT and process consulting. After earning his bachelor's degree in electrical engineering at the Institute of Technology, Banaras Hindu University (Varanasi) in 1992, he joined Infosys, which was then embarking on a dramatic growth curve based on off-shoring software development. After six years as a project manager with Infosys, Sharma joined PriceWaterhouseCoopers (USA), where he provided technology consulting to Fortune 500 companies. He then earned his MBA at the University of Michigan, and—after receiving his degree in 2004—joined the William Davidson Institute.

Returning to our shared authorial voice, together we have deep theoretical grounding, extensive practical experience, and strong ongoing relationships with many of the most innovative offshoring companies in the world. It's this knowledge base and experience that we bring together in *The Services Shift*.

What You'll Find in This Book

We've already introduced the important distinction between out-sourcing and offshoring, mainly talking at the industry level. In Chapter 1, "Globalization of Services: What, Why, and When," we'll dig deeper into these phenomena, giving examples at two levels: industries and companies. We'll provide several tools for you to use as you think about your own company's place in the global services community. We'll explain that the current (and exploding!) wave of services globalization is simply the next logical step in the evolution of international trade, which began with the extraction and exploitation of natural resources, continued through the rationalization of manufacturing around the world—a process that continues today—and now is expanding rapidly into the services sector.

We economists sometimes take for granted certain theories and principles that business practitioners, pundits, and laypeople either don't understand or simply don't buy into. With that potential gulf in mind, we provide some basic economic rationales for why international trade and investment are "good," in the sense of creating comparative advantages for nations, and better returns on capital for individual investors.

Yes, change inevitably causes pain and dislocation for workers in particular industries or sectors. One of the paradoxical aspects of globalization is that the *gains* it creates tend to be spread across large numbers of individuals, whereas the *pain* it generates tends to be localized in smaller groups of workers, companies, or communities. When millions of Wal-Mart shoppers save $10 each on their running shoes, that's a huge collective benefit to those shoppers. Meanwhile, a running-shoe factory closes somewhere in the United States, creating dislocations and pain for the people who worked in that factory, and for the surrounding community. When viewed systematically, in almost all cases, the total gains from trade outweigh the losses. It's just that the losses are more easily identified and observed.

The domestic U.S. press has taken notice, often casting this phenomenon in terms of "American jobs lost." But this is the wrong lens through which to observe trade. The right question is, *where can and should specific tasks be located to achieve the best combination of cost and performance?* Yes, the jobs that are associated with these tasks might move. But locating *the right tasks in the right place* also leads to faster product development, stronger companies in the "offshoring" nations, better returns for investors in those companies, and rising demand in those nations.

In other words, offshoring—done right—leads to an enhanced standard of living in both developed and developing countries. To be sure, change is uncomfortable, and this provides a ready hook for polemicists. But change is also necessary for growth and improvement.

As we make clear in Chapter 1, managers don't have the luxury of putting their strategies on hold to await the outcome of a national policy debate. They have to improve their firms *today,* along lines that have already been proven to work, or they will fall behind to those who *do* make those compelling changes.

Chapter 2, "The Economics and Drivers of Offshoring," provides a framework for analyzing and understanding offshoring opportunities and discusses why the globalization of services is occurring *now*.

In the first part of Chapter 2, we look briefly at two economic frameworks that are helpful in understanding and assessing offshoring opportunities. The first is the value chain, introduced by Michael Porter in 1985. The value chain framework allows the analyst to look inside the "black box" of a firm—breaking it into a sequence of functions or tasks. Porter's insight was that competitive advantage arises from capabilities at the *function/task* level, not at the *firm* level.

The second framework is "transaction costs economics," or TCE, which explains why and where firm boundaries exist. This, in turn, helps shed light on why firms perform some tasks themselves locally, "outsource" some tasks to other firms, and source some from remote locations. As businesses, suppliers, customers, and technologies evolve, the transactions costs involved in moving tasks across firm or geographic boundaries also change, thus affecting the sourcing options and payoffs facing firms.

The chapter then revisits the outsourcing/offshoring decision and, using TCE, discusses the factors that make a task more or less likely to be a candidate for being transferred across a firm or geographic boundary.

In Chapter 1, we explain why trade in services has become more like trade in manufactured goods in recent years (production and consumption have become separable by geography). In Chapter 2, we show how trade in services *differs* in important ways from trade in manufactured goods.

Why? First, services tend to be much more labor intensive than manufacturing. This means that low-wage countries have an even greater advantage in services than they traditionally have had in manufacturing. Second, new (and vocal) categories of workers have become vulnerable to offshoring. Third, trade in services tends to be *synchronous*—that is, happening in real time—which makes this new kind of trade highly visible. And fourth, within the firm, offshoring tends to happen at the task level, and activities sourced remotely remain closely connected to activities retained at home. This means that a service activity that has been offshored—for example, accounting, collections, or product design—still interacts with the company's remaining employees every day.

Still, not all services lend themselves to offshoring. There are still whole categories of jobs that will remain off limits to offshoring, at least for the time being—and in some cases, forever. (Your local barber, your police officer, and your elementary school teacher are probably immune to offshoring.) Certain kinds of jobs near the beating heart of the company—the core competencies—are probably "safe." But changing technologies call for a continual reexamination of what is possible. Radiologists once assumed that they were safe, and it's now clear that they are not.

The chapter concludes with a discussion of what we call the "Five Drivers of Globalization" in the services sector, and explains why those drivers are likely to intensify in the future:

- The economic liberalization in developing countries, which has resulted in 1) lower barriers to economic engagement, 2) higher growth rates in those countries, and 3) increased attention from global firms that are under pressure to generate higher growth rates of their own
- The digitization of business processes, which makes many more business activities "moveable"
- Rapid improvements in quality and reductions in cost across a range of computing and telecom services, which again permit and encourage "task mobility"

- Growing capabilities around the globe
- The emergence of a global business culture, based largely on the practices of leading U.S. and European companies, which makes an ever-larger number of geographic contexts congenial to those companies

In Chapter 3, "Making It Real," we present a framework intended to help you establish realistic sourcing goals for your organization and to implement these goals. Firms pursue offshoring for a variety of reasons, including efficiency, enhancement, and transformation. The first part of the chapter discusses how these approaches differ and why it is imperative that you be clear and realistic about establishing your offshoring goals. These goals influence the entire offshoring journey—which tasks/processes to start with, the type of sourcing partner to work with, the risks encountered, and the expected benefits.

The chapter then discusses the differences between offshoring tasks (for example, operating a call center and managing accounts payable) and offshoring entire processes (for example, hire-to-retire HR management or purchase-to-pay sourcing operations). Task offshoring tends to be cost and best-practice focused, whereas process offshoring is closely linked with reengineering. In some situations, successful process transformation leads to business performance benefits of 10 to 20 times those from labor cost savings.

The chapter then describes in detail how companies go about identifying, documenting, and migrating activities offshore. We walk you through an eight-step process that takes companies from activity identification to implementation, calling on tools such as detailed process mapping, IT systems implementation, risk mitigation, monitoring, process migration, and post-switchover integration.

Let's assume you're interested in offshoring, but you're not sure of your range of choices in the global marketplace. Chapter 4, "The Supply Side," explores outsourcing options today. It begins with an overview of the offshoring universe—size, growth rates, types of activities, and so on. The chapter then discusses how we got here—starting with the Tata Group's initial software exports in 1973 and continuing (in a milestone format) up to the present.

We then present a typology of offshoring business models:

- The captives of global firms such as Motorola, American Express, and Microsoft
- Organizations affiliated with global outsourcing firms, such as Accenture, IBM, and Convergys
- Firms affiliated with offshore software firms, such as TCS, Infosys, and Wipro
- Independent firms, such as ITTIAM, EvalueServe, and Teleradiology Solutions, Inc.

Obviously, offshoring involves all different kinds of firms. Yes, you have the huge software firms that have gotten into the back-office business. And you have the U.S. Fortune 100 firms that are rushing over in large numbers, as well. (IBM now has 53,000 people, or 17.6 percent of its global workforce,[6] in India, and has described India as a linchpin in its strategy to serve the "globally integrated enterprise.") But you also have a host of very small firms in niche roles—market research, medical transcription, and so on. You also have reconfigurations within this cast of characters—for example, GE's spin-out of Genpact (from captive to independent), and R.R. Donnelley's recent acquisition of Office Tiger (from independent to captive).

Today, much of this activity is centered in India. But more and more countries are playing, or trying to play, in the offshoring game. China and the Philippines are already important offshore destinations, and countries such as Hungary, Russia, Morocco, Brazil, South Africa, and Mauritius are gaining ground.

What do these different kinds of firms, in their different geographies, mean for *you*, as a contemporary manager? How do you choose a partner, and what signals should you look for in a successful offshoring relationship?

Chapter 5, "Shifting Skill Sets," explores what this all means for how you manage and organize your firm. We start with the fact that offshoring is a *hands-on activity*. Moving tasks from one geography to another creates both enormous challenges and impressive opportunities for companies. Managers need very specific skill sets to make offshoring work—and those skills often differ from those required in the non-outsourced, non-offshored world.

For example, international skills (language skills, cultural awareness, an understanding of how the global business community functions) were once a "nice to have." Today, for offshoring companies, they are indispensable resources. Where such skills were once confined to the executive suite or in the "international division," they are now required deep down in many different parts of the offshoring organization. At almost every level, people need to understand how to communicate and manage across cultures. They need to be skilled at anticipating and managing risk, and they need to be effective communicators—enabling them to head off the backlash that is often inherent in offshoring, or to contain and offset that backlash when it does arise.

At the same time, strong IT and industrial engineering skills are needed—not only to reengineer, migrate, and manage far-flung operations, but also to develop and maintain the IT systems that are required to manage a geographically dispersed operation.

The chapter presents a framework with which to consider the types of management responsibilities that lead to success. We then draw on detailed interviews with dozens of offshoring firms to illustrate how the key success factors for managers change when an organization embraces global sourcing.

From the opening chapters of *The Services Shift*, we underscore our political agnosticism about offshoring. Because there's no point in arguing with the tide—we assert—managers should focus on *understanding* and *exploiting* this growing trend. In Chapter 6, "The Services Shift: Policy Implications," we adopt a broader policy perspective. Offshoring has led to a flurry of policy initiatives, in both developing and developed countries. What are the general approaches, and what do these mean for managers?

In developing countries, policies have focused on investment in education (sometimes primary, and sometimes advanced technical), telecom deregulation, export-processing zones, general incentives for foreign investment, and—in some cases—a broad-based reform of the commercial code. Obviously, these policies are intended to be "offshoring friendly," and many have proven very successful.

In the developed world, most policy initiatives are aimed at slowing or regulating the offshoring choice. In the United States, for example, at least 33 state legislatures have debated anti-offshoring legislation, and the U.S. Senate has actually passed laws setting limits on offshoring. We argue that for at least three reasons, these policies are generally misguided, in both the short and long term. First, as noted earlier, the savings associated with offshoring tend to be so huge, and companies are under such extraordinary pressure to improve their margins, that managers have little choice but to seek out these opportunities, even when they are frowned upon in the political arena.

Second, the offshore migration of activities is simply too hard to spot to allow for effective regulation. Even when governments try to regulate offshoring, they have almost no ability to monitor, much less enforce, such regulations. Moving a 250-person factory is one thing; moving four customer-care positions or hiring an engineer in China (even though one was available in Michigan) is quite another.

Third, as explained in Chapter 1, all the evidence suggests that for the developed world, inhibiting offshoring only *reduces* long-term incomes. Countries that open up their economies tend to grow faster; countries that throw up protectionist walls tend to grow more slowly. Anti-offshoring policies may be politically appealing in the short term, but they are a bad economic prescription for long-term growth or high standards of living.

The only feasible policy responses to the pain and dislocations caused by offshoring—we argue—are to focus on 1) minimizing costs to affected workers, and 2) hastening their transition to new sectors. Much has been made in the U.S. media about transition and adjustment programs that haven't worked. We point to examples of adjustment processes that *are* effective and *do* add value.

And finally, in Chapter 7, "Looking Ahead," we look to the future. What is the next big thing in the globalization of services? And what does that mean for managers today?

First, we reiterate some of the points made in earlier chapters. Offshoring will become a much more truly global activity. Other countries will "gain on" India as they figure out their own unique niches and competitive advantages.

Second, globalization will come to many more services—both high value added (R&D, product design, legal and advisory work) and more personalized services (tutoring for your child, life coaching, personal scheduling).

Third, globalization of services will grow strongly in the non-IT realm. Instead of servicing clients from a distance, new firms will bring clients to the developing world. We are already seeing the beginnings of this trend with so-called "medical tourism" and retirement communities in low-cost countries.

Fourth, business-process multinationals will play an ever more important role. Companies such as Tata Consultancy Services, Infosys, Wipro, and Genpact are growing at astounding rates; all are likely to have more than 100,000 employees within a few years. They will be well positioned to offer the equivalent of "standardized parts" for knowledge work.[7] As this happens, ever-greater numbers of firms in the developed world will be compelled to conceive of their traditional back-office processes as standardized utilities.

Introductions have their perils. Boiling down the contents of our book into a few short pages—as we've tried to do here, to give you a sense of what's coming—leads to a pretty dense result. Don't be daunted; in subsequent chapters, we will do our best to make some-times-complicated ideas accessible, and *useful*. The services shift is creating an enormously fertile ground of opportunity; our goal is to make you feel at home on that ground.

Endnotes

[1] The trade-to-GDP ratio is calculated as (exports + imports) / GDP. It provides a rough measure of the role trade flows play in an economy. Source: Economic Report of the President: 2008, Table B-1.

[2] Peter Koudal, "Growing the Global Corporation: Global Investment Trends of U.S. Manufacturers," Deloitte Research, 2005.

[3] Company Facts, VISICU, http://visicu.com/index_flash.asp (accessed on February 21, 2008).

[4] Data from "NASSCOM Strategic Review" (2008) and from "Tata Consultancy Services: High Technology in a Low-Income Country" (2000), by Robert E. Kennedy, Harvard Business School Case # 700-092.

[5] "Nasscom-McKinsey Report 2005: Extending India's Leadership of the Global IT and BPO Industries," NASSCOM, December 2005, p. 30, 33.

[6] Paul McDougall, "IBM Head Count In India Tops 50,000," *InformationWeek* (Feb 2007), www.informationweek.com/story/showArticle.jhtml?articleID=197002525.

[7] I first heard this phrase from John Sviokla, a former colleague at Harvard Business School and currently Vice-Chairman and Director of Innovation and Research for Diamond Management, a leading technology strategy consulting firm.

1

Globalization of Services: What, Why, and When

Let's assume you're a senior decision maker at a company somewhere in the developed world. Let's assume further that your company is engaged in providing *services* of some sort or another. But let's not be too restrictive in our definition of "providing services." Even if your company is primarily a manufacturer, it almost certainly provides an extensive menu of services—both within the company, and between your company and its customers and vendors.

Now consider the following quote:

> If you sit at a desk and process paper and computer files, I can move your job to India. I can definitely do it cheaper. I can probably do it faster and more accurately. It's a whole new world out there, and most U.S. firms have no idea what's about to hit them.[1]

This provocative assertion comes from Raman Roy, former president and CEO of a company called Spectramind eServices, one of the Indian pioneers in the fast-moving universe of IT-enabled services. He made that comment in April 2002, shortly before Spectramind was bought by Wipro Technologies—an Indian IT service provider that today employs 72,000 people, runs 53 development centers around the globe, is the world's largest independent R&D services provider, and serves as a strategic partner to five of the top ten most innovative companies in the world.[2]

Do you think people such as Raman Roy and companies such as Wipro are irrelevant to your future, or to your company's future? Do you think your industry will somehow be exempted from Roy's prediction—which in the intervening years has already been proven accurate, many times over?

If so, you're probably wrong.

Three "Safe" Industries Meet Offshoring

We've all heard stories about manufacturing moving offshore, from the developed world to the developing world. Unless you were one of those unfortunate workers whose factory job moved away, this process likely seemed distant and, vaguely, to make some sense: As the economy develops and the workforce becomes better educated, low-skill manufacturing jobs move offshore so that workers in the developed world are freed up to do higher "value-added" activities, many of these in services.

But not just *any* service jobs. As noted in the introduction, call centers and similarly low-skill, back-office service operations are now moving offshore. In our roles as consumers, we've learned that the person who's calling about the late payment on the MasterCard or conducting the market research isn't necessarily calling from around the corner. We've learned to listen for the soft accents, the determination to "stick to the script," the feigned enthusiasm about the local sports team, and so on. And going in the other direction, when we phone a call center looking for help, we've learned to gauge whether the person we're talking to has a command of the English language—let alone a command of the technology in question.

So like many routine manufacturing jobs, many lower-skill-content service jobs are now vulnerable to being offshored. (Many already have; more will be in the near future.) But what about higher-skill-content service jobs? Are they "safe"?

Not necessarily. Let's look at three industries that might seem invulnerable to offshoring, but aren't: equity research, legal services, and clinical trials and drug development.

Equity Research

Where *are* the "safe" jobs? How about on Wall Street: the beating heart of the U.S. domestic economy?

Not really. A large number of white-collar jobs in equity research have already been offshored. Equity research—which involves evaluating both the financial performance and business strategies of publicly traded companies—today is not only being conducted in its traditional Wall Street hub, but also offshore, in India. The large investment banks, including JPMorgan Chase and Goldman Sachs, employ equity analysts in India both for cost savings and for their ability to cover international companies that are difficult for domestic (United States) analysts to research.[3]

Many offshore equity research analysts work in "captive" operations, meaning they are employed directly by the investment banks. However, a growing share work for third-party vendors—some in large broadline offshore-services providers (Infosys's Progeon, ICICI's Pipal Research) and others in small, independent companies (Copal Partners, Rathis).

Legal Research

Roughly the same pattern emerges in the legal-services field, where both large law firms and small, third-party vendors are using offshore lawyers and paralegals for tasks such as database management, due diligence, and patent applications.[4] True, the majority of complex legal work still requires face-to-face interaction, but law firms and service providers are migrating many well-defined, repetitive tasks to low-cost, high-labor-supply locations. This migration has been accelerated by the digitization of legal databases, research resources, and filing systems that allow attorneys to complete and submit documents from anywhere in the world.

As in the other cases cited earlier, *almost all forces are pushing in the direction of offshoring these white-collar service jobs.* In addition to realizing significant cost savings through the use of offshore legal support, law firms are finding it makes sense to move labor-intensive paperwork to low-cost locations, thereby freeing up home office employees for higher-value-added activities. The result? According to trend-spotting Forrester Research, something like 29,000 legal jobs were scheduled to be offshored by 2008.[5] Surely that is only the first wave of legal jobs that will be decamping in the next few years.

Clinical Trials and Drug Development

Emerging service-based knowledge industries such as pharmaceutical clinical trials and biotech research—once the exclusive turf of the developed world—are now flourishing in countries throughout the world. The therapy or drug that a decade ago would have been developed close to home, today is being developed on the other side of the world—literally.

This move has been driven by numerous factors, including cost, talent, and population resources (that is, "bodies"). From a cost perspective, developing a single drug for a large pharmaceutical company can cost nearly $900 million today (a total that is likely to climb to $1.5 billion by 2010), with as much as 40 percent of this money being spent on clinical trials.[6] Clinical trials are labor intensive—people have to hand out the drugs, people have to take the drugs, and people have to monitor, record, and report on the effects that the drugs have on the people who take them.

People is the operative word.

As a result, pharmaceutical companies have been aggressive in utilizing third-party contract research organizations (CROs) to manage and create tasks ranging from clinical trials to drug development. The CROs themselves are thoroughly global in their orientation. One leading company, Quintiles, has multiple offices on every continent, drawing upon resources from various global markets depending on project need. Drug maker Eli Lilly—the pride of Indianapolis, Indiana, deep in America's heartland—conducts 50 percent of its clinical trials outside the United States, using both its own "captive" organization and working with third-party vendors.[7] Lilly's decisions to offshore clinical research are driven not just by costs, but by the desire to access local talent, such as doctors and statisticians, and to gain access to abundant population resources for clinical evaluation. As Lilly's executive vice-president of science and technology, Steven Paul, noted in a recent *BusinessWeek* interview:

> It's not just cost, here. Let me be very clear. It's availability of patients. The medical systems in some of these countries are very sophisticated. The number of patients available for some of these trials is very substantial. There is infrastructure.[8]

Even tasks higher up the value chain, including original biomedical research, can be done in global locations with direct links to large multinationals. The government of Singapore, for example, recently developed Biopolis, an enormous, collaborative biomedical office park that seeks to employ 2,000 researchers in its first phase alone.[9] Biopolis has already recruited leading researchers from research institutions such as MIT and Stanford, while also signing tenant agreements with pharmaceutical companies such as Novartis. Similarly, clustered scientific communities such as Biotechnology Ireland and the still-emerging Genome Valley in India have been designed to create world-class research centers *and* move the research closer to where both existing and future biotechnology manufacturing will happen.

Both clinical trials and biomedical research highlight the *minimal importance of geography* for many activities. With the emerging availability of top talent in countries around the world, knowledge industries will thrive in locations that are continuously linked electronically. These have traditionally been in the United States, Europe, and

Japan. But in the future, they could be almost anywhere that has the right technological and legal infrastructure, combined with the right people.

In short, there is nothing special about clinical trials or advanced medical research that requires these services to be performed "onshore." As a result, they are already moving offshore.

Four Industries in India—and Elsewhere

To gain another perspective on the services shift, let's look at the country that's currently at the center of the offshoring revolution—India—and dig down into four industries (information technology and IT-enabled services, medical transcription, teleradiology, and medical tourism) in which Indian companies have taken on tasks that they couldn't have performed even a few years back.

Current estimates are that Indians export around *$40.8 billion* of services each year. Other large software and business process out-sourcing (BPO) services exporters include Ireland ($8.3 billion), Canada ($7.0 billion), the Philippines ($4.9 billion), and Israel ($3.0 billion).[10] Note that the top three sourcing locations for offshoring are all countries in which fluent English is spoken by a large percentage of the population. Note, too, that of these countries, India has by far the largest labor pool and the lowest wage rates. And, finally, note that India is on the other side of the world from the United States, so assuming an appropriate workflow in a given industry, Indians can be working while Americans are sleeping.

As you'll see, many other countries are knocking on the off-shoring door; for the moment, however, India has combined its lin-guistic, economic, and geographic advantages to give itself a commanding lead over its "upstart" rivals.

Industry Case-in-Point #1: IT/ITES

Most U.S. managers are aware that India has earned itself a major position in the Information Technology/Information Technology Enabled Services (IT/ITES) sector. Nevertheless, the specifics can be startling:

- NASSCOM, India's IT trade association, reported that in 2006, 1.3 million individuals in India worked in IT (software) and ITES (business process outsourcing), with the majority of these workers supporting global multinationals. These numbers are increasing rapidly (see Table 1.1).

TABLE 1.1   Employment in India Exports

Sector	FY 2004	FY 2005	FY 2006	FY 2007 (estimated)
IT Services	215,000	297,000	398,000	562,000
ITES-BPO	216,000	316,000	415,000	545,000
Engineering Services and R&D and Software Products	81,000	93,000	115,000	144,000
Domestic Market (including user organizations)	318,000	352,000	365,000	378,000
TOTAL	830,000	1,058,000	1,293,000	1,630,000

Source: NASSCOM [11]

- Between 2004 and 2007, the total software and services exports by the Indian IT/ITES sector more than doubled: from $16.7 billion to $39.7 billion (see Table 1.2).
- In addition to the large Indian and Western IT service providers (for example, IBM, EDS, Wipro, Infosys, etc.), at least 150 companies have set up independent, "captive" organizations for business process outsourcing.
- The emergence of more than 3,000 small (that is, revenues of less than $100 million) Indian IT service providers suggests that small to mid-size businesses in the United States and other developed countries (that is, not just the big multinationals) are using India for various IT-related tasks and services.

TABLE 1.2   Exports by Sector (in USD Billion)

	FY 2004	FY 2005	FY 2006	FY 2007 (estimated)
IT Services	10.4	13.5	17.8	23.7
Exports	7.3	10.0	13.3	18.1
Domestic	3.1	3.5	4.5	5.6
ITES-BPO	3.4	5.2	7.2	9.5
Exports	3.1	4.6	6.3	8.3
Domestic	0.3	0.6	0.9	1.2
Engineering Services and R&D, Software Products	2.9	3.9	5.3	6.5
Exports	2.5	3.1	4.0	4.9
Domestic	0.4	0.8	1.3	1.6
Total Software and Services Revenue				
Exports	16.7	22.6	30.3	39.7
Domestic	12.9	17.7	23.6	31.3

Source: NASSCOM[12]

A leading Indian player in the global IT/ITES strategic offshoring arena is Infosys Technologies Ltd. Founded in 1981 and headquartered in Bangalore, Infosys today has a presence in more than 20 countries, and employs more than 75,000 people worldwide.

Infosys delivers a wide variety of services—application development and maintenance, enterprise quality, infrastructure, packaged application, product engineering, and systems integration—to customers in a broad range of industries, including aerospace, high technology, retailing, banking, and others. It serves more than 500 global customers, including companies such as Nordstrom, DHL, and JPMorgan Chase.

Over the past few years, Infosys has grown aggressively—from $100 million in revenues in 1999 to just over $3 billion in 2007[13]: a compound growth rate of more than 53 percent!

Industry Case-in-Point #2: Medical Transcription

When you visit a physician in the United States, that visit is likely to generate a tape or digital recording that serves both as the doctor's notes on the visit and as a roadmap for subsequent examinations and treatments. (Sometimes the doctor makes the tape in real time, with you in the office; sometimes he or she waits until the visit is over.) But in order for those audio records to be useful to the physician, they have to be translated into a text format, either through an automated transcription process or manually—that is, by people listening through headphones and typing on keyboards.

In the 1990s, it was assumed that some combination of the electronic medical record (EMR) and the rapidly evolving field of speech recognition (SR) software would replace nearly all people-based medical transcription by the turn of the century. So far, though, these technologies have had only limited impact, in large part because they are prone to errors, and medical errors can be costly, or even deadly. (Market penetration is something like 5 to 8 percent for EMR, and 1 percent or less for SR.) As a result, the demand for transcription services continues to be robust.

Today, the medical transcription industry is estimated to have revenues of around $25 billion per year, with an annual growth rate of between 10 and 15 percent. In the 1990s, the American Association for Medical Transcription (AAMT) estimated the number of medical transcriptionists at 250,000; currently, that number is somewhere between 350,000 and 400,000 full-time workers, with part-timers pushing the total closer to 500,000.[14] The increasing need for documentation to support reimbursement, the imperatives of risk management, and the need for ever more data are all fueling the growth of medical transcription. As a result, continued significant growth is foreseen for this industry in the near future; mostly centered around Medical Transcription Service Organizations (MTSOs).

Nevertheless, it remains a highly fragmented industry, populated by one massive company (with revenues at $400 million), three or four companies with revenues each of between $100 million and $200 million, a handful of companies in the $10 million to $100 million range, and a couple of handfuls of companies in the $3 million to $10 million range (see Table 1.3 below).

TABLE 1.3   Medical Transcription Companies

Employees	Total Number
Full Time	350,000–400,000
Including Part Time	500,000
Companies (by Revenue)	**Number of Companies**
$400 million	1
$100–$200 million	3–4
$10–$100 million	Some
$3–$10 million	~20
$500,000–$3 million	More than 200

The combined revenues of all these $10 million–to–$400 million companies total between $800 million and $900 million. The remaining $24.1 billion (in other words, the vast majority) is divided among internal transcription departments, individual contract medical transcriptionists, "mom & pop" transcription companies, and the 200 or so companies with revenues ranging from $500,000 to $3 million.[15]

Medical transcription outsourcing first gained a toehold (and earned a lot of media attention) in India in the 1995–1997 period, well before "BPO" entered the business vocabulary. Although the Indian medical transcription industry went through a rough patch at the turn of the century, it has rebounded and is expected to reach $647 million by 2010, when it will employ around 52,000 Indians.[16]

Meanwhile, U.S.-based MTSOs are building their offshore capabilities. The reasons are compelling. For one thing, the median age of

U.S. transcriptionists is close to 50, and young workers are not entering the industry fast enough to replace those who are leaving. Even
more compelling, a transcriptionist in the United States earns between
$31,000 and $36,000[17]; in India, he or she makes between $5,000 and
$12,000.[18] As a result, U.S.-based MTSOs are acquiring smaller Indian
offshore vendors to gain access to these low-cost transcriptionists.
Today, Indian units of large U.S. players account for almost 70 percent[19] of Indian medical transcription offshoring revenues. These large
players include CBay, Spheris, Spryance, Acusis, and Heartland.

CBay, for example, is an Indian-funded firm with 1700 transcriptionists, editors, and managers located in the Indian cities of Bangalore, Hyderabad, and Mumbai. The Indian staff listens to digital
sound files that arrive via the Internet, prepares written reports, has
them edited, and returns the completed files in 12–24 hours.[20] The
firm maintains its 170-person staff in Baltimore, Maryland that handles most direct interactions with clients: sales, marketing, customer
service, and so on.[21]

We should not give the impression that India has cornered the
market on the offshored U.S. medical transcription industry. At least 30
medical transcription companies in the Philippines[22] (for example) currently service the U.S. market. Although their share of the overall market today is less than 1 percent, projections indicate that this number
will grow significantly, and that medical transcription will become a
major source of employment in the country—a fact that has prompted
the Filipino government to establish medical transcription certification
guidelines and requirements. Re-creating the pattern established in
India, U.S. companies such as MxSecure have begun building up their
capacity in the Philippines.[23]

Industry Case-in-Point #3: Teleradiology

Let's look at another example from the health-services industry,
with the understanding that medical services are no different from
most corporate business processes. In other words, they aren't "rooted"

by much of anything. "As health care becomes digitized," the *New England Journal of Medicine* recently editorialized, "many activities ranging from diagnostic imaging to the manipulation of laparoscopic instruments, are rendered borderless."[24]

The same could be said about most nonmedical services. Can a given service be digitized? Can it be done without a face-to-face interaction? If so, it probably can be offshored.

The field of radiology (that is, the use of imaging technologies to diagnose, and sometimes treat, disease) has already learned this lesson. Offshore teleradiology is a rapidly emerging industry that today services hundreds of U.S. hospitals. In a traditional hospital, a radiologist is kept on call all night, and is woken up when necessary to review images in urgent situations. Depending on the volume, he or she may become sleep-deprived—and therefore more likely to make mistakes—and is subject to constant interruption in busy periods. Although the radiologist is on site, he or she actually has very little interaction with the patient, and may only speak to the medical staff by phone.

Teleradiology turns all of this on its head. Simply stated, teleradiology involves the electronic transmission of radiological images—such as X-rays, CTs (computed tomograms), and MRIs (magnetic resonance images)—from one location to another, for the purposes of interpretation and/or consultation. Through the use of virtual private networks (VPNs), standard telephone lines, satellite connections, or wide area networks (WANs), X-rays taken at midnight in a U.S. hospital can be read by radiologists on the other side of the earth—places such as Israel, Australia, and India—where it is the middle of the day. These remote radiologists review the image and send their opinions back electronically. Turnaround tends to be less than an hour, which is often quicker than onsite radiologists.

The United States currently faces a shortage of radiologists, with something like 20 percent of radiology vacancies in hospitals going unfilled.[25] Meanwhile, the demand for scans is skyrocketing, due in part to the increasing diagnostic effectiveness of medical imagery, and also in part because of the imaging needs of an aging U.S. population.

Teleradiology helps allay the shortage of U.S.-based radiologists, which is exacerbated during overnight shifts. It also does so at a salary that is, depending on location, significantly cheaper than the $365,000 average for an American radiologist.[26] (U.S.-certified radiologists in India, for example, cost around $28,000.[27]) And under the right circumstances, it produces *better* results.

Consider the example of Teleradiology Solutions, a U.S.-based company that employs radiologists in Bangalore and Delhi, India, as well as in Illinois, Georgia, Massachusetts, and Connecticut. The company was founded in 2002 to provide U.S. hospitals with services during the graveyard shift (known in the medical profession as "nighthawk" services), and also to provide coverage during overflow periods and when U.S.-based radiologists go on vacation or a leave of absence. Teleradiology Solutions was the first company in India to provide U.S. hospitals with teleradiological services,[28] and is today a leader in the imaging markets field. It provides preliminary interpretation of all noninvasive imaging modalities, including CAT scans, MRIs, ultrasounds, nuclear medicine studies, and conventional plain films—all with a turnaround time of less than 30 minutes, when necessary.

Besides emergency reporting, Teleradiology Solutions also covers a wide range of elective reporting, such as outpatient brain/spine/musculoskeletal MRI studies, and 3D post-processing for CT/MR angiography (heart-exam imagery) and colonoscopies.

A company we'll return to at regular intervals in this book is Wipro Technologies, one of the most successful of the Indian software-services firms. Wipro specializes in a broad range of offshored services, one of the more interesting of which is its Global Radiology Centre (GRC). The GRC, which is based in Bangalore, India, is staffed by MD radiologists from Wipro's clinical partners. It provides high-end 3D image processing, radiology reporting, and oncology treatment planning services to its global clients, and is also involved in clinical trials, as described earlier in the chapter (see Figure 1.1).

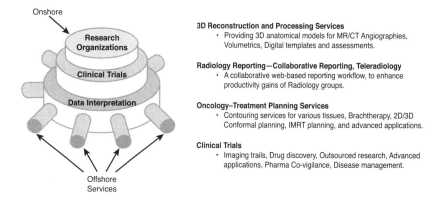

Figure 1.1   Wipro has developed an integrated model to move some activities offshore.

Source: Wipro[29]

Since its inception in April 2003, the GRC has delivered more than 30,000 3D processed studies and more than 5,000 radiology reports (as of August 2007). The Bangalore-based radiologists work on advanced analysis and processing workstations in a secure, HIPAA-compliant facility, and their assessments are delivered via encrypted virtual private networks.[30]

By most accounts, the services delivered by the GRC have contributed to faster turnaround times, increased clinical productivity, lower health-care costs, and minimized exploratory surgery needs. Because its radiologists are under less time pressure than their U.S. counterparts, and because they work on state-of-the-art equipment, the GRC maximizes the information derived from diagnostic imaging exams—which, in turn, helps interpreting radiologists and referring physicians visualize a patient's anatomy more comprehensively and realistically.

In other words, the GRC's output is not only "good enough"; in some ways, it is *better than* (as well as far cheaper than) the output of onsite American radiologists working under less favorable conditions.

Industry Case-in-Point #4: Medical Tourism

Our final Indian industry case study involves the phenomenon of medical tourism (also known as "health tourism"). Simply stated, this involves a person in need of a non-urgent medical procedure going overseas to have that procedure done. In many cases, the trip includes recuperation and leisure activities, which is the "tourism" component.

Medical tourism is far from a new concept. Since the days of the ancient Greeks (when pilgrims visited Epidauria, home of the healing god Asklepios), people have traveled in search of cures. Some 200 million people have visited the French city of Lourdes since miracles started being reported there in the mid-nineteenth century—and because the Roman Catholic Church has officially recognized 68 miraculous healings that have occurred there.[31]

Today, we can point to more mundane forces at work in support of medical tourism. Travel has become easier and cheaper. Developing countries have gradually increased their standards of sanitation (especially where they cater to Western tourists). Consumers in countries with nationalized health care are sometimes required to wait months or years for elective procedures in their home countries. If they agree to go abroad for treatment, they can arrange to have their elective surgeries on a schedule that's convenient to them. Some procedures, such as cosmetic surgeries, may not be covered by health plans, forcing the consumer to be more cost-conscious than usual.

Which brings us to the most compelling factor of all behind the rising phenomenon of medical tourism: cost differentials (see Table 1.4). Depending on the procedure in question, it may be only a *tenth* as expensive to get treatment in a less-developed country. Even after the costs of plane tickets, hotel rooms, and "pure" tourism, in many cases medical tourism is cheaper than treatment at home.

TABLE 1.4   Medical Tourism Cost Differentials

Treatment	U.S./U.K.	India/Others
Heart bypass	$130,000	$10,000
Heart valve replacement	$160,000	$9,000
Angioplasty	$57,000	$11,000
Hysterectomy	$20,000	$3,000
Knee replacement	$40,000	$8,500
Hip replacement	$43,000	$9,000
Spinal fusion	$62,000	$5,500
Root canal	$750	$260

Source: Woodman, *Patients Beyond Borders*, p. 7–8.

Although major U.S. companies have not yet embraced the medical tourism concept, small businesses in the United States—particularly hard-pressed by skyrocketing health-care costs—have begun encouraging their employees to have certain procedures performed overseas. This has led to the birth of a new boutique "concierge" industry in the United States, which matches the employees of U.S. companies with appropriate physicians overseas and makes all of the necessary travel arrangements.[32]

Who's providing the services? In India, the biggest player is Apollo Hospitals Group.[33] In fact, Apollo is the largest private hospital group in Asia, with 37 hospitals, 7,000 beds, and partnerships with hospitals in Kuwait, Sri Lanka, and Nigeria. Established as a public limited company in 1979, Apollo today has annual revenues in excess of $180 million, with an annual growth rate of approximately 20 percent. Although local patients constitute something like 90 percent of Apollo's customers, Apollo also serves "medical tourists," with patients flying to India for a surgery, followed by a vacation/recovery period.

Since 2001, Apollo has treated approximately 95,000 foreign patients. The company has established marketing offices in London and Dubai to attract clientele from the United Kingdom and the United Arab Emirates. (It also treats patients from less-developed countries, such as Bangladesh, when local treatment is not available.)

Working with the Indian tourism council, Apollo has sponsored "roadshows" across Britain, highlighting its treatments and services.

Cyril Parry, a 59-year-old from South Wales in the U.K., recounts his experience with Apollo as follows:

> I had the Birmingham Hip Resurfacing (BHR) procedure at Apollo Hospitals, Chennai, India with a British-trained surgeon of a long-standing, decade of experience in BHR. The operation was a truly great job. Air-conditioned room, en suite bathroom for eleven days, two personal nurses night and day seeing to my needs, clean thin scar, could not have been better. I am thrilled beyond words!
>
> Should I tell you the price? All expenses including new passport, visas, two return tickets, ambulance to airport for return journey, cardiac check-up, all for less than £5,000. Only wished I had done it years back, I would have saved myself untold agony. Cheers, my dears!

Apollo has been successful in attracting private equity to fund its expansion over the years. A recent McKinsey study is optimistic about the industry's future, pegging annual Indian medical tourism growth in a recent five-year period at 25 percent,[34] and predicting that the industry soon will bring approximately $2 billion in annual revenues to India.

As in our previous industry examples, we should stress that India is not the only player in medical tourism. At least a dozen other countries are actively promoting themselves as destinations for medical tourists, including Cuba, Costa Rica, Hungary, Israel, Jordan, Lithuania, Malaysia, Thailand, Belgium, Poland, Singapore, and South Africa. In fact, officials in Thailand and Malaysia reported that their countries treated more than 600,000 medical tourists in 2003.[35]

Economics 101: Why Trade and Invest?

We've spent some time looking at several interesting industries that are affected by the services shift: equity research, legal research, and clinical trials and drug development. We've also looked at the phenomenon from the Indian side of the planet: How do companies in an emerging country such as India perceive and act on opportunities to provide services to developed countries such as the United States, the U.K., and Germany?

Now let's go down a level deeper, and—with our economists' hats on—look at some of the dynamics that underlie these relationships. To state the question simply, why do companies trade and invest on a global scale today? And if those kinds of investments cause pain and dislocation at the local level—such as we've seen in the United States in recent years—why should the most powerful economy in the world put up with this kind of upset? The answer, economists will tell you, is that *trade and investment is what creates wealth in the first place,* both for countries and companies.

History shows that embracing the global economy is crucial to economic growth in rich countries, and for development in poor ones. If we scan the list of the world's most successful economies over the past half-century, including the United States, Germany, France, Japan, China, Chile, and South Korea, we find that encouraging cross-border trade and investment flows have been central to each country's economic strategy in every case. At the other extreme, countries that have resisted globalization have generally lagged behind their more open neighbors. This less happy group would include Afghanistan, Burma, China prior to 1978, India prior to 1991, Tanzania, the USSR prior to 1989, Venezuela, and Zimbabwe after 1997.

What lies behind this difference? International trade and investment are integral to a country's economic growth because they *increase the productivity of local resources.* This invariably leads to increased productivity, higher wages, and a higher standard of living. Put another way, free trade encourages a country to focus on those things it does relatively well, and to stop doing things it does poorly (a dynamic that economists refer to as "comparative advantage"). A country's standard of living can rise only when the efficiency with which it uses its resources (people, capital, etc.) improves. Trade—

along with education, investment, and technological progress—are important drivers of productivity growth. Trade allows highly productive sectors to sell into a market that goes beyond national borders, thereby increasing output and incomes in these sectors. They expand by drawing resources (workers, investment) from sectors with relatively lower productivity.

Trade has a second important benefit. Because it increases the range and quality of options available to local consumers, it forces local producers to improve their offerings in order to compete more effectively. Although this pressure is inconvenient for local producers, it has clear benefits for consumers. Countries that have lowered their tariff barriers and increased the intensity of competition in the local market often see rapid improvements in productivity as local producers rush to upgrade their products and processes.

Much of the discussion around trade policy revolves around the fate of specific workers who are displaced from trade-exposed industries. For example, one common refrain among media pundits goes something like this: "How are North Carolina textile workers supposed to compete with Sri Lankan workers making one dollar a day?"

Although this argument makes sense intuitively—and actually does capture the legitimate plight of those North Carolina workers—framing the issue this way ignores the wider benefits of trade. When a country increases trade, *everyone* in that country benefits from the cheaper goods now available from abroad. If millions of people now have access to a wider variety of cheaper goods, we have to offset these gains against the losses to displaced workers.[36]

With trade, everyone benefits from cheaper goods—thereby raising purchasing power and real incomes. Competition from abroad also creates pressure on local producers to improve their productivity. The cost and productivity effects benefit everyone. Take restaurant workers, for example. U.S. bartenders and wait staff earn 50 to 70 times more than their counterparts in India. Is this because they work 50 times as hard, or are 50 times more productive? Of course not.

The U.S. workers enjoy high wages because *the overall U.S. economy is 50 to 70 times more productive than India's.* The only way to raise overall productivity is to undergo the process of dislocation and reallocation of productive resources. This is painful, and no one denies that a displaced textile worker is likely to be individually worse off because of increased trade. But those costs are vastly outweighed by the cost, quality, and income improvements for society as a whole.

Most of the think tanks and strategy firms that have studied the economics of offshoring have arrived at the same fundamental conclusions: that although offshoring inevitably hurts a relatively small number of U.S. workers, the overall macroeconomic gains to the U.S. economy are enormous. Here are a few examples:

- Catherine Mann, an economist who has worked on the President's Council of Economic Advisors, has written that U.S. GDP growth between 1995–2002 would have been lower by 0.3% annually (2.1% total, or approximately $200 billion) without foreign offshoring.[37] This may sound like a small percentage, but when applied to the huge base of the U.S. GDP, it's actually a huge sum in absolute terms.

- McKinsey estimates that for every dollar of U.S. services activity that is offshored, a global gain of $1.46 is generated, with $1.13 accruing to the United States. Within the $1.13 pie, American consumers and shareholders gain, while some individual workers of the offshored activity lose ground.[38]

- A study by the Information Technology Association of America states that 2008 U.S. GDP will be $124.2 billion higher as a result of global sourcing of IT products and devices. The study also found that by 2008, the economic benefits gained from global job sourcing in this sector will spur the creation of 317,000 net new jobs.[39]

Another way to look at the offshoring phenomenon, and its associated costs and benefits, is to put it in the context of the larger U.S. economy. As suggested by Table 1.5, outsourcing and offshoring do indeed lead to a relatively small number of layoffs, but the real story is one of *task reorganization* rather than a net loss of jobs:

TABLE 1.5   The U.S. Job Market

Total U.S. employment	137 million
Annual job switches	35 million
Involuntary job switches	15 million
High-end estimate of "offshored" jobs	250,000
Percentage of U.S. layoffs from offshoring	Less than 2 percent

Sources: Forrester, Brookings[40]

Like increased international trade, foreign direct investment (FDI) also generates a broad array of benefits. In addition to providing capital to fund investment, direct investors (that is, those investing directly in firms or physical assets, as opposed to publicly traded securities) typically provide technology, links to supply and distribution chains, and management. All of these factors increase the productivity of local resources, and thus raise wages and improve the standard of living. Much of China's export growth over the past two decades has been fueled by foreign-invested production facilities. Yes, investment capital was necessary, but other factors were just as important. Nearly all of the relevant research confirms that recipient countries realize many and varied benefits from FDI.

Of course, numerous factors influence a country's standard of living. These include historical factors, the lack or abundance of natural resources, proximity to developed country markets, and so on. Although most of these factors are fixed, and therefore beyond the control of a given country, trade and investment policy are *decision variables*. (Countries are free to do the right thing, or the wrong thing, when it comes to trade policy.) Practical experience as well as numerous academic studies indicate that openness to international trade and investment flows is a critical ingredient for development.

Why Managers Need to Understand—and Embrace—Offshoring

Let's continue our quick tour through the economics that lie behind offshoring, winding up with the compelling reasons why nearly all companies should consider global sourcing for at least some tasks.

The global economy is in the midst of a vast transformation. Globalization can be measured in many ways—in terms of government policies, actual trade and investment flows, and so on—and nearly every measure shows that economic linkages among countries have become more extensive. Here, we review three measures that illustrate this changing picture.

The first measure has already been introduced: a country's "openness" to international trade and investment. This methodology was first suggested by Sachs and Warner (1994), and later updated by Kennedy (2000). Seven factors were used to calculate a "policy openness" index for 192 countries. These factors include average tariff rates, regulatory restrictions on FDI, the presence or absence of a two-tiered foreign exchange system, and others.

Figure 1.2 charts the global shares of market GDP, purchasing power parity GDP, and population among countries that are considered open to the global economy. This doesn't mean that all, or even most, citizens in these countries are engaged in global commerce; it simply means that their national governments are not erecting significant obstacles that prevent them from doing so. As the figure illustrates, the share of global population living in open economies remained fairly steady from the early 1960s through the mid-1980s. Then, starting around 1986 and accelerating in the early 1990s, dozens of countries implemented programs of economic liberalization that deregulated domestic markets and lowered barriers to trade and investment. In the short span of only *13 years* (1985–1998), the percentage of people living in "open" economies (the bottom line in the chart) rose dramatically: from 23 percent to 78 percent.

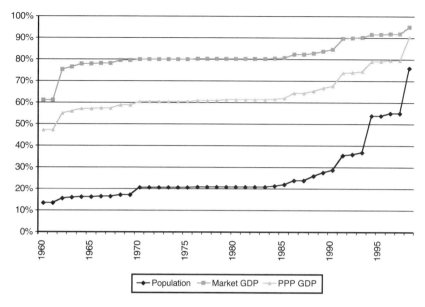

Figure 1.2   Global openness shares[41]

Measures of trade and foreign direct investment as a percentage of economic activity follow a similar pattern. Since the end of World War II, global GDP growth has averaged around 3.7 percent, with wide variation across countries and regions of the world. Global trade has grown at a 7.2-percent compound annual rate, and foreign direct investment (FDI) flows have grown at a 9.6-percent rate. Measured as a percentage of country or global economic output, exports and imports have steadily increased (see Figure 1.3). A similar pattern is evident with foreign direct investment. While the year-to-year flows of FDI are quite volatile, the cumulative stock of FDI has shown a steady increase since 1960. The rate of increase appears to have accelerated since the early 1980s.

Will these trends reverse themselves? Anything is possible, but a significant turning back of the clock seems unlikely. The consensus among development professionals and the vast majority of national economic policymakers is that relatively free prices, investment in education, decentralized capital allocation, and openness to the global economy are the best paths out of poverty for poor countries.

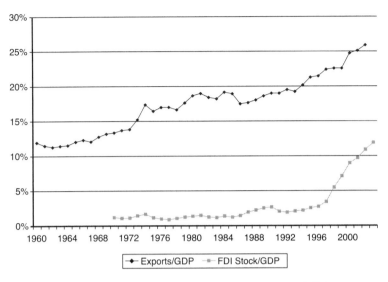

Figure 1.3   Global merchandise exports and stock of FDI as a percentage of GDP

Source: World Bank Trade Statistics 1960-2005

After decades of stop-go policy experimentation, the overwhelming majority of low- and middle-income countries have implemented programs of economic liberalization. For those that stay the course, the future looks brighter than the recent past.

But what exactly does this brighter future look like? Each year, the World Bank publishes an in-depth study titled "Global Economic Prospects and the Developing Countries." This study explores a variety of issues facing developing countries and, based on current and anticipated policies, projects GDP growth by income group and region. Table 1.6 is adapted from the 2002 edition of this study.

As of 2000, high-income countries accounted for about 78 percent of global GDP, and were forecast to grow at their historical rate of 2.6 percent in the decades to come. This came as no surprise. The projections for the low- and middle-income countries, however, were a revelation. The World Bank projected that low- and middle-income

TABLE 1.6   GDP Growth by Income Level and Region

	GDP Growth 1974-1998	Projected GDP Growth	GDP Share 1998	GDP Share 2025	% of Increased Growth
High-Income Countries	2.6%	2.6%	78.0%	62.6%	52.3%
Low- and Middle-Income Countries	3.6	5.5	22.0	37.4	47.7
East Asia and Pacific	6.9	7.5	6.3	17.9	25.6
South Asia	5.3	5.9	2.0	3.7	4.9
Latin American and Caribbean	2.9	4.4	7.0	9.0	10.4
Central Europe/Central Asia	1.4	5.2	3.7	5.8	7.2
Middle East and North Africa	1.9	3.7	1.9	2.0	2.1
Sub-Saharan Africa	2.3	4.2	1.1	1.3	1.5

Source: World Development Report, 2002.

countries would grow at more than *twice* the rate of high-income countries (5.5 percent versus 2.6 percent). In addition, the study predicted that low-income countries in every geographic region would outperform the high-income countries as a group. In other words, for the first time in at least 75 years, the World Bank was predicting *an across-the-board convergence in income levels*.

So here's where the manager contemplating offshoring begins to have "skin in the game." These projections indicate that *nearly half of global GDP growth over the next 25 years will occur in developing countries.* As a group, these countries will grow their share of global GDP from 22 percent to 37 percent. This is a development that few international firms can afford to ignore!

Goldman Sachs offered an additional perspective in a widely influential October 2003 study that changed the way many managers viewed the future of the global economy. "Dreaming with BRICs: The Path to 2050"[42] projected economic growth for the six largest economies (the "G6," which includes the United States, Japan, Germany, the U.K., France, and Italy) and for four large developing countries it labeled the "BRICs" (Brazil, Russia, India, and China). The study built an economic model that considered current economic policies, capital accumulation, demographics, and technical innovation.

The conclusions of the Goldman Sachs study prompted many leading companies in the developed world to undertake a fundamental reassessment of their emerging-market strategies in many leading companies. Briefly stated, the study concluded the following:

- Over the next 50 years, the BRICs will become a much larger force in the world economy. Of today's G6, only the United States and Japan will remain among the six largest economies in 2050.
- As early as 2009, incremental GDP growth in the BRICs will exceed growth in the G6.
- Total GDP for the BRICs will surpass the current G6 by 2039.
- The list of the world's largest economies will look much different in 2050. Many of the largest economies will no longer be among the richest. This will make strategic planning and choices much more complex for international firms.

The Goldman Sachs study projected that the United States will continue to have the highest per-capita GDP but that China will become the largest economy, with India a close third and every other country far behind. The study also projected development paths for individual countries. All four BRICs are projected to close the per-capita GDP gap with today's leaders, with Russia forecast to catch and surpass Germany by the end of the period. Figure 1.4 summarizes the current and projected GDP measures for a selection of countries.

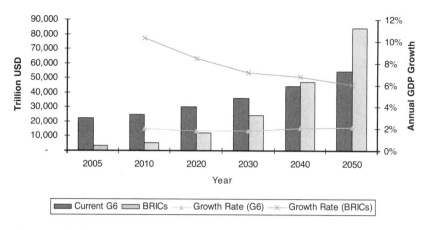

Figure 1.4   Current and projected GDP measures

What's the bottom line for managers today?

The global economy has undergone substantial changes in the past 20 years. It is likely to change *even more* over the next 50 years. The engines of growth in the new global economy are increasingly located in developing countries. How managers seize these opportunities and manage the challenges these trends create will determine the success or failure of their companies, and of their careers.

Summing Up: The Compelling Case for the Services Shift

Today's business environment is one of increasing competitive intensity, on a global scale, creating staggering new challenges for managers.

It's an environment characterized by *increased volatility* and *greater uncertainty.* The average product lifecycle is shrinking, meaning that companies need to bring more products to market, and do it faster. Consumers are becoming more demanding, insisting on more value at lower price points. There is a growing need to continually come up with something *new* (product or service or market) or something *better* (efficiencies, product features, customization, personalization etc.).

Meanwhile, new technologies and business models are lowering barriers to entry, introducing disruptive changes, and creating asymmetric competition. Competitive intensity has increased as technological innovation has accelerated. According to a global survey of corporate executives conducted by McKinsey, 85 percent of respondents described the business environment in which their companies operate as either "more competitive" (45 percent) or "much more competitive" (40 percent) than it was five years ago. The report noted that this competitive intensity is increasing for small as well as big companies, and across all industrial sectors.[43]

Meanwhile, the speed, efficiency, and global nature of financial markets generates a steady drumbeat of demand for greater shareholder value, trimmer balance sheets, and stronger bottom lines.

In short, companies are compelled to deliver along multiple and seemingly contradictory dimensions. They have to be better *and* cheaper *and* faster—all at the same time!

Here's where the phenomenon that we refer to as the "services shift" can, and should, come into play.

We contend that most of these forces compel companies to look offshore for solutions to at least some of their problems. From a defensive standpoint, they need to lower their costs to compete—and offshoring certainly offers that prospect. But offshoring also allows companies to be proactive in shaping their futures: by improving the quality of products and services, developing new offerings, and—over the long term—creating toeholds in the economies and markets that will be most important years and decades down the road.

Endnotes

[1] Personal interview with Raman Roy, Founder and CEO of Spectramind eServices, Gurgaon, India, April 2002.

[2] "Wipro Fact File," Wipro, www.wipro.com/aboutus/fact_file.htm (accessed on February 12, 2008).

[3] Anjali Cordeiro. "Wall Street Looks to India to Boost Equity Research Ops." Dow Jones Newswires, February 13, 2006.

[4] Eric Bellman and Nathan Koppel, "Legal Services Enter Outsourcing Domain." *Wall Street Journal.* September 28, 2005.

[5] John C. McCarthy, "Near-Term Growth of Offshoring Accelerating," Forrester Research, May 2004.

[6] Faiz Kermani, "Patient Recruitment for Clinical Trials," whitepaper for Chiltern International and Piribo, Ltd, 2005, p. 4.

[7] Michael Arndt, "Lilly's Labs Go Global," *BusinessWeek Online* (Jan 2006), http://aol.businessweek.com/print/magazine/content/06_05/b3969416.htm? chan=gl.

[8] Michael Arndt, "Lilly's Labs Go Global," *BusinessWeek Online* (Jan 2006), http://aol.businessweek.com/print/magazine/content/06_05/b3969416.htm? chan=gl.

[9] David Tong, "Singapore's Reply to Offshoring—Build Biopolis, Create New Jobs," *San Francisco Chronicle*, April 18, 2004.

[10] "Strategic Review 2007: Annual Review of the Indian IT-BPO Sectors," NASSCOM, Feb 2007.

[11] "Strategic Review 2007: Annual Review of the Indian IT-BPO Sectors," NASSCOM, Feb 2007, p. 146.

[12] "Indian IT Industry Factsheet (2008)," NASSCOM, www.nasscom.in/upload/ 5216/Strategic_Review_Feb2008.pdf.

[13] "Infosys Annual Report 2006–2007," Infosys, 2007.

[14] "Medical Transcription—Predicting the Future," Akshaya—Kerala IT Mission, India, 2003.

[15] "Medical Transcription—Predicting the Future," Akshaya—Kerala IT Mission, India, 2003.

[16] "The U.S. Medical Transcription Industry: Perspective on Outsourcing and Offshoring," Research and Markets ValueNotes, May 2006.

[17] "AAMT Answers Frequently Asked Questions About Medical Transcription," American Association of Medical Transcription, 2003.

[18] Julekha Dash, "Tough Passage to India," *Baltimore Business Journal* (July 1, 2005).

[19] "The U.S. Medical Transcription Industry: Perspective on Outsourcing and Offshoring," Research and Markets ValueNotes, May 2006.

[20] Julekha Dash, "Tough Passage to India," *Baltimore Business Journal* (July 1, 2005).

[21] "About CBay," CBay Systems, www.cbaysystems.com/us/about/index.htm (accessed on February 21, 2008).

[22] "Offshore Medical Transcription Outsourcing Service(s) Philippines," MedScript Asia, 2008.

[23] Alexander Villafania, "U.S. medical transcription firm to open office in RP," INQUIRER.net, July 04, 2007, http://newsinfo.inquirer.net/breakingnews/infotech/view_article.php?article_id=74796.

[24] Robert Wachter, "The Dis-location of U.S. Medicine—the Implication of Medical Outsourcing," *The New England Journal of Medicine* (February 16, 2006).

[25] Henry J. Aaron and William B. Schwartz, *Can We Say No?: The Challenge of Rationing Health Care* (Brookings Institution Press, 2005), p. 85.

[26] 2007 AMGA Physician Compensation Survey, CEJKA Physician Search, www.cejkasearch.com/compensation/amga_physician_compensation_survey.htm, accessed on February 19, 2008.

[27] Robert Kennedy, "IT-Enabled Services (F): Teleradiology Solutions, Inc." Case Study, Michigan Business School, September 6, 2003.

[28] Teleradiology Solutions Overview, Teleradiology Solutions, www.telradsol.com/about_us.html, accessed on February 19, 2008.

[29] Personal interview with Achaih Palekanda, Wipro, September 5, 2007.

[30] In addition to its many other provisions, the U.S. Health Insurance Portability and Accountability Act of 1996 (HIPAA) established privacy standards. See http://aspe.hhs.gov/admnsimp/pl104191.htm.

[31] Lourdes, Wikipedia. Retrieved February 21, 2008 from http://en.wikipedia.org/wiki/Lourdes.

[32] Walecia Konrad, "Employers make a push for 'medical tourism,'" *FSB* (May 2007), http://money.cnn.com/magazines/fsb/fsb_archive/2007/05/01/100003808/index.htm (accessed on February 19, 2008).

[33] K. Janiga and R. E. Kennedy, "Going Global (D): Apollo Hospitals," Case Study, Michigan Ross School of Business, August 2004.

[34] "Healthcare in India: The Road Ahead" Confederation of Indian Industry and McKinsey & Co., 2002.

[35] Jeff Pope, "The Globalization of Medicine: The Emerging Market of Medical Tourists—Estimates, Challenges and Prospects," http://sbus.montclair.edu/cib/Conference%20CD/Section%2013.pdf.

[36] Pankaj Ghemawat and Ken A. Mark, "The Real Wal-Mart Effect," HBS Working Knowledge, August 2006.

[37] Catherine Mann, "Globalization of IT Services and White Collar Jobs: The Next Wave of Productivity Growth." International Economics Policy Briefs, December 2003.

[38] Martin Baily and Diana Farrell, "Exploding the Myths of Offshoring," *McKinsey Quarterly* (July 2004).

[39] Andrea Bierce, et. al., "The Real Offshoring Question," *Executive Agenda* (Third Quarter, 2004).

[40] L. Brainard and R. E. Litan, "'Offshoring' Service Jobs: Bane or Boon—and What to Do?" Brookings Institution Policy, Brief No. 132, April 2004.

[41] R. E. Kennedy, "The Global Business Environment," Case Study, Michigan Ross School of Business, August 2004.

[42] Wilson, Dominic, Purushothaman, and Roopa, "Dreaming with BRICs: The Path to 2050," Goldman Sachs Global Economics Paper No. 99, October 2003.

[43] "The McKinsey Global Survey of Business Executives: Confidence Index," *McKinsey Quarterly* (April 2006).

2

The Economics and Drivers of Offshoring

Business today is tougher, faster, more global, and more competitive.

Companies are being forced to be *really good* at what they do. They have to be more effective, more efficient, and more innovative. They have to beat their competition based on some combination of cost and quality.

In this chapter, we dig more deeply into exactly how that's done in the context of a service business. We also look more systematically at the drivers that lie behind the globalization of the services sector today. What's pushing businesses to go outside their traditional boundaries and geographies? Are those forces here to stay, or are they reversible? Are they likely to wane, or intensify?

First, though, we explore two conceptual tools—value chain and transaction cost economics—that will help you understand and embrace the move of services outside the walls of your company, possibly to the other side of the world.

Putting on the Economist's Hat

We want to maintain a practical orientation in this book. Even if we see an opportunity to dive into a corner of economics that we find theoretically interesting, we mostly will resist that temptation.

That said, it makes sense at this point to take a brief look at two economic frameworks—the value chain and transaction cost economics—which, taken together, provide a useful perspective with which to consider your firm and its opportunities to offshore and/or outsource. These frameworks provide insight into issues such as the following: How does your firm create value? Are there opportunities to create value by moving activities across firm or geographic boundaries? If so, how should you identify activities, select partners, and manage risks?

The Value Chain: The Firm as a Sequence of Linked Activities

As consumers and customers, we buy products and services that we believe will enhance our lives in some way. By and large, we don't think a lot about what's involved in *producing* a good or service; we just want the value that's inherent in it.

Similarly, as employees and employers, we generally focus on performing our jobs in a way that helps deliver value to our customers, be they consumers in retail stores or corporate customers in a larger chain of value creation. Again, despite being touched by firms (our own and others) on a daily basis, we tend not to think about how the activities within firms are linked, or how each creates value—either by itself or through its linkages with other activities. But when we begin contemplating moving some aspect of our enterprise offshore, it's important to focus more closely on the process of value creation.

One way to think about how firms create and capture value is a framework originally developed by Harvard Professor Michael Porter. The value chain approach was first presented in Porter's 1985 book *Competitive Advantage*.[1]

Prior to the emergence of the value-chain approach, strategic analysis generally looked at the firm as a single unit. The analyst would consider a firm's strengths, weaknesses, opportunities, and threats: the so-called SWOT analysis. This approach relied on impressions (that is, "I think we're good at service"), but because the typical firm encompassed such a broad range of activities, it was difficult to know what specific activities to focus on, what data to gather, or what analysis to perform in order to reveal the sources of competitive advantage.

Porter's central insight was that a firm is actually a system of interconnected activities, with both physical and information linkages. A firm's competitive position in the marketplace results from superior or inferior performance in specific activities. With this perspective as a starting point, activity-level performance can be explored analytically, and strategies can be formulated to improve the firm's position.

As illustrated in Figure 2.1, the framework splits a firm's activities into primary and support activities.

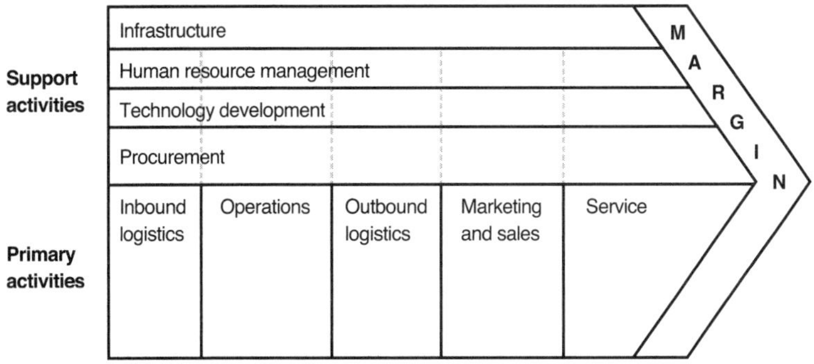

Figure 2.1   The generic value chain

Source: *Competitive Advantage: Creating and Sustaining Superior Performance*, p. 37.

Primary activities are the steps that directly impact the product/service that customers care about. In a manufacturing firm, these include inbound logistics, operations, outbound logistics (distribution), marketing and sales, and service. Support activities are those that provide the background necessary for the effective and efficient operation of the firm, but which do not impact the main product/service directly. Support activities typically include human resources, information technology, and accounting.

Value chain analysis posits that competitive advantage occurs at the activity (or functional) level. The analysis and strategy formulation process consists of three distinct steps:

- Breaking down the firm's key functions into primary and support activities.
- Assessing the potential for adding value in each activity. This generally involves benchmarking against best-practice competitors and determining sources of superior or inferior performance.
- Formulating strategies that focus on key activities which enable companies to sustain a competitive advantage. This generally involves strategies to lower costs or create a differentiation for which customers are willing to pay a premium.

The value chain framework provides several insights. First, *competitive advantage results from superior performance in specific activities*. In most industries, one or a few activities are "core"—that is, they are the keys to competitive advantage. The value-chain approach argues that managers should *focus their efforts on improving performance in core activities*, meanwhile making sure that other, non-core activities are performed at an acceptable level. These non-core activities are good candidates for outsourcing, particularly if there are outside firms that specialize in these non-core activities (for example, ADP in payroll processing, EDS in running data centers, and Hewitt Associates in managing human resources processes).

A second insight, implied earlier, is that *there are two generic sources of competitive advantage: low cost and differentiation*. Firms can win in the marketplace either by offering standard products at the lowest cost or by distinguishing their products in such a way that customers are willing to pay a premium for them. Again, cost strategies and differentiation take place at the activity level.

An often-overlooked extension of this insight is that a firm should select one overarching strategy (low cost or differentiated) and configure all activities to support this strategy—that is, bring them into alignment. Stated the other way around, if a firm focuses some of its activities on lowering costs and others on creating differentiation, the result is likely to be a strategic muddle.

Wal-Mart, for example, has extraordinarily low costs because it has configured all its activities to minimize costs. The firm has massive scale in logistics and distribution, offers low-cost generic products, and invests little in its stores or merchandising. As you will see later, there are many situations where moving an activity offshore or to a third party can dramatically cut costs.

Apple, on the other hand, follows a differentiation strategy. The computer and consumer-electronics maker focuses relentlessly on product design and the user experience. Much of its logistics, manufacturing, and service functions are outsourced to third parties. Apple spends heavily to differentiate its products, and the experience of recent years—iPods, iTunes, iPhones, and so on—shows that customers are willing to pay for this.

The third insight from the value chain framework is that *firms should focus on a few key activities*—and specifically, those that provide competitive advantage. Other activities, typically support activities, are less important and can be moved away.

Why is this perspective important for our purposes? Because once you examine your company as a series of interlinked activities—some of which it is better at than others—you can see quickly that you don't need to perform *all* of the tasks in the series in order to create value. Let's look at two common examples—janitorial and food services—as shown in Figure 2.2.

All companies have to keep their physical premises clean; many also decide that for one reason or the another—lack of local resources, efficiency, and so on—they need to offer onsite food

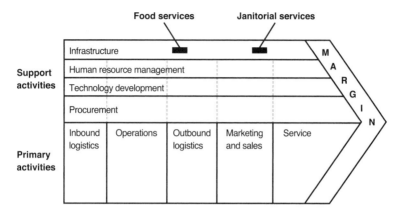

Figure 2.2   Two support activities within the firm's value chain

options for their employees. For most companies, though, these tasks are not considered primary, value-creating activities (nor do they tend to play to the strengths of companies outside of these specialized fields). As a result, they often are outsourced to the lowest bidder on a contract basis, with certain quality expectations being specified in the contracting phase. Since the 1980s, there has been a trend toward outsourcing activities that firms view as non-core—food service, data center operations, service, and so on.

Thinking through Transaction Cost Economics

Because some tasks can be handled more effectively and at a lower cost by outsiders, managers have to decide which tasks are best performed internally, and which should be outsourced. Ronald Coase is one of many economists who have looked at this fundamental make-or-buy decision; his work in the field of "transaction cost economics" earned him a Nobel Prize in Economics in 1991.

Coase first laid out the fundamentals of transactions costs economics (TCE) in a 1937 paper titled "The Nature of the Firm,"[2] in which he explored why some economic transactions occur inside of firms whereas others are mediated by the market. The theory was greatly extended by University of California, Berkeley economist Oliver Williamson in a series of books and articles, most notably

Market and Hierarchies: Analysis and Antitrust Implications (1975)[3] and *The Economic Institutions of Capitalism: Firms, Markets, Relational Contracting* (1985).[4] TCE explores the factors that influence whether transactions take place inside of firms or across firm boundaries—sometimes referred to as the internalization/externalization decision.

The basic tradeoff is that market-mediated transactions provide powerful incentives for efficiency and performance, but often incur significant transaction costs. Performing an activity internally generally lowers transaction costs, but often means 1) higher administrative costs, and 2) fewer or less-powerful incentives for performance.

Traditional economics focused merely on the cost of producing and distributing products. The insight provided by Coase and Williamson is that firms incur other significant costs when engaging in market-mediated transactions. *It is the total cost of exchange—production plus transaction costs—that should determine where an activity should take place.*

Transaction costs fall into three broad categories:

- **Search and information costs**—These are incurred as the firm determines what its options are, if goods are available in the marketplace, who has the lowest price, and who has the best reputation. In some markets, search costs are quite high. Consider real estate and dating services: People pay tens of thousands of dollars to the intermediaries who have information on homes and potential spouses.

  With offshoring, even if the potential for savings exists, many firms incur significant search costs to evaluate potential geographies, find potential suppliers, evaluate their capabilities and reputations, evaluate options, and so on. These costs are declining as intermediaries arise and information sources are created. For most firms, however, they are still high.

- **Bargaining costs**—These are incurred in the process of coming to an acceptable agreement with the other party. This might include communication and travel costs, costs incurred while bargaining (such as legal or consulting fees), the possibility that negotiation tactics kill your value-creating deal, and the costs of drawing up an appropriate contract.

In the context of outsourcing, these contracts are referred to as **service level agreements (SLAs)** and can be quite detailed. We return to SLAs in Chapter 3, "Making It Real."

- **Policing and enforcement costs**—These are the costs inherent in making sure the other party sticks to the terms of the contract (monitoring), and of taking appropriate action—often through the legal system—when it doesn't.

TCE is based on two departures from traditional economic thinking. Traditional economic models assume both *perfect information* and *easy enforcement*. Any practicing manager will quickly point out that neither assumption is realistic—and in fact, Williamson questioned them both. First, he introduced the idea of **bounded rationality**, which refers to the fact that people have limited memories and limited ability to process information. This implies that information is costly to gather and, even when available, may not be used to reach optimal decisions. Consider the game of chess. Even though all the rules and options are known before the game starts, no person is capable of flawlessly analyzing every option that might occur in the course of the game.

Managers face the same problem. No matter how hard they work, they never can have all the relevant information, nor can they know all the consequences of every possible course of action.

Even if an executive knows that offshoring makes sense, he or she is not likely to know all potential suppliers, each supplier's capabilities and reputation, and the range and probability of all potential outcomes (for example, great performance, stolen data, takeovers of one or both parties, financial stress, etc.).

Williamson's second departure from classical economics involves **opportunism**. This refers to the possibility that people will act in a self-interested way, taking advantage of unforeseen circumstances that provide the chance to exploit the other party. Opportunism is generally a larger problem when transacting across firms. True, it frequently occurs inside firms, as well, but in that context it can be countered more easily with administrative procedures.

An example of opportunism is holdup. Imagine that a firm outsources its accounting functions. As soon as the in-house accounting staff is let go, the firm's bargaining power vis-à-vis the supplier may be greatly weakened. The opportunistic supplier firm may take the earliest possible opportunity to renegotiate for better terms.

When you combine limited information, bounded rationality, and the fear of opportunistic behavior, you can see why firms worry about being held up—and they might invest significant resources to avoid bad outcomes.

The real explanatory power of TCE comes from three variables that can be used to describe any transaction. They are *frequency*, *uncertainty*, and *asset specificity*. According to TCE, these three variables (alone or in combination) determine whether transactions costs will be lowest in a market or in a hierarchy.

- **Frequency**—If the transaction or activity is needed only infrequently, it is most likely to be purchased on the market. Consider legal work, management consultancy, or an IPO. Few operating firms would create internal capabilities in these areas because it would be difficult to justify the investment. Each involves specialized skills that are employed infrequently. In these cases, it makes sense to put these resources in a focused firm that can service whatever demand arises, rather than having dedicated resources in a particular operating firm.

- **Uncertainty**—A second important variable is how difficult it is to foresee all possible factors that might affect a transaction. One obvious factor is the length of time over which the transaction takes place. A second is the range of outcomes. Purchasing a gallon of milk has low uncertainty: You pay for the milk, take it home, and determine whether it's good or not good. A ten-year equipment lease, by contrast, has many uncertainties. Many factors could change over the ten years, including technology, the financial condition of one or both parties, and the presence or absence of alternative uses. Long-lived transactions are likely to occur inside the firm—or, if they are moved across firm boundaries, they tend to incur higher costs of contracting, monitoring, and enforcing contract provisions.

Uncertainty about the range of outcomes can work both ways. On the one hand, uncertainty creates room for opportunistic behavior, which tends to raise transactions costs—thus seeming to call for inside-the-firm provision. On the other hand, some types of uncertainty create the opportunity for shared services (say, a call center) that allows the uncertainty about an individual firm's demand to be diversified by being pooled across several firms.

- **Asset specificity**—This applies to those situations in which an asset is much more valuable in one transaction than in any alternative use. For example, an auto parts supplier may be asked to locate next to an assembly plant. The supplier incurs large capital costs to build and equip the factory. If the assembly plant owner goes out of business or attempts to renegotiate, the supplier has few options. Because the managers of the supplier are presumably forward-looking and realize this possibility, they will demand contract provisions to protect them.

To summarize this point: Transaction-specific assets make internal provision more likely.

We hope it is clear that the value chain and TCE frameworks translate rather directly to decisions regarding whether to outsource and/or offshore. Activities that are non-core, transaction oriented (as opposed to long-lived), involve relatively low uncertainty, and do not involve transaction-specific assets are strong candidates for outsourcing. Activities such as answering customer queries in a call center, managing accounts payable and receivable, and human resources administration fit these criteria well.

Any of these features can be overcome with some bargaining and contracting effort. In many cases, the savings from going offshore are large enough to overcome even substantial transactions costs.

From its original articulation more than a half-century ago, TCE has focused on cost minimization. This is more than just "good housekeeping"; in fact, the cost-minimization perspective inherent in TCE has profound implications for managers. Oliver Williamson, mentioned earlier, has argued that cost minimization and operational efficiency of the firm—which he calls "economizing"—are actually more important to business strategy than formal "strategizing." For example, Williamson describes why two firms in the same industry with the same technology and the same customers can often differ dramatically in profitability. As he puts it, it's

> ...not because the managers in one are working harder than managers in the other. Instead, managers in the two firms are working equally hard but one is working smarter—better organization form; better internal incentives and controls; better alignment of the contractual interfaces.[5]

The best longitudinal data on the growth of transaction costs, as summarized in Table 2.1, seem to validate Coase and Williamson's arguments, and strongly suggest that the traditional economic notion of costs being primarily *production*-related is a badly antiquated view.

TABLE 2.1   The Rise of Transactions Costs[6]

Year	Transaction Costs from Private Sector	Transaction Costs from Public Sector	Total Transaction Cost Sector in % of U.S. GDP
1870	22.5%	3.6%	26.1%
1890	29.1%	3.6%	32.7%
1910	31.5%	3.7%	35.2%
1930	38.2%	8.2%	46.3%
1950	40.3%	10.9%	51.2%
1970	40.8%	13.9%	54.7%

In other words, the 100-year trend toward increased transaction costs between 1870 and 1970 both underscores the centrality of *transactions* in the American economic system and the large-scale shift to a (transaction-intensive) service economy. This trend helps validate Williamson's conclusion that the companies that best manage transactions costs are most likely to be successful.

Outsourcing and Offshoring: Digging Deeper

Now let's return to the real, rough-and-tumble world of outsourcing and offshoring. As we've already noted, companies don't have to perform all of the activities that ultimately are required to create value for their customers. Firms can partner with other companies (very often, established vendors) and *outsource* some of these activities to them.

At the same time, in the increasingly globalized context of business, the power of analyzing your firm's sourcing options using the value chain and TCE frameworks is only growing. Firms are no longer constrained to perform all value-creating activities within the borders of their home countries. Some of these activities can be located *offshore* (outside the national borders of the firm's home country) to places where they can be carried out most effectively. Phrased slightly differently, for many service companies, *new sources of value are likely to be found outside the boundaries of the firm and the nation.*

Firms that decide to pursue those new sources of value generally face two key decisions, as represented in Figure 2.3.

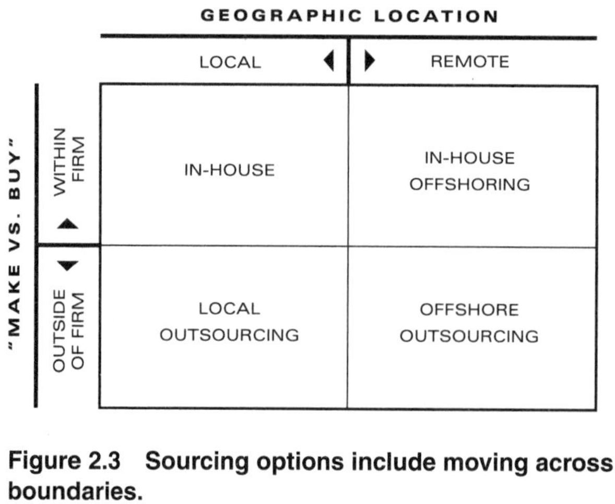

GEOGRAPHIC LOCATION

	LOCAL ◀ ▶	REMOTE
WITHIN FIRM	IN-HOUSE	IN-HOUSE OFFSHORING
OUTSIDE OF FIRM	LOCAL OUTSOURCING	OFFSHORE OUTSOURCING

"MAKE VS. BUY"

Figure 2.3   Sourcing options include moving across firm *or* geographic boundaries.

The first is the "make or buy" decision: Do you perform the activity within the firm, or do you outsource it to another firm? The second relates to the geographic location: Should the activity be located "locally" (that is, within the same country) or remotely (abroad)?

The several ways that companies answer these questions lead to different sourcing options, including the following:

- Performing the activity locally and in-house
- Moving to remote provision but keeping the activity in-house
- Outsourcing it locally
- Outsourcing it to a remote location

For example, General Electric might choose to perform research on a new plastic in its laboratory in Connecticut (in-house), contract with a vendor in Connecticut to build its supply-chain application (local outsourcing), conduct R&D in its own center in India (in-house offshoring), and procure finance and accounting (F&A) services from a vendor in China (offshore outsourcing).

Note, too, that a company can use different options for different activities; it also can use multiple options for the same activity. Dell, for example, operates call centers globally, as well as procures these services from vendors across the world. According to Romi Malhotra, who runs Dell's India operations, global outsourcing enables Dell to manage the seasonality that is inherent in the company's customer-service workload. It also helps the company benchmark and fix its costs, broaden its experience and knowledge base, and mitigate geographical risk.[7]

With our two-by-two of the basic outsourcing and offshoring options in mind, let's now look at each of these phenomena in greater detail.

Outsourcing: Moving Across Firm Boundaries

Outsourcing is the contracting out of specific corporate tasks to an external company or person. Almost every organization engages with external parties—commonly called third-party providers or service providers—to perform at least some of its tasks. Outsourcing can occur either onsite (for example, janitorial and food services), at a remote location (for example, payroll processing by ADP), or in the case of certain support functions, both.

Typically, the function being outsourced is considered non-core to the business. Looking back to an example cited earlier, janitorial services are nowhere near the core of the performance of a financial-services firm. (Will excellent in-house performance in janitorial services give JPMorgan Chase a competitive advantage today or in the future? No.)

Every company's motivations for outsourcing are different. As implied by the value chain analysis presented earlier in the chapter, some companies outsource low-value activities so that they can focus their resources on higher-value and more critical tasks. Others outsource higher-value activities that require a specific skill set—such as deep or broad corporate legal skills—that they don't have, and don't particularly want to develop, within the firm. (For example, most companies below a certain size have trouble covering the entire waterfront of corporate legal questions, and very few can cover all those areas in depth.) Still others, such as Dell, outsource to absorb seasonality in demand for the activity: You may not want to hire additional employees to help you out with that holiday-related jump in demand.

Although it's a safe bet that outsourcing in one form or another has been around as long as people have been doing business, only recently have firms started contracting out important-but-non-core business processes such as payroll and billing—most often to specialized vendors who make those processes their own core activity. As noted in Chapter 1, "Globalization of Services: What, Why, and When," information technology outsourcing (ITO) and business process outsourcing (BPO) have been growing rapidly in recent years.

ITO gained momentum in July 1989 when Eastman Kodak—then a Fortune 20 company—decided to outsource much of its IT function. Kodak handed over its entire data center, microcomputer operations, telecommunications, and data networks to a group of third-party providers (including IBM, Digital Equipment Corp., and Businessland) in a ten-year, $250-million deal. This move marked a dramatic departure from the traditional corporate stance of close, in-house control of IT. With the Kodak experience and similar precedents in mind, more and more companies started considering ITO a viable strategic option, and in the ensuing two decades, the ITO deals have become larger and more complex. P&G outsourced its IT infrastructure management to H-P in a ten-year deal worth $3 billion. Du-Pont signed a similar deal with Convergys for $1.1 billion.

Just as one shoe never fits all, there's almost no chance that outsourcing will prove to be a solution to all, or even most, of your competitive problems. The key questions, therefore, are *why* and *when* you should outsource, and the answers will vary depending on the activity or process you are looking at, and the strategic and operational pressures facing your firm and the industry. Broadly speaking, outsourcing can help you reduce distractions and focus your resources on your core competencies, get access to additional financial resources by lowering your operating costs and investment needs, and tap into external capabilities.

If you are exploring the outsourcing of a particular activity, consider the following factors.

Business Importance

Evaluate the contribution that this process makes toward your business strategy and competitiveness. This evaluation should address such questions as the following:

- **Does it give you a competitive advantage?** If the afore-mentioned Apple—which aims to make sophisticated technology comprehensible to mere mortals—asked itself this question about, say, product design, the answer would be a clear "yes." If Shell Oil asked itself the same question, the answer would not be so clear-cut.

- **Is the process unique/proprietary to you?** A pharmaceutical company would be unlikely to outsource an activity if, by so doing, it would reveal confidential information about its drug formulations, current research programs, and so on. Similarly, an insurance company wouldn't outsource back-office functions if that would risk revealing the proprietary algorithms it uses to screen applications and set rates.

- **Does it involve sensitive business information?** As noted, you don't want your competitors to know where you're going next. In addition, you and your colleagues have a deep understanding of your business context—a perspective that potential vendors are unlikely to have. If an activity requires reservoirs of what might be called "tacit knowledge," it's an unlikely candidate for outsourcing.

If the answer to any of these three questions is "yes," you probably *don't* want to outsource the process—at least not entirely, or precipitously.

Process Characteristics

Some processes are easier to outsource than others. When considering the feasibility of outsourcing, you should think through the defining characteristics of the proposed activity. Remember that to outsource successfully, you need to be able both to *specify your expectations* and *monitor what the vendor delivers*. In many, many cases, this is more easily said than done!

Following are some additional factors to take into consideration, as you approach the challenge of outsourcing:

- Making the financial/business case—Early on, of course, you have to work the numbers that support (or don't support) outsourcing. You have to identify the strategic and operational

Delta Outsources as a Key Element of Its Emergence from Bankruptcy

Delta Airlines filed for Chapter 11 bankruptcy protection in September 2005. Its strategy to work its way out of bankruptcy focused on reduce operating costs and boosting revenue while maintaining service levels to stay competitive. One of the restructuring initiatives involved the consolidation and outsourcing of its finance and accounting activities—previously spread across 11 European locations. Accenture won the business in 2006 with a proposal to service the airline from Prague (Czech Republic). Delta also outsourced its data center operations, customer reservations, business record-keeping, flight management, and maintenance-tracking systems to IBM that same year.

These moves, among others, saved Delta more than $3 billion annually and allowed the airline to emerge from bankruptcy after 19 months of restructuring.

returns—as well as the risks—and build a business case. Beware of the human tendency to emphasize the positive when it comes to a change of this potential importance. Just how real *are* those potential gains? In the same spirit, what can go wrong? What impact would these failures have on the business?

- **Separability**—Not all processes are easily moved across firm boundaries. At the risk of stating the obvious, processes don't take place in a vacuum; there are almost always upstream and downstream linkages with other processes, both in-house and external. A process for approving the purchase of a part from a vendor, for example, may involve purchasing, product management, engineering, inventory management, and so on. If this is the case, outsourcing one piece of the process (for example, inventory management) might be difficult.

As a rule, for a process to be outsourced successfully, it must have limited and well-defined interfaces to other processes. You should recognize that *some phases of an activity may be more separable than others.* For example, it may be difficult or impossible to separate the process of researching and drafting a

Backsourcing: Going in the Opposite Direction

Here's another wildcard to consider: Outsourcing is reversible. Not everything that you outsource needs to remain with vendors forever. Deals may not work out, or your priorities may change. We call the reversal of an outsourcing decision "backsourcing" (that is, bringing it back home).

Backsourcing doesn't necessarily imply a failed outsourcing. In some cases, companies that outsource learn a great deal of useful information about the outsourced function, and eventually feel that they can "repatriate" that function and perform it themselves in a way that creates a competitive advantage. In other cases, the outsourcing company acquires new capabilities—oftentimes through a merger or acquisition—which prompts a revisiting of the outsourcing decision.

In one of the largest outsourcing contracts to date, financial services giant JPMorgan Chase signed a $5 billion, seven-year IT outsourcing agreement with IBM at the end of 2002. It was intended to transform JPMorgan Chase's technology infrastructure through "absolute costs savings, increased cost variability, access to the best research and innovation, and improved service levels."[8]

Two years later, however, following its merger with Bank One, JPMorgan Chase terminated the outsourcing pact with IBM, a decision that effectively backsourced most of the company's IT services within the JPMorgan Chase umbrella again. The merger with Bank One enabled JPMorgan Chase to acquire new operational expertise, prompting the company to "switch from IBM to self-sufficiency to take advantage of Bank One's cost-cutting know-how."[9] The world had changed, and JPMorgan Chase now appeared to have the capability in-house to save more money and deliver higher-quality processes than by using an external party.

report—which tends to involve lots of interviewing and collaborative work. Once the report is developed, however, the copyediting and proofreading phases are likely to be more separable, and therefore easier to outsource. Stated the other way around, outsourcing of processes with low separability tends to generate increased interaction costs, confusion, and finger pointing!

- **Transferability**—To be able to move a process across a firm boundary (to a vendor), you also have to be able to transfer the capacity to *run* that process. Again, because your company is so familiar with the task at hand, you and your colleagues may underestimate its complexity, requiring regular applications of experience and judgment. Complexity does not automatically disqualify a task from being outsourced; it simply means that documentation of the process—and of the active transferable knowledge—must be addressed carefully. If the knowledge is "all in the head" of the employees who currently run the process (so-called tacit knowledge), that knowledge somehow has to be gotten out of their heads and into process documentation. Offshoring firms are very good at documenting processes. If you choose to outsource, your in-house experts on operational specifics will be crucial during the transition of the process to the vendor. Those with the tacit knowledge often find this transfer process threatening, so it is important to manage communications and expectations carefully.

- **Manageability**—When you outsource, you enter into a legal contract with the vendor. This means that you have to be able to represent the service levels that you need to get out of this contractual relationship, which once again means that the process and its desired outcomes must be well defined.

  Consider two functions: writing software and an executive secretary supporting senior-level managers. It is relatively easy to specify how a new piece of software is supposed to work. A project manager defines the data a program will use, how this data will be manipulated, and what will happen with the information generated (for example, specific reports or data feeds that must be produced). The specification would further indicate what hardware and operating systems would be used and what programs the new software must interact with. A large software program may be complicated, but producing the documentation of how the program should perform and determining whether the code delivered performs according to spec are relatively straightforward.

  Now consider how you would specify and monitor performance by an executive assistant. Drafting a complete list of responsibilities would be difficult (be friendly, stay one step ahead of your boss, exercise good judgment about whether to pass through "urgent" phone calls when he is in a meeting). It would be even more difficult to accurately monitor the assistant's performance analytically. At the end of the year, the executive is either pleased with the assistant's performance, or not. The executive would not say, "You were friendly on 183 days, but fell below standard on 57 days." Because of these differences in the ability to specify and monitor performance, many firms outsource software engineering, whereas few outsource support for executive-level assistants.

- **Market capabilities**—Before taking the outsourcing plunge, you need to assess the likelihood that the market can actually deliver the processes you are planning to outsource. How many vendors can deliver the solutions? From what locations? How well?

  To a certain extent, this is a question of market maturity. (In an immature market, the demand may be out in front of the supply.) Giant companies such as American Express and General Electric can reshape the market by creating more or less dependent entities to which they outsource specific functions—and then wait for the marketplace to catch up. If and when vendors proliferate and become competitive, the giants can shift to more arm's length relationships, or perhaps even spin out their previously captive operations—as GE did with its India operation in January 2005, creating Genpact. For companies that are not giants, of course, this is an unrealistic scenario. If the suppliers aren't out there, and if you aren't in a position to call them into being, then it's simply too soon to attempt to outsource this particular function.

- **Organizational/soft issues**—Organizational, cultural, and other "soft" issues can impact outsourcing substantially. Outsourcing may lead to big changes—and, of course, change can be disruptive and difficult. In fact, understanding and managing the organizational issues around change well may be the most important contributor to ensuring the success of your outsourcing effort.

  Outsourcing to keep up with booming demand will be much less disruptive than outsourcing to cut costs during a slump. Workers with marketable skills, such as accountants, software engineers, and graphic artists, will likely be much less disturbed by outsourcing than those with few marketable skills, such as payments clerks or shop stewards in an auto components plant.

Outsourcing is not simply an economic transaction. Formulating a change-management strategy is often an important step. In all cases, both a transparent process and a clear senior management commitment to that process—aimed at educating and creating allies—are extremely important.

Offshoring: Moving Across Geographical Boundaries

As we've all heard countless times, the world is getting smaller. But one relatively unheralded aspect of this process of global change is that developing regions around the world are acquiring new capabilities. As a result, the best place to locate a particular business process may no longer be in your home country.

Simply stated, **offshoring** means the procurement of goods or services across national boundaries. The entity providing the service can be either a corporate subsidiary (captive offshoring) or an external vendor (offshore outsourcing). It's worth noting that even as offshoring gains momentum, the term itself seems to be gradually losing some ground to alternative labels—for instance, global delivery—in part because business processes are increasingly serviced from points all around the world (leading people to question the meaning of a "shore"), and in part because some companies are attempting to sidestep the negative publicity associated with offshoring. For simplicity's sake, we'll stick with "offshoring" here and throughout this book, but it's worth keeping your ear out for the evolving terminology of offshoring.

Though manufacturing companies have long procured both raw materials and finished products from overseas, procuring services from offshore is a relatively new phenomenon. Offshoring in services has historically been difficult because of the formerly insuperable barrier of geography. But the key drivers of globalization—including increasingly sophisticated and ever-cheaper technology, economic liberalization, growing global talent, and many others—have significantly whittled away at the geography barrier. (We'll return to these drivers shortly.) For the first time in history, sophisticated service providers have to ask themselves 1) whether the labor, processes, and technology they utilize for service provision have to be located close to customers, or if they can be accessed remotely, and 2) what degree of managerial control is required over the task. In more and more cases, those service providers are choosing to access resources in low-cost countries. This is offshoring.

General Electric, often a trendsetter, started offshoring its IT functions in the early 1990s. As the business landscape got increasingly more competitive due to globalization, GE began looking outside of North America for growth and competitive advantage, particularly in India. In September 1989, CEO Jack Welch was on a visit to India to sell airplane engines and plastics to the government. During a breakfast meeting, Sam Pitroda, chief technology adviser to the prime minister of India, had another agenda and suggested that GE consider buying software from India.

> I gave him my presentation and I said, "Jack, give me a $10 million dollar software order. I will use it to quick start software export in India." So Jack said, "Fine. In 30 days I will have 12 GE executives coming to India. You show them around and convince them." In 30 days, ten people came. My chief of staff organized many meetings and Jack and the ten person team gave us a $10 million order.[10]

Pleased with the initial work performed out of India, GE began contracting out IT software work to Indian vendors such as Wipro, TCS, and Infosys in 1991. The result: millions of dollars in savings.[11]

Other companies quickly followed suit. In the next significant wave, business process services went offshore when large multinationals such as GE, American Express, and British Airways set up their own offshore business-process subsidiaries. More recently, companies have moved significantly more complex tasks that require the application of decision rules—such as processing insurance claims and conducting clinical trials—offshore. Today, most companies above a certain threshold of size and complexity are engaged in offshoring in one form or another.

Why are they doing so? You already know the most obvious and compelling answer: *cost savings.* The opportunity to arbitrage (that is, buy low, sell high) wage rates is compelling, and because labor constitutes a large part of services, cost advantages can be significant. For example, you can hire software engineers in India at about 20 percent of the rate you would pay in the United States. According to a study published in the *Journal of Corporate Accounting & Finance*, companies that have "aggressively farmed out specific IT and HR tasks to India, Malaysia, Pakistan, Singapore, Ireland, South Africa, and Australia have claimed cost savings of 50–75 percent, even after considering the additional overhead involved in managing a global process."[12]

The study goes on to hint at both some of the challenges inherent in offshoring as well another fundamental argument in favor of it: "While firms now fear a loss of control or less reliable information from outsourcing [offshoring], what they are likely to wind up with is improved state-of-the-art processes."

As offshoring matures, in other words, firms are realizing that the potential advantages go far beyond cost savings (see Table 2.2). In many cases, offshoring enables a company to draw on resources from a more talented (as well as a cheaper) labor pool. In other words, if high school graduates are providing customer service in your call centers now, you could probably hire a college graduate in the Philippines who would provide better service at half the cost.

TABLE 2.2   Three Approaches to Offshoring

Offshoring What?	Notes	Examples
Business process as is	Continue to run the process in a similar manner, but take it offshore.	Medical transcription, call centers
As-is business process with the intent of reengineering	Take the process offshore but reengineer it to make it more efficient and effective.	Insurance claims, clinical drug trials
Innovation and research	Source global talent to carry out your high-end and innovation activities.	R&D, product development

This, in turn, means that *offshoring can act as a trigger for the reengineering of a wide range of business processes.* More than simply a cost-saver, offshoring also could be your gateway to global talent.

When is offshoring appropriate? One way to answer that question is by identifying several factors that work *against* successful offshoring:

- **The need for physical proximity**—Certain kinds of activities (having your hair cut, directing traffic, teaching kindergartners, and so on) require a physical presence. There are many corporate equivalents, many of which are related to the physical needs and comforts of employees, but others of which are in higher-level realms that require the elusive ingredient of "face time" (either peer-to-peer or hierarchical).

- **Restrictive regulatory requirements**—Some local, regional, or national regulations are specifically aimed at hindering offshoring (and the job losses that are presumed to be related to it). The local-content regulations governing certain manufacturing sectors are a case in point. Other regulations restrict offshoring accidentally or incidentally. Take radiology, an example cited in Chapter 1. Although there's nothing that says that medical-imaging data can't be sent halfway around the world and interpreted there, most U.S. states require that radiology reports be signed by a doctor with a license to operate in that state, and it may be hard to find such licensed doctors in an offshore location.

- **The need for in-person contact**—Despite recent advances in virtual-conferencing technologies, some kinds of work simply have to be done in person. CEOs and their general counsels, for example, need to be in close proximity and regular contact. Although this is obviously an extreme case, there are many other compelling examples throughout most organizations. And even among scrupulously law-abiding companies, there are certain kinds of activities for which you may not want a paper or electronic trail. (Early-stage brainstorming might be one. Asking for legal advice on a *Foreign Corrupt Practices Act* issue is another.) Again, in such cases, face-to-face contact may be a prerequisite for doing business.

- **The need for dense information exchange**—This is an extension of the previous point. Some activities are so information-rich that they require extensive personal interaction just to establish a common ground for moving forward. If the continuing contacts tend to be information-rich, unstructured, and random (in terms of time), the activity is an unlikely candidate for offshoring.

With the preceding cautions in mind, it's possible to map out the activities that your company currently performs in terms of what degree of *change* is needed, and how offshoring might meet that need for change. We consider the "how to" specifics in the next chapter.

At the same time, of course, it's important to note that there is an array of new costs associated with offshoring (such as management overhead, infrastructure, training, travel, etc.), as well as risks (such as communications breakdowns, attenuated supply lines, cultural gulfs, etc.), all of which could make these benefits somewhat less attractive to companies in specific circumstances. These topics, too, are addressed in Chapter 3.

The Key Drivers of Services Globalization

You've seen how more and more services are being outsourced and offshored. But because either process tends to require a significant organizational commitment, it's fair to ask the following question: *To what extent is this phenomenon self-limiting or rooted in today's particular market circumstances?*

To answer that question, it's important to understand exactly what's driving services globalization today. We can point to five such "drivers":

- An ongoing global market liberalization
- The digitization of business processes
- The low cost and high speed of computing and telecom
- Growing capabilities around the globe
- The rise of a global business culture

We explored the first of these five drivers, global market liberalization, in Chapter 1. As we noted there, in the amazingly short span of only *13 years,* the percentage of people around the world living in "open" economies rose dramatically: from 23 percent in 1985 to 78 percent in 1998. When borders become more open to economic interactions, increased flow of goods and services across those borders is practically inevitable.

Now let's look more closely at the other four drivers.

Driver #2: The Digitization of Business Processes

The explosion in outsourcing and offshoring is in large part the result of the digitization of a wide range of business processes, including payroll, procurement, customer support, and many others. A dependence on paper effectively roots a business in geography; conversely, the shift from paper to electronic formats makes geography far less relevant.

When one of the authors (Kennedy) worked as an operations manager at Chase Manhattan Bank in the mid-1980s, 70 to 90 percent of client and transaction records were kept in paper files. Expensive Wall Street office space was filled with filing cabinets so that these records were accessible on short notice. A major initiative in 1985–86 was to design a system that allowed remote storage—in New Jersey! A major constraint on this initiative was the effort involved in loading these records onto trucks, transporting them through the Holland tunnel, and storing them in Hoboken. At one point, the estimate was that the bank would have to add around 70 staff and make 50–70 daily roundtrips through the tunnel to support the effort. But it was worth it because of real estate savings.

Compare that with the situation today. More than 90 percent of customer and transaction records are in electronic databases—no banker's boxes, no loading dock staff, and no trucks. Once the information is electronic, it can be almost instantly transmitted to New Jersey, or to India. The options available to operating managers have expanded tremendously, and smart managers are seizing those options.

It's worth noting that the majority of business correspondence is already electronic (see Figure 2.4). This is especially true within the walls of the company: A survey by technology market intelligence provider IDC indicates that *70 percent* of document exchange between employees is already electronic, underscoring the declining importance of geography.[13]

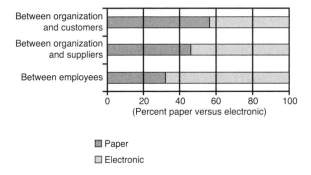

□ Paper
□ Electronic

Figure 2.4   Most communications are now digital: percentage of documents exchanged between organization and customers, suppliers, and employees that are paper versus electronic.

Source: IDC, 2005.

IDC research further suggests that effective document management is correlated with organizations that exhibit above-average growth and are most responsive to flexible market conditions. This stands to reason: Companies that digitize payroll checks, invoices, procurement orders, accounts payable records, and so on are likely to be more accurate and cost-effective. In other words, the same good habits that make a company more competitive domestically help position that company for effective offshoring.

Driver #3: The Low Cost and High Speed of Computing and Telecom

This driver—the increasing availability of high-speed Internet and low-cost telecom—is closely related to the driver just cited. Of course, we're all familiar with the phenomenon of the Internet, but it's worth reminding ourselves that no modern technological advance has ever been embraced as quickly (see Figure 2.5).

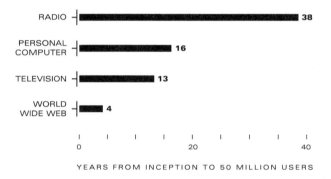

Figure 2.5   Adoption rate for new technologies

Source: *Economist*, Global Policy Forum[14]

The global installation of fiber-optic cable lines during the 1990s by corporations such as Lucent and Global Crossing provided the entire planet with the telecommunications infrastructure necessary for broadband Internet access and inexpensive international connections. In fact, those pioneering companies probably did *too* good a job: Many analysts believe that the current worldwide glut of fiber-optic cable will continue to drive down the already low costs of international communications.

The cost of international telephone calls has dropped every year since 1988, often by double-digit annual percentages.[15] In the same period, the *volume* of international calls has soared. The future looks the same, only more so: With the emergence of Voice over Internet Protocol (VoIP), the cost of international telephony will move even further down to negligible levels. All of this bodes well for the future of offshoring.

What about the personal computer (PC)—the workhorse that pulls the sled of global technological integration? Between 1995 and 2005, the average PC has become much more powerful—with 30 times the memory and a processor that is 15 times as powerful. At the same time, the prices of both desktop and notebook computers have fallen by more than 50 percent. (See Table 2.3 and Figure 2.6.)

TABLE 2.3   Technology's Relentless Advance

Year	Average Desktop Price	Average Notebook Price	Typical Specs
1995	$1,926	$2,819	386DX processor, 35MB–55MB memory
1998	$1,619	$2,395	66MHz processor, 120MB–355MB memory
2000	$1,306	$2,167	133MHz processor, 650MB memory
2001	$1,163	$1,876	233MHz processor, 1.5GB memory
2005	$801	$1,256	1GHz processor, 15GB memory

Source: Yahoo! News[16]

The presence of powerful computers on desktops and laptops around the world ensures that a wide range of individuals and companies can take advantage of the digitization of business processes cited previously. It also means that more and more activities can be located almost anywhere in the world.

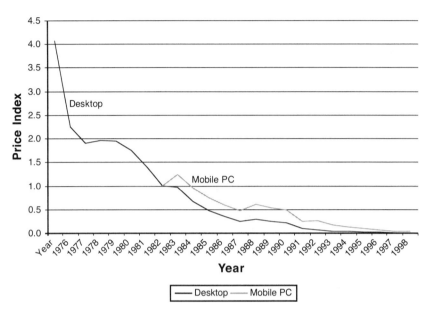

Figure 2.6   Price index (adjusted for quality): desktop computer and mobile laptop

Source: Berndt, Dulberger, and Rappaport[17]

Driver #4: Growing Capabilities Around the Globe

For most of the second half of the twentieth century, much of the world's managerial, engineering, and technical wisdom resided in the developed world, and particularly in the United States, Europe, and Japan. The status quo was reinforced by the fact that the world's leading centers of learning were in those same countries, particularly in the United States. Talented young people from around the world did their undergraduate and graduate studies at one of the United States' many distinguished universities. Many wound up staying in the United States, leading to recurrent complaints about the "brain drain" from the developing to the developed worlds. To cite just one case in point, Rajat Gupta—the former managing director of McKinsey—was an Indian national who went to Harvard for his MBA. Gupta took his first job post-graduation at the McKinsey office in New York, and built the business into an international consulting powerhouse.

In recent years, however, this picture has changed dramatically. Take management education, for example. It's no longer necessary to attend an elite school in the United States to obtain an elite MBA degree. The 2005 MBA rankings from the *Economist Intelligence Unit* identified a Spanish school (IESE at the University of Navarra) as the world's top MBA program, and ten out of the top 25 programs in that particular ranking were located outside the United States. In that same year, the average GMAT score for the entering class at the elite Indian Institute of Management (IIM) in Ahmedabad, India, was 750 (of a possible 800); compared with Harvard's average of 707, and Northwestern's 700.[18] True, the IIM draws from a far larger pool of applicants (more than 100,000), but it also boasts an even higher "yield" than Harvard Business School: In 2004, 100 percent of those admitted to IIM enrolled![19]

What about the output of these newly elite schools? In 2005, 81 percent of the IIM's newly minted MBAs elected to stay in Asia, despite skills that were in great demand in both the United States and Europe. One reason was that the top recruiters at IIM that year included traditional American MBA employers such as Lehman Brothers, Procter & Gamble, and IBM, along with top regional businesses such as Alghanim Industries, Hindustan Lever, and ICICI Bank.[20] Local opportunities put forward by some the world's best companies make it possible—even compelling—for top students to make their careers in their home countries.

IIM is still exceptional, but it is by no means the exception. At the new Indian School of Business (ISB), which includes McKinsey's Gupta as a founder, students who receive offers from multinationals around the world are increasingly choosing to stay domestic in India. As the ISB career office puts it:

> An interesting trend that was witnessed this year at the ISB was that an increased number of students have chosen to opt for domestic offers over international offers. Yashraj Erande, Class of 2006, said, "I was offered a very interesting job by a

U.S.-based technology company. But I knew I wanted to be closer to home, working in the increasingly challenging and versatile business environment, and hence I chose a job offer which gave me a chance to play a pivotal role in India."[21]

The emergence of strong educational and employment opportunities around the world has also converged with new immigration restrictions in the United States in the wake of the terrorist attacks of September 11, 2001. Between 1998 and 2000, visas issued by the United States to foreign students grew by around 13 percent. Between 2001 and 2003, by contrast, student visas plummeted 28 percent.

Meanwhile, there has been a significant drop in American students enrolled in graduate engineering programs over the last two decades (see Figure 2.7). Between 1983 and 2001, graduate school enrollments saw a decline of 21 percent from U.S.-born students,[22] while foreign-student enrollment increased 89 percent.

Additionally, rapidly expanding service firms from emerging economies such as India's Infosys and TCS are aggressively recruiting American students from American companies to work in both the United States and India. Tata added more than 30,000 employees in 2006, with more than 1,000 of them coming from the United States.[23]

What's the upshot? Increasingly, companies that want to recruit and retain the best possible talent have to look all over the world for that talent. In many cases, they will win in the sometimes ferocious competition for that talent only if they can provide compelling local employment opportunities—that is, great jobs in India for Indians, great jobs in China for the Chinese, and so on. And to an extent not seen for at least a century or two, American companies may be compelled to look overseas for great young recruits. Again, this has significant implications for the future of outsourcing and offshoring.

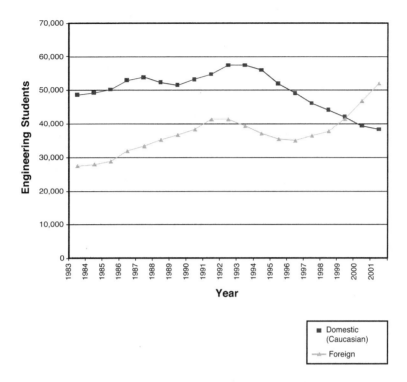

Figure 2.7   Graduate Engineering Students, by national origin

Source: National Science Foundation.

Driver #5: The Rise of a Global Business Culture

Just as the *knowledge* that drove business for many decades resided mainly in Western countries, so did the *culture* of business, broadly defined. This, too, is changing.

Take language, for example. For many years, China's efforts to increase its trade in services have been hampered by its relative lack of competent English-language speakers. But this challenge was identified as a priority by the Chinese government more than a decade ago, and since the mid-1990s, school children in China have been required to learn English starting in primary school. To be sure, there is reason to be skeptical about the overall efficacy of such programs. (An equivalent push in Japan in prior decades was notably unsuccessful.) But the sheer numbers of young people involved will almost certainly lead to literally millions of young Chinese being able to speak the language of global commerce, and thereby being equipped to compete more directly with their counterparts in the United States, India, Ireland, and so on for global service jobs.

The point deserves underscoring. British Finance Minister (and more recently, Prime Minister) Gordon Brown observed in 2005 that within 20 years, the number of English speakers in China would exceed the number of speakers of English as a first language in all of the rest of the world combined.[24]

And of course, the Chinese aren't the only newcomers embracing the "language of business." The British Council estimates that by 2015, 3 billion people—in other words, almost half of the world's total population—will speak more or less fluent English.[25]

TABLE 2.4   An Emerging Global Business Culture

	1980	1990	2002
English language as first or second language (million)	700	950	1,600
Share of international business correspondence	55%	62%	70%
Percentage of emerging-market graduates going home within five years	20%	38%	56%
Number of countries with more than $500 million in venture capital funding	4	12	44

Source: Various sources.[26]

Of course, language is only one of many manifestations of the emergence of a global business culture. Money also talks—and increasingly, the money that fuels new businesses can be found all over the world. Venture capital, for example, has expanded far beyond its original outposts in Silicon Valley, New York, Boston, and the Midwest, and today is a global industry—a trend that is accelerating at a rapid pace.[27]

India and China are today the largest VC destinations outside the United States and Western Europe; each has passed the $1 billion mark in VC investments. According to TSJ Media—a research firm that tracks India's VC market—the first quarter of 2006 saw an infusion of $1.4 billion in VC and private equity in India. This was *three and a half times* as much as was invested in India only a year earlier.[28]

"There is a good chance the next Hotmail or Skype could come from India," says Danish VC pioneer Morten Lund, who was an early investor in Skype. "More money, more international thinking, and the self-confidence to dare to do 'invented here' stuff."[29] In fact, VC investment in India and China now equals that in the U.K., and is higher than in either France or Germany. Key implication is that venture capitalists now see India, China, and some countries in Eastern Europe as a source of innovation and new business products and models.

The Five Drivers: Powerful, and Here to Stay

So there you have it: the five drivers. They exert a powerful influence on global business, and they are only going to increase in importance.

Think back to the discussion of transaction cost economics (TCE) earlier in this chapter. The drivers of globalization suggest the need to both find new ways to work smarter—as prescribed by Oliver Williamson—and be able to adapt the organization structurally and culturally to align with innovative ways to increase efficiency.

For service companies, the drivers of globalization—especially technology and economic liberalization—have led to serious reevaluation of the boundaries of the firm. Much of the historical theory of the firm assumed that the underlying issue of information (access, cost, quality) would force firms to perform most activities in-house. With technology such as the Internet and ubiquitous telephony greatly reducing the information barrier with parties outside the firm, the boundary of the firm has evolved significantly.

To cycle back to the question we asked at the opening of this chapter, is the globalization of services simply a fad, or is it likely to be a permanent and growing phenomenon (and therefore worthy of your careful scrutiny)? The answer to that question grows directly out of our five drivers. Of those five, only the first (the ongoing global market liberalization) can be considered "reversible" in any significant way. Yes, it's conceivable that one or more of the recently liberalized economies—put under some sort of serious social or political strain—could slip back into the kind of static, centralized economic model that characterized their past. Conceivable, but unlikely, because liberalization creates its own momentum. Twenty five years ago, Eastern Europe, most of Africa, and much of Asia was made up of state-controlled economies, with few interactions with the global economy. In those days, moving away from globalization was no big deal because the "global economy" consisted largely of Western Europe, North America, Japan, and a few other outposts such as Taiwan, Hong Kong, and Singapore.

Today, most countries in all three regions are "open" to the global economy. Countries that backslide—such as Zimbabwe and Venezuela—do so largely on their own. Global multinationals are not too concerned, because dozens of other countries are in waiting to take their place, as both consumers and workers in the new global economy.

Our other four drivers (the digitization of business processes, the low cost and high speed of computing and telecom, growing capabilities around the globe, and the rise of a global business culture) exist more or less outside the realm of public policy and legislative fiat. The first two are *technology*-focused, and history suggests that once a technological genie is let out of the bottle, it can't be stuffed back in.

The second two are *people*-focused, and once people have acquired skills and a new (self-interested) way of looking at the world, they are unlikely to be led back into the old, unproductive ways of doing things. Ask almost anyone you meet in Eastern Europe: Like the rest of the world, they want to live in the present, and the future.

Do you need still more data to convince you of the power and irreversibility of offshoring, and its applicability to the services sector? Consider the following:

- Seventy percent of major U.S. companies have begun off-shoring at least some of their business processes.[30]
- Twenty percent of Fortune 500 companies have R&D facilities in India.[31]
- GE has filed 95 patents out of its R&D center in Bangalore.[32]
- Thirty-three percent of Fortune 500 companies have "captive" IT operations in India.[33]
- In India, the ratio of commercial service exports to merchandise exports has increased from 25 percent to 39 percent in the period from 1990 to 2003.[34]

In short, the globalization of services is here to stay, and is only likely to accelerate in the future.

Endnotes

[1] Michael E. Porter, *Competitive Advantage: Creating and Sustaining Superior Performance* (NY: Free Press, 1985).

[2] R. H. Coase, "The Nature of the Firm," *Economica*, New Series, Vol. 4, No. 16 (Nov 1937), pp. 386–405.

[3] Oliver E. Williamson, *Markets and Hierarchies: Analysis and Antitrust Implications* (NY: Free Press, 1975).

[4] Oliver Williamson, *The Economic Institutions of Capitalism* (NY: Free Press, 1985).

[5] Oliver Williamson, "Strategizing, Economizing, and Economic Organization," *Strategic Management Journal*, Vol. 12, Winter 1991, pp. 75–94.

[6] S. Engerman and R. Gallman, eds., *Long-Term Factors in American Economic Growth* (University of Chicago Press, 1986), "Measuring the Transactions Sector in the American Economy," p. 121.

[7] Noshir F. Kaka, "Running a Customer Service Center in India," *McKinsey Business Technology: Our Point of View*, 2006, www.mckinsey.com/clientservice/bto/pointofview/pdf/MoIT8_Dell_F.pdf.

[8] "JPMorgan Chase Signs with IBM for IT Infrastructure Services Transformation," IBM Press Release, December 2002, www-03.ibm.com/press/us/en/pressrelease/381.wss.

[9] Paul Strassman, "Why JPMorgan Chase Really Dropped IBM," *Baseline Magazine* (January 13, 2005).

[10] Speech given by Sam Pitroda (May 7, 2004), *The Cook Report on Internet*, September–October 2004.

[11] Jay Solomon and Kathryn Kranhold, "Western Exposure in India's Outsourcing Boom, GE Played a Starring Role," *The Wall Street Journal* (March 2005) http://online.wsj.com/article/SB111151806639186539.html.

[12] J. Richard Anderson and Richard N. Vita, "Should You Outsource Accounting and Finance?" *Journal of Corporate Accounting & Finance*, Volume 17, Issue 6, pp. 11–15.

[13] Angèle Boyd, "Information Management: A Critical Success Factor for Financial Services Firms" IDC White Paper, March 2005, http://a1851.g.akamaitech.net/f/1851/2996/24h/cacheB.xerox.com/downloads/usa/en/n/nr_IDCFinancial ServicesWhitePaper.pdf.

[14] Benjamin Holt, "Timing the Spread of Technologies" (graph), Global Policy Forum, July 1999, www.globalpolicy.org/globaliz/charts/techsp2.htm.

[15] "Telegeography 2005: Executive Summary," Telegeography, 2005, p. 13.

[16] Gregg Keizer, "Windows System Requirements—1990–2006: More for Less," Yahoo! News, May 19, 2006.

[17] Ernst R. Berndt, Ellen R. Dulberger, and Neal J. Rappaport, "Price and Quality of Desktop and Mobile Personal Computers: A Quarter Century of History," National Bureau of Economic Research (paper presented at the conference on Price, Output and Productivity Measurement), Summer Institute 2000.

[18] 2005 Full-Time MBA Profiles, *BusinessWeek*, www.businessweek.com/bschools/rankings/full_time_mba_profiles/.

[19] 2004 B-School Profiles and Rankings, *BusinessWeek*, www.businessweek.com/bschools/04/full_time_profiles/iima.htm.

[20] 2005 Full-Time MBA Profiles, *BusinessWeek*, www.businessweek.com/bschools/rankings/full_time_mba_profiles/.

[21] "ISB Achieves Its Best Ever Placements Results," Indian School of Business, www.isb.edu/placements2006/index.html.

[22] www.cra.org/wp/index.php?cat=18 (only includes U.S.-born Caucasian students, not Black, Hispanic, or Asian).

[23] Diane Lewis, "India Tech Firms Seeks US Talent in Offshoring Twist," *Boston Globe* (May 30, 2006).

[24] Tania Braningan, "Let China Learn English, Says Brown," *Guardian Unlimited* (February 22, 2005).

[25] Jonathan Adams and Max Hirsch, "English for Everyone," *Newsweek* (Aug 15, 2007), www.newsweek.com/id/32295.

[26] Robert Kennedy, "Understanding Offshoring and the Global Reorganization of Work," presentation at Diamond Exchange, May 2006.

[27] "Transition—Global Venture Capital Insights Report, 2006," Ernst & Young.

[28] "India—All Aboard," *Red Herring* (June 5, 2006).

[29] "India—All Aboard," *Red Herring* (June 5, 2006).

[30] Candace Lombardi, "Survey: Software Companies Increasing Offshoring Work" CNET News.com, January 12, 2007, www.news.com/Survey-Software-companies-increasing-offshoring-work/2100-1022_3-6149703.html.

[31] *Executive Agenda,* A.T. Kearney, Vol. VII, No. 4, Fourth Quarter 2004, www.atkearney.com/shared_res/pdf/ea74_pharmaExplores_S.pdf.

[32] *Executive Agenda,* A.T. Kearney, Vol. VII, No. 4, Fourth Quarter 2004, www.atkearney.com/shared_res/pdf/ea74_pharmaExplores_S.pdf.

[33] Manish Subramanian and Bhuwan Atri, "Captives in India: A Research Study," *Infosys* (February 2006), p. 3, www.infosys.com/global-sourcing/white-papers/captives-research-v2.pdf.

[34] World Development Indicators, *The World Bank*, 2007.

3

Making It Real

As you start on your sourcing journey, it is important to define your goals and expectations. This may sound self-evident, but a clear definition of what you hope to achieve through offshoring may be more elusive than you might think. For example:

- Are you looking primarily to take costs out of your current operations?
- Do you want to improve operations?
- Is your ultimate goal to change the ways you do business fundamentally, and to create a whole new universe of possibilities?

There's no one "right answer," of course. But the goal you set for your business will point toward the type of sourcing deal you should pursue, and will define the relationship you ultimately enter into with your service delivery provider.

It is also important to note that some of these needs and expectations are interrelated, and likely to evolve over time. For example, once you transform your business operations, you may want to focus on taking costs out of the newly designed processes. Or, after initially focusing on costs, you may realize that the reengineering of processes can provide additional returns. As needs and expectations evolve, your sourcing partners and the type of arrangements you enter into may change dramatically.

In this chapter, we look first at the three distinctive (but interrelated) goals you may choose to pursue through offshoring. Then we consider the important distinction between *tasks* and *processes* in the definitional process. And for the balance of the chapter, we present an eight-step roadmap for successful service offshoring.

Three Distinct Sets of Goals

It is critically important to align your sourcing strategy with your business goals. Linda Cohen and Allie Young of the Gartner Group provide a concise summary of the possibilities[1] (see Figure 3.1). They argue that there is a range of business value to be created—but in order for an organization to gain higher levels of business value, it must enter into more complex relationships with vendors (or offshore providers). Those relationships can aim primarily at *efficiency, enhancement*, or *transformation*.

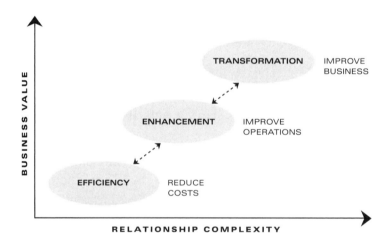

Figure 3.1   Different approaches to sourcing

Goal #1: Efficiency

If your primary goal is to make operations more cost effective by taking costs out of existing processes, you should pursue an efficiency-focused sourcing approach. This approach generally focuses on "commodity-type" processes—in other words, processes that are standardized, well defined, and predictable. Typically, these include processes that are outside your core but are still essential to your organization's success.

The goal of efficiency-focused sourcing is to maintain existing service quality, availability, and consistency while cutting costs, commonly through labor arbitrage (that is, buying your labor cheaper elsewhere). You can either outsource to an offshore vendor or perform the service yourself at the offshore location. If you go the former route, keep in mind that large service providers who specialize in offshore sourcing are likely to be in a position to point you to sources of cost advantage beyond simple labor cost arbitrage, such as reengineering, consolidation, and analytics. (Again, our three goals tend to overlap.)

If you hand over your processes to a vendor, you will enter into a service contract. The terms for these types of contracts are specified in "service level agreements" (SLAs) that lay out the quality and quantity of the service to be delivered. As a rule, the types of processes defined by these contracts are well understood, and outputs can be easily measured and monitored. For example, a call center contract might specify how quickly calls are answered, the average handle time, and minimum customer satisfaction scores. It is also important that these processes have a clear and well-defined interface with other processes that have been retained within the organization (for example, call inquiries and transactions are recorded in a specific customer contact database). When this is the case—easy-to-specify performance combined with standard interfaces—processes are relatively easy to separate and transfer.

Billing, for example, is a back-office function that traditionally has been plagued by underinvestment in staff and technology. Well into the era of the alleged "paperless office," many elements of the billing process continue to be manual and paper-dependent. "Finance and accounting processes," according to the U.S. research firm IDC, "can be breeding grounds for inefficiency, laden with manual and redundant processes, priming them to be outsourced."[2]

This is particularly frustrating to the savvy functional manager, because as he or she well knows, if you manage your receivables cycle well and reduce Days Sales Outstanding (DSO), you can save a *lot* of money. Here's where offshoring comes in. By offshoring their billing processes, many companies have achieved savings of between 30 and 60 percent of operating costs, while also realizing large reductions in working-capital requirements.[3] Outsourcing can allow you both to leverage the vendor's technology investments and access their best practices in billing—about which they're almost certainly thinking more intensively and creatively than you are.

Other common targets for efficiency sourcing include check processing, mainframe and network operations, and desktop computing support. Handing over these activities to a partner provider can help you save not just costs, but also valuable management bandwidth. Think about that for a moment: Instead of spending your managers' time on the operational details of these support processes, you can focus them on other issues that are far more critical to your organization.

Of course, not all companies are in a position to profit from efficiency sourcing. But we strongly suggest that you look sideways in your industry, and see if your competitors *are* finding such savings. If so, you almost certainly need to get into the game—or risk being left behind.

Goal #2: Enhancement

You should enter into an enhancement sourcing effort if your primary aim is to improve the way your current business processes are carried out. The key idea here is that by moving to a better technology platform, reengineering existing business processes, or otherwise embracing ways to do things better, you can improve your operational performance and outcomes. Here, your primary focus is not on cost reduction, but on process improvement—which often leads to reduced costs, along with higher quality, increased availability, and other good outcomes.

As you work with an external provider on the enhancement of your existing operations, the relationship between you and that provider becomes critically important. You will have to work together effectively, freely sharing knowledge and ideas. As a result, these relationships tend to be far more complex than those that are created in the context of efficiency-focused sourcing. Your partner needs to fully understand your business goals and process-outcome expectations, in part because it may be hard to exhaustively specify requirements or performance metrics at the very beginning of the engagement. Those goals and expectations will likely evolve over time, as you work with the vendor and analyze the process and its inherent possibilities. Similarly, specific scope and functionalities can only emerge over time—and are likely to evolve over time, as well.

Your contract terms should focus on operational outcomes and improvements. The contract and governance needs for enhancement relationships are more complex; you need models that will keep the deal current as the business environment changes, as well as provide incentives to the service provider for delivering continuous value improvements beyond those originally specified. Remember: Because a high level of trust between you and your partner is essential, a close alignment of your interests is critically important.

What's a promising ground for enhancement sourcing? Consider working with specialist vendors to reengineer and improve your Human Resource (HR) processes. Diageo, a $7 billion premium beverage company with 22,000 employees around the world, worked with Deloitte to that end.[4] Rapid growth and expansion into new market segments had left Diageo with a fragmented HR function. In November 2002, the company embarked on an HR overhaul aimed at unifying and streamlining processes, better aligning HR to business needs, and reducing costs.

The overall cost-cutting target for the initiative was 20 percent. A migration from PeopleSoft to an SAP-based HR model with self-service capabilities emerged as the central part of the initiative. Diageo worked closely with Deloitte as it pursued three goals: SAP HR skills, integrated program management, and improved change methodologies.

Diageo and Deloitte worked together to establish a strong governance structure and three dedicated teams focused on process, systems, and data; organization and people; and implementation. Together, they designed and implemented a "virtual HR service center" that substantially reduced the need for call centers. Something like 25 percent of the existing HR workforce was let go—and yet, employees had greatly improved access to quality information, including 24/7 access to forms, policies, and job openings. Meanwhile, the HR professionals who were retained had much clearer roles and responsibilities, and HR developed generally better relationships with line-of-business managers, in large part because they had time to better align their recruiting, staffing, and performance management with business needs.

One key point to take away from this story is that Diageo and Deloitte worked closely together—and *invented* together. As they discovered broken processes in unexpected places, they navigated through scope changes and found additional value to their mutual benefit.

Other target areas for enhancement sourcing include the reengineering of back office processes such as the development and management of ERP systems, the industrialization of cottage-industry processes such as medical transcription, and insurance claim processing.

Goal #3: Transformation

If you want to fundamentally change the way your business works, or if you want to acquire new business capabilities, you will need to look to *transformational* sourcing. This is aimed at achieving rapid, sustainable, step-change in enterprise-level performance, often through bundling technology, consulting, and outsourcing. The point is to dramatically improve the competitiveness of the organization by creating new value and new revenues, outmaneuvering the competition, and changing the very basis on which your corporation operates.

Even more so than with enhancement sourcing, a business transformation outsourcing (BTO) project assumes that the specific services to be provided can't be defined precisely at the beginning of the project. Instead, a final goal is established (for example, "productivity improvements of 20 percent by the end of Year Three"). After agreeing upon this type of high-level strategic goal (and perhaps defining some interim milestones), the customer and vendor jointly define existing baselines and establish satisfactory ways of measuring progress toward that goal.

The stakes in transformational outsourcing can be enormous. A successful initiative can drive dramatic business improvements; conversely, a failure may put the entire corporate agenda at risk. Transformational outsourcing therefore requires a very close partnership, and assumes the most complex kind of relationship between the service provider and the service recipient. You and your vendor will have to interact intensively, invest in each other extensively, renegotiate the contract(s) continuously, and trust each other intimately. You have to be prepared to engage in a long-term relationship, most likely based on gain-sharing, equity-sharing, or a joint-venture model.

One successful example of transformation outsourcing is IBM's relationship with Bharti Enterprises, a leading telecom provider in India. IBM is providing IT services, software, and hardware to Bharti, as well as consolidated data-center assets, help desks, and enhanced data-recovery capabilities. In this relationship, IBM is rewarded based upon Bharti's revenue: As Bharti's revenue increases, so does IBM's compensation for the project.[5]

In November 2005, Wachovia announced that it had signed a seven-year agreement with Genpact to establish an offshore operation to support Wachovia's BPO efforts.[6] Although the terms of the agreement were not included in that press release, the relationship was much closer than the typical customer-supplier relationship. Wachovia picked up a seven percent stake in its Indian partner, which in return received a gain-sharing deal, ensuring that the incentives of both parties would be aligned.

A number of service providers purport to deliver "generic" transformation services. For example, EDS's end-to-end Call Center Outsourcing solution for communications-service providers offers to transform customer-service performance along multiple dimensions: effectiveness, efficiencies, cost impact, revenue, and so on. EDS claims that the solution transforms call-center operations and optimizes the infrastructure, while at the same time improving call handling, workforce management, and effective agent cost. And in fact, telecommunication operators that have teamed with EDS report that churn rates have declined by five percent, customer lifetime value has increased by 15 percent, and customer satisfaction rankings have improved between 50 and 80 percent.[7]

In a transformational relationship—which may or may not involve offshoring, by the way—contracts and governance can be hugely complex. You and your vendor are essentially joined at the hip. Be prepared to approach your entire business in dramatically new ways, to be flexible as conditions change, and to be very close to your vendor.

Tasks Versus Processes

Now let's move to the second major focus of this chapter: the difference between *tasks* and *processes,* and how you can use that difference to your offshoring advantage. We first review some basic organizational theory and then explain how that theory relates to offshoring.

Business tasks—such as outbound calls in a call center, medical transcription, and desktop support—are relatively easy to define and understand. They reside within a functional area and can be specified in detail. Tasks have clear sets of inputs, well-defined information requirements, and explicit instructions for processing.

Figure 3.2 represents various tasks in the finance and procurement departments of a typical company.

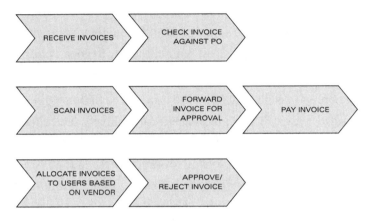

Figure 3.2   A selection of tasks in finance and procurement

You could outsource one or more of these individual tasks—for example, matching invoices to purchase orders—and done well, that outsourcing could create efficiencies and save money. And in fact, both the outsourcing and offshoring of work on a task basis have grown substantially in recent years, with companies looking for cost advantage and access to best practice.

As discussed earlier in this chapter, task outsourcing tends to work best when performance is easily specified and when interfaces to the rest of the organization are well defined. This is the realm of efficiency outsourcing, typified by call centers, medical transcription, payments processing, and insurance claims processing.

But there are several problems with this narrow "task" view. First, it fosters within the vendor a narrow, and likely sub-optimal, view of servicing your firm and, ultimately, your customers. Within the vendor, there are only limited linkages to your firm. This chopped-up and disaggregated approach allows for only very limited visibility of key measures such as defects, costs, and time needed to service the customer (which in this case would translate into "pay supplier invoices"). Because the task approach leads to a limited understanding of how various tasks relate to each other—for example, the fact that invoices need to be scanned before they can be forwarded for approval—the overall work flow design is often inefficient. It may lead to a series of local optimums, but not necessarily to good end-to-end performance.

This phenomenon is illustrated by the experience that one global services firm had with a British pharmaceutical company. The client had asked the vendor to manage its accounts payable task (matching invoices to purchase orders, resolving discrepancies, and making timely payment). Prior to the engagement, average payment time was more than 45 days, which meant the client missed out on the standard two percent discount it would have received if it had paid within 28 days. For reasons internal to the client, the vendor was asked not to get involved with the purchasing operation or intake of invoices.

In a procedure known as "process mapping" (discussed at length later in the chapter), the vendor identified an end-to-end processing time of 21 days (with an additional 24 days outside its control). The vendor applied Six Sigma and lean analysis to the tasks it inherited, and was able to reduce processing time to eight days on average, an improvement of 62 percent. But payables still averaged 32 days, with only 35 percent of payments qualifying for the 28-day discount.

After several attempts to broaden the mandate were rebuffed, the vendor did an end-to-end analysis on its own and identified the problem as a mail drop location at one of the least efficient post offices in London—causing, on average, a nine-day delay, with wide variation. This bottleneck was followed by an inefficient scanning and invoice filing process that was controlled by the purchasing department, and which averaged another 15 days. After some delicate discussions, the vendor convinced the client to "experiment" with a different drop location, and to cede control of the scanning and filing process. This cut a week off average acceptance times, and 12 days off of scanning and filing (19 of the pre-intervention 24 days). In other words, expanding the intervention allowed processing time to be reduced from 45 days to 13 days, and for on-time payments to go from less than 10 percent to more than 90 percent. On a $3 billion annual purchasing budget, this led to savings of more than $40 million.[8]

Similarly, a focus within the vendor on discrete tasks may limit investments in productivity-enhancing technologies such as automation and optical character recognition (OCR), even though these investments have the potential to contribute significantly to increased productivity and customer value. And finally, when the focus is on individual tasks, neither the customer nor the vendor is focusing on key business outcomes such as productivity, controllership, and value optimization. In most cases, this leaves a lot of value on the table.

The remedy? It is often useful to think of a series of related tasks as a *business process*, which can then be managed and optimized as a whole. **Business processes** (as we use the term) are streams of activity that flow through, around, and across an organization's functional boundaries. Stated slightly differently, business processes take place across a range of functional silos. People performing a process-related activity within the confines of one of those silos rarely have the opportunity to examine the broader business process that their activity supports.

How do you identify a business process? First, business processes *are typically supported by an operational system*. For example, the billing business process is supported by a billing system; the same is true for the purchasing and ordering processes.

Second, business processes *typically generate (or collect) unique measurements to gauge organizational performance*. These metrics can be a direct result of the process, or they can be derived from the process outcome. For example, the "sales ordering" business process supports numerous reports and analytics, such as customer profitability and sales rep performance.

Third, business processes *are usually triggered by an input, and result in output that needs to be monitored.* For example, an accepted proposal is input to the ordering process, which results in a sales order and its metrics. In most organizations, you can identify a series of business processes, in which outputs from one process become inputs to the next.

Depending upon the nature of the business, you can categorize processes in various ways. For example, a business process can be decomposed into several "subprocesses," which together contribute to what might be called a "super-process." In fact, the analysis of business processes typically includes the mapping of processes and subprocesses all the way down to the level of individual activities.

As you map out these processes, tracking how they "hopscotch" from one functional area to another, you begin to see clearly that the *coordination* of the tasks and dependencies between the individual tasks is extremely important. Unfortunately, the brilliant execution of individual tasks is not enough to ensure superior process performance. Any such isolated brilliance is likely to be swamped and obscured by underperformance elsewhere. Errors in a particular task—such as keypunch errors—will drag down other tasks. Idle time between tasks drags down the performance of the overall process, even though no particular task's owner feels responsible.

This is a key point, both in terms of general management theory and our outsourcing focus: In many cases, *it is the wait time between various tasks in the process that makes the overall process time consuming and inefficient.* For example, consider Figure 3.3, which summarizes an accounts-payable process that was reengineered by Genpact.

To summarize this diagram's main point, the total processing time required for an individual invoice was less than one hour, but the

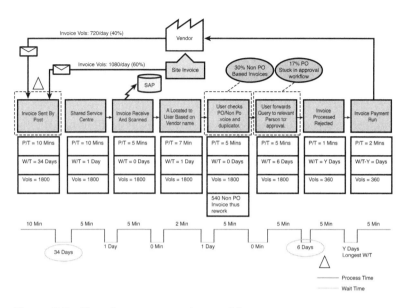

Figure 3.3   Mapping an accounts payable process

elapsed calendar time that it took to process an invoice was *more than 40 days*. Why the long wait? It reflected both the inefficient workflow design and the outmoded technologies that were used in the process. Individual tasks were being carried out with relative efficiency—for example, managers within each function "batched up" work orders to minimize labor hours. This makes sense for each functional manager, but the overall result is a highly inefficient global process. The optimal approach here is to work to optimize the entire process (as measured by time to pay, accuracy, and cost), even if it leads to higher costs for some specific tasks.

In fact, the "power of processes" can provide you with much greater returns than merely cutting costs out of tasks. In many cases, the process view yields *10 to 20 times* the simple labor cost savings that can be realized through the task-based view. The term "the power of processes" was coined by Genpact's Tiger Tyagarajan and used effectively to sell its vision of high impact offshore outsourcing.

Example: The Procure-to-Pay Process

Let's look at one typical business process—procurement—from end to end, and explore its outsourcing potential. We'll start at 50,000 feet and then move down to specifics.

Traditionally, organizations have viewed procurement as a transactional overhead function. Today, many organizations face the seemingly incompatible goals of reducing costs while improving performance, so they are taking a closer look at sourcing. In fact, effective procurement is increasingly being perceived as a strategic asset—one that can add value to a business and improve its bottom line. In the course of this rethinking, many companies discover to their dismay that a number of factors are working to prevent them from optimizing their procurement advantage: multiple fragmented purchasing groups within the organization, legacy tools and technology, nonuniform processes, and others.

The remedy, they discover, is to take an end-to-end view of the whole process and to design "procure-to-pay" (or "source-to-pay") business processes. By taking a broader view of the process, firms are lowering the cost of goods and services purchased by aggregating purchasing power and improving their "spend" management, as well as reducing operating expenses through automation, process improvement, and labor cost savings. Designing a process that integrates purchase order, general ledger, and accounts payable systems can lead to improved controls and increased compliance. It can also lead to better tracking, reporting, and management of important activities such as spend analysis, supplier and category management, purchase-order processing, compliance management, and invoice processing.

Figure 3.4 presents one firm's sourcing-to-procure-to-pay process—which spans three major functions and nine activities. In a *task* view of the world, each task, or even each function, would be optimized on its own. A *process* view looks at all nine tasks as a group and optimizes overall performance.

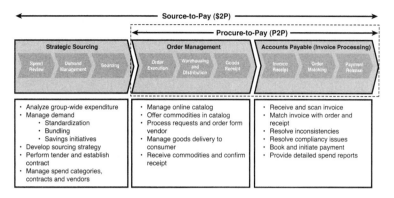

Figure 3.4 The procure-to-pay process spans several distinct functions.

Let's inject some real numbers into this somewhat theoretical discussion. The following summary is derived from the real-life experience of a company—call it Acme World Services—that went through exactly the kind of review of its procure-to-pay (P2P) procedures described previously. At the outset of the review, Acme had a 40-day accounts-payable cycle time, although the actual processing time per transaction added up to less than one hour, with each transaction costing approximately $20 (on a fully loaded basis). Fifty people worked on various aspects of P2P at Acme, costing the company around $3.5 million a year in staffing costs. They processed about $1 billion in annual payments, with about 60 percent of all invoices being paid on time.

After carefully mapping out the P2P process, the company decided to move it offshore. The offshore cost was about $2.2 million, or 38 percent below the onshore cost. The move offshore was followed by some moderate reengineering that took employment down to 40 people, which further reduced costs to $1.8 million. Acme had now saved nearly half of its initial costs.

This was good news, but far better news followed. In addition to cutting costs, the reengineering led to both a reduction in error rates and faster cycle times, reducing the average payable from 60 days to 25 days. Based on this faster payment rate, the company was able to negotiate a two percent fast-payment discount from its suppliers.

This amounted to an additional *$20 million* in annual cash flow. If you scan these numbers again, you realize that the "process savings" ($20 million) were more than *ten times* the direct labor savings ($1.8 million). In addition, the process savings were sustainable, and would scale up automatically as the firm grew. Finally, the new "process view" IT systems allowed for much better tracking of individual transactions all the way through the system, which in turn enabled better error identification and analysis of individual employee's performance. That is Tyagarajan's "power of processes."

The bottom line: When you look to move activities offshore, think *process* rather than task. Think about the *end-to-end* flow of work, rather than isolated islands of tasks. The rewards can be enormous.

Putting Theory into Action: An Eight-Step Process

So far, we've provided few specifics as to how to "make it real"— the subject of this chapter. Let's address those specifics now. In the following pages, we lay out an eight-step process for effective outsourcing/offshoring. Those steps (which we'll cast as imperatives) are as follows:

1. Identify the tasks.
2. Map the process(es).
3. Decode the relevant technology and infrastructure.
4. Identify and mitigate risks.
5. Select a vendor.
6. Select a geography.
7. Migrate your operations.
8. Integrate your operations.

Let's look at these steps one at a time, with the understanding that many of them overlap, and in some cases, run concurrently.

Identify the Tasks

The value chain analysis presented in Chapter 2, "The Economics and Drivers of Offshoring," as well as the examples provided in this chapter, argue convincingly for taking an *activity-* or process-based view of the business. Transaction-cost economics helps us understand the type of activities we can look to outsource: Those that are infrequent, reasonably well defined, non-asset-specific, and not at the core of the business.

How do you, as a manager, identify the tasks or processes that might be good candidates for outsourcing and/or offshoring? In Figure 3.5, we present a well-known industry "decomposition" framework—developed by EquaTerra—to help you in practice. The process decomposition compass applies to both tasks and business processes.

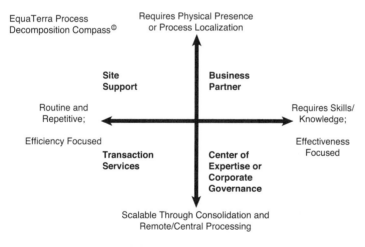

Figure 3.5   Determining your sourcing options using EquaTerra's process decomposition compass

As shown in Figure 3.5, you should consider two primary parameters to help identify activities with high potential for offshoring or outsourcing. First, along the horizontal axis of the compass, consider whether the tasks are routine and repetitive in nature—and are thereby *efficiency* focused—or whether they require knowledge and skills, and are thus *effectiveness* focused. Second, along the vertical axis of the compass, consider whether tasks from various parts of the organization can be co-located, or whether the requirements of physical presence or local processing prevent co-location—and, thus, consolidation—by you or your vendor.

Depending on 1) the nature of the task under consideration, and 2) its mapping along these two dimensions, you can decide on the optimum sourcing mechanism. For example, a task may require physical presence and local processing. If this particular task is efficiency focused—such as in-person desktop support—you should consider site support. On the other hand, if this task requires specialized skills or knowledge, such as legal counsel, you may seek local services from a business partner. Scalable processes that are efficiency focused—such as outbound calls—are ripe for outsourcing as a transaction service, whereas those that are knowledge intensive should be organized into a center of expertise.

Figure 3.6 depicts the "outsourceability" of an activity, based on where it maps to the compass.

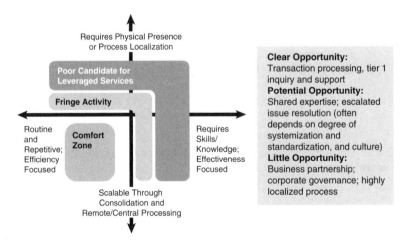

Figure 3.6   Location on the compass reveals candidates for off-shoring/outsourcing.

Activities that fall within the "comfort zone" are prime candidates for outsourcing and/or offshoring, whereas those in the area are not—either because they are best delivered as localized processes or because they are effectiveness- (that is, knowledge-) focused.

To bring this framework a little closer to earth, let's consider the example of typical HR processes in an organization. They are mapped in Figure 3.7.

Figure 3.7   HR processes mapped onto the decomposition compass

Processes such as payroll, rewards administration, and vendor management are prime candidates for outsourcing and/or offshoring. These activities are well defined, they can be aggregated, consolidated, and serviced centrally. On the other hand, activities such as

HR strategy, workforce planning, and talent management are 1) critical to the business, and 2) localized within units of the firm. As a result, it tends to be difficult to outsource/offshore these activities.

Obviously, these types of diagrams require extensive unpacking to be useful. There are three appendixes to help you do that:

- **Appendix 3A**—Provides a set of questions to help you determine whether a given process is efficiency focused or effectiveness focused, and another set of questions to determine whether a process is standardized or customized
- **Appendix 3B**—Provides a set of questions to help you assess the feasibility, value, and risk of potential outsourcing efforts
- **Appendix 3C**—Provides a set of questions to help you assess the "offshoreability" of selected processes

Map the Process(es)

"Process mapping," introduced earlier, is just what it sounds like: a technique whereby you visually display exactly what happens across the collection of activities that together create value. It helps you comprehend and document the existing workflow as well as identify linkages to other tasks and processes, IT dependencies, reporting and control opportunities, and bottlenecks.

Mapping begins with an exploration of the various components of a process:

- **Logic**—What is the purpose and goal of this set of activities?
- **Handoffs**—What are the different entities involved, and how do activities get transferred between them?
- **Milestones**—What are the key landmarks in the process?
- **Time**—How much time does each activity take? How long are the lags between actions?
- **Cost**—How much does it cost to carry out each various activity?
- **Value added**—How much value does a particular activity add to the overall process?
- **Relationships**—How are different activities and efforts related, and to what extent are they dependent on each other?

Typically, process mapping occurs on three levels. The *macro* level is the least detailed, often depicting between 5 and 15 critical steps in the process. It allows you to capture the big picture, and defines the scope of the process.

At the *functional* level, you capture more detailed information on the activities being performed and the value being added to the process. It can be used, for example, to calculate process, cycle, wait, and move times, as well as process costs.

Task maps represent the worm's-eye view, providing you with extensive detail about how a particular activity is carried out.

You and your colleagues are in the best position to decide exactly how to represent and capture activity on these three levels. In most cases, a working group will employ a simple toolkit (see the following sidebar) and start at the macro level. When it is time to drill down to produce specific functional or task maps, it is often necessary to bring in functional or IT specialists to provide the detailed inputs.

Now let's apply this toolkit. A macro mapping of a typical customer order process might look something like what's shown in Figure 3.8. Note, in particular, the flow of activities across functional lines and departments.

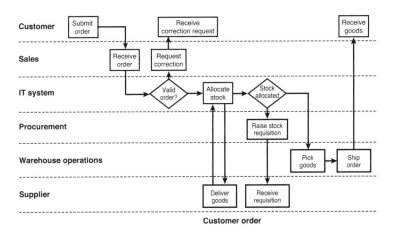

Figure 3.8   Customer order process map

A Sample Toolkit for a Process Map

Type	Representation	Example
Activity	Box	Submit Order
Review/Decision	Diamond	Valid Order?
Process flow	Arrow	Purchase Order
Storage	Triangle	Documents
Delay	Big D	Waiting for Information
Start/Stop	Oval	Stop

If we dove down to the functional level, we would start to explode each of the activities in this process map. A functional mapping would specify what forms are filled out, who does each task, what information is needed to make a decision, what decisions can be made, where the information goes for each option, and so on.

The task-level mapping involves everything someone would need to know to re-create the process. In other words, a *huge* amount of information is required, and this mapping is typically performed by industrial or software engineers and pulled together in thick binders. These include the following items:

- What data is entered into which fields of which screens
- Database structures, index fields, and feeds
- Technical information on data interchanges

- Waiting times
- Release conditions
- Specific reports produced

As a manager, it is unlikely that you will be producing process maps yourself. They are, however, a critical step in the move toward optimizing your operations. It is important that you ensure this process is undertaken—either by your organization, your advisory firm, or your vendor. Further, it is not enough to ensure that some sort of process mapping has occurred and that big binders have been assembled. Your organization has to *own* those binders. It must be knowledgeable about and comfortable with the results. Anything less, and you will be setting yourself up for failure.

Decode the Relevant Technology and Infrastructure

As you embark upon the sourcing journey for your business processes, it is important to have in hand a good understanding of your underlying information technology (IT) applications and infrastructure. Your core enterprise applications—which may be embedded in legacy, proprietary, and commercial enterprise systems—play a key role in your business operations, and the prominence of technology within business processes will only increase in coming years.

Reengineering efforts typically revolve around the design, installation, and operation of an Enterprise Resource Planning system such as SAP, BAAN, or Oracle. These systems provide a platform on which functions or process-specific applications can be implemented. The ERP system provides a foundation that facilitates firm-wide (or cross-firm) data sharing, process tracking, and reporting. ERP systems have great potential, but they require huge upfront effort.

It's often helpful to think in terms of a "value stack" and of linkages between business services and IT applications and infrastructure. (See the left side of Figure 3.9.) IT applications are supported by underlying IT infrastructure, and business process logic is encoded in these applications. Although in most cases IT infrastructure delivers little or no direct business value, you do require a solid, stable, and enabling IT infrastructure.

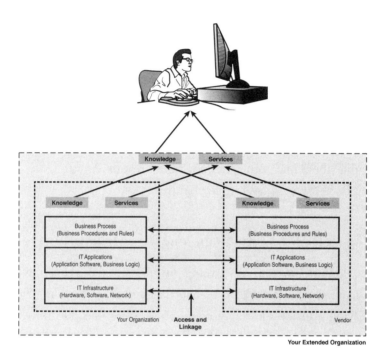

Figure 3.9   Success depends on seamlessly linking value stacks with your vendor.

The point of putting that entire expensive IT infrastructure in place, of course, is to gain the ability to run the applications that are relevant to your business. Applications enable efficient and innovative business processes, and eventually these processes provide value—knowledge and services—to the end business user.

As you consider outsourcing or offshoring your business processes, you need to confirm that your underlying information technology applications and infrastructure can support this strategy. Distributing individual "chunks" of your business across a variety of vendors and geographies will require access to, and linkages among, value stacks. Only a seamless technological interface between your systems and those of the vendor can ensure that the end business user feels that all your services are being provided by a single player: *you*.

As suggested by Figure 3.9, your vendors will need ready access to your systems and applications as they deliver your business services.

In many cases, this may be as simple as giving them remote access into your systems. For example, you can provide the vendor who is carrying out benefits administration on your behalf access to your mainframe-based HR application. To enable the extended enterprise and move work beyond boundaries, however, you may also need to invest in new systems and technologies. For example, companies such as mortgage lenders that deal with a high volume of paper-based transactions need a robust document imaging and management system to be able to "move" documents offsite (or off-shore) easily. Standardizing the technology environment on well-accepted industry platforms, such as web-based services, goes a long way toward facilitating easier integration with your partners and suppliers. Robust document management and workflow systems bring many benefits: better transaction tracking, faster retrieval of documents, and smoother handoffs.

In most cases, outsourcing and offshoring are dependent on the creation and maintenance of compatible systems—for both you and your vendor. This is one reason why there's been a long-term trend away from proprietary IT systems and toward industry-standard platforms such as SAP and PeopleSoft. It is not the executive's responsibility to master these details—but your IT organization must be directed to move to vendor-compatible systems and to work with vendors to manage system security and performance.

A vendor's standard set of service offerings may not work well in your environment, or may require costly and time-consuming system changes/upgrades. An IT expert or offshore advisory firm should be able to alert you to these implications in advance—but be prepared for surprises.

Meanwhile, your in-house IT group has to be aware of your sourcing expectations and manage the underlying technology platform to support these needs. Involve that group actively in your planning and decision-making process. They can help enormously with data security and business continuity, and also help put controls and audit trails in place to ensure security and monitoring.

According to studies conducted by EquaTerra, organizations must address critical elements of their enterprise software applications while pursuing business process outsourcing.[9] These include the following:

- Measuring and benchmarking current cost levels, and estimating the true savings potential of outsourcing.
- Determining how underlying IT systems enable or constrain business process performance, and how outsourcing will impact performance levels.
- Defining a way to compare and contrast your own software environment with that provided by the vendor.
- Understanding the capabilities of your enterprise software environment as it relates to outsourcing management and governance.
- Defining the outsourcing scope from the perspective of the enterprise software environment. This requires you to map business process elements being outsourced against the underlying software applications support.

Identify and Mitigate Risks

Moving organizational activities and business processes outside the firm and/or national boundaries exposes you to new sets of risks, some of which arise in realms that are strategic to your business. Especially in light of the increasing regulatory scrutiny and negative public sentiment about "moving jobs" offshore, it's critical that you identify, understand, and proactively mitigate these risks.

You need to ensure "observability" and "alignment of incentives" as processes are moved to a remote location and/or serviced by an external vendor. At the same time, it is important to note that there may be risks and competitive disadvantages in *not* leveraging global and market delivery capabilities optimally. This is a note that we sound throughout this section: Yes, there are risks inherent in jumping into global service delivery. But there are different risks inherent in *not* jumping in.

Let's explore some of the key risks that you should consider as you embark on a global service delivery journey. We organize our discussion of these risks into five broad categories:

- Geographic and location risks
- Migration risks
- Business operations risk
- Customer, employee, and capabilities risks
- The risk of holdup

Geographic/Location Risk

The mere act of crossing a geographic boundary creates some specific challenges. These include dealing with the potential for political unrest; adverse changes in regulations and/or the exchange rate; differences in legal, cultural, and economic institutions; missing complementary firms and enabling clusters/ecosystem; the inability to enforce a previously agreed upon contract through the legal system; and the capabilities of local talent.

Of course, these risks vary, depending on the particular location and its experience as a center for global service delivery. In general, though, it's important to recognize that carrying out operations in a distant geography can, and does, create different challenges than those you are accustomed to at home.

For example, moving service activities to India creates an exposure to any potential conflict between India and Pakistan, and to Muslim-Hindu unrest. But similar issues arise in other offshore locations.

The regulatory regime is also an important factor. As you will see in Chapter 6, "The Services Shift: Policy Implications," many developing countries have created tax or regulatory incentives for foreign firms to establish service delivery centers. In some countries, such as India, these incentives are well established and unlikely to be reversed. In others, the "sustainability" of the incentives is open to question.

Fluctuations in the value of local currencies present another macro challenge. In early 2008, the India rupee appreciated by more than six percent against the U.S. dollar, raising costs and squeezing margins for India-based offshore providers. And if that happens, the impact may not be felt only by your vendor. Shrinking supplier margins may result in a drop in quality of service and lack of investment in continuous improvement by the supplier—which will, ultimately, impact your business.

The regulatory situation regarding protection of consumer data, firms' intellectual property, and trade secrets varies from country to country. Although security breaches can occur anywhere, they attract disproportionate attention when they occur offshore. In 2005, several employees of Mphasis—a leading Indian outsourcing company later acquired by EDS—were arrested for allegedly stealing Citibank customers' PIN numbers and using the information to pilfer an estimated $350,000 from those U.S. customers. The incident received widespread attention in the global press.[10] Of course, such breaches can also occur when you outsource domestically, but these incidents often don't hit the press. (That same year, more than 40 million credit card numbers were accessed by a computer hacker at a processing center in Tucson operated by CardSystems Solutions Inc.[11]) Security risks are everywhere, and need to be managed everywhere. The good news is that, because of customer sensitivity, offshore providers are often more careful about security issues than are domestic captive or outsource vendors.

Cultural issues present yet another challenge, which many firms underestimate. Conseco—which sells life, health, and annuity policies to middle-income clients—moved 800 call center positions to India in 2001 in an effort to save costs. The firm's then-CEO proclaimed, "I'm convinced there's better customer service in India.

Conseco was focused on cost savings and apparently skimped on cultural training and accent neutralization. Cultural differences between Conseco's customers and Indian employees—for whom checkbooks and insurance were new concepts—presented challenges. Eventually, Conseco had to move the customer service operations back to the Midwest.[12]

Optimistic cost savings projections based on labor-cost differentials are often more difficult to realize than expected. Increased interaction requirements—due to lack of well-defined service content and process standardization, the need for greater judgment, and codependence with other tasks—can contribute to some of the "invisible" costs.

Migration Risk

Transitioning processes exposes you to migration risk; that is, what happens during the process relocation that might impact your business operations. As a part of the risk assessment, you need to identify and examine each transition activity and its associated risks and their impact on service continuity.

Do you and your service provider have the necessary capabilities to transition the process? Do you have a common understanding and a plan in place? How much experience does the vendor have in transitioning processes?

Transition planning requires anticipating issues that may arise during process transition and devising proactive solutions. Most firms choose to run the "to-be-transitioned" activities in parallel until the remote operation passes several quantitative "tests," such as call answer times, data-entry error rates, or accuracy and response times for customer inquiries.

A successful migration requires detailed planning and monitoring to ensure smooth cutover on the technology, infrastructure, and knowledge dimensions of your operation.

A poor transition can lead to new business issues. Cogent Road, a firm that provides web software to mortgage companies, found that a software project outsourced to Calcutta took twice as long as planned. Also, quality and customer satisfaction levels were low due to the language barrier and 12-hour time difference between India and its San Diego headquarters. Cogent's conclusion: Going forward, the firm will keep core processes close to home and will only outsource/offshore only if "it's not a 'mission critical' project," declares marketing vice president William DiPaolo.[13]

Business Operations Risk

Carrying out operations at a new location, through a new provider, exposes you to business operations risk. Will your business processes continue to be serviced as required? Will customers notice a change in quality—for example, encountering a thick accent that is difficult to understand? Will the service turnaround time be negatively impacted? Can the operations scale up and down according to the business needs?

Operational risks manifest themselves in terms of slippage on time, cost, and quality of service. Operations may be disrupted due to lack of adequate understanding by the vendor (or offshore team), lack of vendor capabilities to deliver services as promised, or the vendor's inability to scale up the operations as needed by the business.

Several companies that faced operational challenges after transitioning processes have brought them back. Lehman Brothers stopped outsourcing its IT help desk to a leading Indian services provider due to poor quality of service, bringing the help-desk function back in-house. One research report concluded, "in terms of helpdesk, Indian firms could not provide the level of quality and services Lehman needs."[14] Shop Direct moved 250 jobs to India when it opened a call center in Bangalore in March 2002, aimed at dealing with orders and customer inquiries. Service-quality challenges, however, soon forced the company to move the jobs back to its call centers in the U.K.[15]

Operational challenges are not limited to ensuring current quality and service levels. They are also related to being able to exploit the potential for continual improvement and expanding capabilities by leveraging a global delivery model. Whereas five years ago, the focus of most sales engagements was immediate cost savings, the leading offshore vendors now focus more on continual improvement.

Customer, Employee, and Capability Risk

Outsourcing and offshoring pose considerable brand risk—particularly when outsourcing relates to customer service and other functions that contribute significantly to a company's public image. A poorly managed sourcing relationship can lead to unhappy customers and dilute a company's brand.

Your brand reflects the emotional connection that your customers have with your company. Such a connection can take years to build, and can be broken in seconds. Every interaction—whether by phone, email, or chat—impacts your customer and his or her lifetime value to your firm.

To minimize the public's anger about offshoring, and by extension to protect their brand, companies have become more transparent about offshoring. Some are even giving customers the option to choose where they want to get serviced. E-Loan—an online auto, mortgage, and home-equity lender—is letting customers decide between having their loans processed overseas or in the United States. "We don't think we can force that efficiency onto consumers because of the patriotic and privacy issues that are legitimately raised," said Chris Larsen, chief executive of E-Loan. Customers who choose the offshore option get faster service—as much as two days faster. In the first six weeks of the program, 85 percent of E-Loan customers opted for offshore processing, versus the 15 percent who chose the U.S.-based service.[16]

Some topics are more sensitive than others. Surveys reveal little pushback to international call centers for technology support and survey work. On the other hand, there is much reluctance to discuss health or credit information with international workers.

You may also face challenges from within your organization. Adding capacity offshore is easy to justify, and will likely meet little employee resistance during boom times. But when a transition occurs during a downturn, employee concerns come to the fore and many react emotionally. In these situations, a detailed communication plan and change-management strategy are key. Workers should know why activities are being transitioned, and what this means for them. In most such cases, silence "feels worse" than bad news.

Finally, you need capabilities to govern an outsourcing relationship and to manage across distances. Can you work with the vendor to deliver quality services within cost and on time? Can you manage and integrate distributed processes, and get people to work together across time zones? Do you have processes and tools that enable global delivery?

Sometimes, you can outsource too much, which can lead to the hollowing-out of your organizational capabilities. If you outsource servicing of a business task completely, you risk losing the capability to execute that task independently in the future. If the activity you are outsourcing is important (although not necessarily core or critical), make sure you retain some operational knowledge and capabilities in-house—typically around ten percent of the task volume.

Holdup and Other Strategic Risks

Working with an external vendor exposes you to a variety of strategic risks. If you become very dependent on a particular vendor, you can face "holdup" by that vendor under the guise of a renegotiation due to "unforeseen circumstances."

Holdup occurs because of the transactions cost issues discussed in Chapter 2. As you move from planning an offshoring/outsourcing relation to actually implementing one, your bargaining power changes. If you shut down your internal operations, make relationship-specific investments, or have poor monitoring of the vendor's performance, you are subject to holdup.

The primary remedy for holdup is to establish the rules for future trade as clearly as possible, and to build in mechanisms that adjust the contract to account for foreseeable but uncertain future conditions. These may include longer-term contracting, "escalator clauses," other market-based re-pricing schemes, or shared investment in dedicated facilities.

Once you outsource, you also face the risk of vendor underperformance. They may perform less work than required, contracted for, or paid for by you, which is summed up in the term "shirking." You can guard against shirking by 1) monitoring to detect underperformance by the vendor, or 2) providing incentive contracting, in which you share the benefits of effort and thus have better aligned incentives.

Remember that while you can outsource your processes and systems, you can't completely outsource the associated risks. In most cases, the liabilities you faced before outsourcing (for example, bad customer data, product quality problems, etc.) will still be yours; an outsourcer is unlikely to accept full liability for consequential damages. On a more positive note, because outsourcing firms typically specialize in the tasks/processes you are moving to them, they typically have much better systems, controls, and processes than you do.

On the other hand, *don't view outsourcing as an insurance policy*. It may be a mechanism for tapping into better processes and controls, but unless a risk is specifically mentioned in the contract, vendors will not price it into their cost model, and they will not compensate you for it if and when it materializes.

Once you have a good understanding of the various risks, you need to come up with a plan to mitigate these risks. Risk management is usually divided into four components: *risk identification, risk analysis, risk response planning,* and *risk monitoring and control.* Essentially, you would identify the potential range of outcomes, consider the likelihood of each and the effect it will have on your business and operations, consider ways you can guard against that risk or steps you can take to mitigate the same, and finally do a cost-benefit analysis to justify risk mitigation.

Select a Vendor

Firms exploring global sourcing options today have an ever-increasing number of potential vendors and geographies to choose from. Similarly, they can select from a wide variety of business models as well as enter into various types of partnerships.

If you decide to *offshore* your tasks, you need to select an offshore destination. *Outsourcing* requires you to select a vendor to partner with. If you decide to *offshore* and *outsource,* you will need to do both. While pursuing offshore outsourcing, some companies select the vendor first and then the location; others decide upon a location and then look for the best vendor to work with in that location. With leading multinational and offshore vendors expanding globally and adding service delivery capacity around the world, chances are good that there's a vendor out there who can help you get to a particular geography of your choice.

For purposes of simplicity, we separate the vendor- and geography-selection processes in this and the following section. In the real world, of course, these two choices are generally part of a single larger decision.

Once you have a good understanding of your sourcing strategy, you can embark upon the process of vendor selection. As noted, a wide variety of vendors provide business process services from across different geographies. Some leverage *scale and breadth* of their operations, whereas others provide *differentiated and niche* services. Multinational service firms such as IBM and Accenture, as well as offshore providers such as TCS and Infosys, are expanding service offerings from offshore. Vendors focused on specific functions (such as Hewitt Associates in HRM) or specific domains (such as ITTIAM in digital signal-processing) offer differentiated skills.

Obviously, selecting a vendor is a critically important decision. Outsourcing almost always touches upon things like strategy formulation, contract negotiation, and employee transfer, and so it tends to be a big investment. In addition, outsourcing can take some time before it begins to pay off. For these reasons and more, you need to assess a vendor thoroughly on what might be called the "Three C's" of outsourcing:

- **Capabilities**—The technical, domain, and geography competence they possess
- **Culture**—Values, vision, and their potential "fit" with your organization
- **Commitment**—The resources they will bring to bear for you

Each of these "Three C's" can be explored along multiple dimensions. In terms of capabilities, for example, you obviously need to review their proven technical competencies, preferably based on relevant projects they have completed successfully in the past. Cultural issues are key: Your partner is a virtual extension of your own business, and you need to make sure they understand your organization and customers. Commitment means, among other things, their ability to sustain the relationship. Are they financially viable and organizationally strong?

Most companies in search of an outsourcing vendor follow some version of the following four steps:

1. Create a vendor-selection team.
2. Short-list appropriate service providers and reach out to them.
3. Evaluate these potential providers.
4. Negotiate the contract.

Create a Vendor-Selection Team

You need to put together an internal team to manage vendor evaluation and selection, and to conduct the negotiation process. Although team composition and size vary based on contract size and complexity, the team generally should consist of a project manager, representatives from the business, a service/process expert, an IT expert, a relationship manager who will be the primary point of contact with the

Multisourcing and Collaborative Partnering

Increasingly, companies are working with multiple vendors and exercising different options simultaneously for sourcing a business process. This management and distribution of business processes across multiple vendors, or between vendor(s) and in house, is commonly referred to as *multisourcing*. This can help eliminate lock-in, provide best-of-breed advantages, and provide access to specialized skills.

Multisourcing can combine different delivery models, including offshore, nearshore (for example, nearby locations such as Mexico, the Caribbean, and Canada), and onshore. Many leading global firms work with multiple vendors in multiple geographies. Citi-Corp, American Express, and Dell all source from both captive and outsourced delivery centers in India. This model allows the firms to better balance variable workloads, and to use outside vendors to benchmark their internal operations. Other well-known examples include ABN Amro splitting a $2.24 billion services sourcing contract between five vendors, and GM dividing its IT outsourcing contract among six vendors.

future service provider, a negotiation expert, and a contracts and legal expert. You can also seek advice from external advisers, and you may choose to make them a part of the selection team.

The team should carry the process through to completion, though some members may need to be involved only at specific times. The team should gather information about the process, such as service baselines and benchmarks, as well as sourcing expectations.

Short-List Appropriate Service Providers and Reach Out to Them

Your team should do an initial screening of potential service providers. To do this scan, consider factors that are important to you and your service needs. These would include their business model (for example, do they provide standard or customized offerings?), their size and geographical footprint (can they support your global operations?), and technology, industry, and service capabilities. Your team should also come up with a standard way to interact with service providers in the selection process—for example, identifying the point of contact, channels of information exchange, schedule of interactions, and so on.

At the same time, your team should come up with a concise statement of your organization's goals and key expectations from sourcing (reduced costs, improved availability, etc.). Depending on the specifics of the proposed contract, the type and amount of information you provide will vary. For example, if you are looking at commodity-type cost efficiencies, you probably don't have to elaborate upon your business strategy. If you're seeking a transformational deal—leading to innovation and best-in-class capabilities—strategy becomes a central consideration. Obviously, as discussed earlier, this should also include all relevant criteria for the proposed contract: general terms and conditions, statement of work, and anticipated service levels. This communication should be sent out to all short-listed vendors.

Evaluate These Potential Providers

The selection team should develop specific, analytical criteria by which to evaluate vendor responses. It may take some effort to arrive at a consensus about criteria to be used, especially as the team consists of members from very different backgrounds, but the broad areas to consider generally include the following:

- **Service delivery capability**—How effectively can the provider meet your service needs? How high up will you be in their overall priority list?

- **Relationship management**—How experienced, strong, and credible is their relationship management interface? How capable/willing are they to work within your governance processes, and adhere to your terms and conditions?

- **Alignment and vision**—As noted earlier, cultural fit is critically important in a services context. They will probably be interacting heavily with your employees and/or customers. Can you work effectively with them? Do they have a good understanding of your business needs and vision?

- **Pricing**—Last but certainly not least, you need to consider the price of service delivery. It is important to consider all costs and hidden charges, such as those involved with transition. Also consider the payment options and flexibility they offer you.

You need to weight these criteria according to the specific needs of the project. For example, alignment and vision become much more important for a long term, end-to-end innovation deal, whereas pricing is the key driver for a commodity-type cost-savings deal.

Based on the responses of the service providers and your criteria, you can select two or three potential providers to examine more closely. Initiate your financial due-diligence process. Invite them to make an in-person presentation at your site. Build in time for sustained technical interactions between the prospective vendor and your team. Make sure that during these discussions, you work with the vendor's relationship manager and solutions experts, as opposed to their sales people. This will help you assess the prospective vendor team along multiple dimensions. How good are they at managing relationships and delivering services to your needs? Are they flexible? Does the record suggest that they are good at managing change?

In most cases, your team should also go and perform vendor site visits. In the case of a potential offshore provider, you'll probably have to travel some distance—but that makes your trip all the more important! While at their facilities, pay special attention to mechanisms they have in place to address security, privacy, and data/IP protection concerns.

Negotiate the Contract

Once you select a vendor to partner with, enter into detailed contract negotiations to develop an appropriate service level agreement (SLA) or similar contract (see Appendix 3D). Secure the best deal for yourself, and at the same time try to make sure that it is a win-win relationship. You need the vendor's best work; make sure the incentives are there for them to service your account at that level.

Select a Geography

While India has long been the leader in IT and IT-enabled services, the phenomenon (as noted earlier) is no longer India-centric. China, Southeast Asia, Central and Eastern Europe, and Latin America have emerged as attractive destinations for global service delivery. In short, offshoring is evolving into global service delivery.

With increasing globalization and improved capabilities in more geographies, managers now have many more options to choose from. It's better to have more choices than fewer—but more choices means you have to put more time into reviewing your options. Where you locate your tasks offshore is likely to be an important decision *over the long term*—that will help determine the quality of skills and capabilities that your company will be able to access over the coming years (or even decades). As you make this decision, you need to consider a whole host of factors, including culture, education, language, talent, quality of life, ease of travel, regulations and legal policies, political stability, risks, and many more.

Among the tools available to you in this key decision are offshore location indexes, published by firms that specialize in analyzing the relative attractiveness of various countries as hubs for global service delivery. One of the most popular of these is A. T. Kearney's Global Services Location Index, issued annually (see Appendix 4A). It measures the viability of countries as offshore destinations based on their financial structure, people skills and availability, and business environment. Kearney expanded the index from 25 countries to 40 in 2005, and then to 50 countries in 2006, reflecting the growing number of countries that are jockeying to become preferred locations for global service delivery.

Indexes such as Kearney's can be a good starting point for assessing the attractiveness of various locations for offshoring. Depending on your company's resources, you may decide to conduct your own analysis, considering such factors as the following:

- **PESTLE**—This acronym stands for the "**Political, Economic, Social, Technological, Legal**, and **Environmental**" components of the outsourcing decision. It can help you understand the "big picture" environment of the country, and the opportunities and threats that lie within it.

- **Demand**—Consider the attractiveness of the domestic market and the strength of the local economy. This is more important if you are considering starting or scaling up your operations in the local market, and not merely using it as a base for global delivery of your business services.

- **Supply**—You need to examine the quantity, quality, and cost of human capital, talent pool, and infrastructure available in that country.

- **Time**—Finally, you need to consider the preceding factors not only as they stand today, but also how they are likely to evolve over time. How will government policies shape infrastructure development? Will current investments in education grow the talent pool adequately in the future?

After you have gained an understanding of the attractiveness of the country, you may further explore the "fit" of the country with your organizational needs. Again, this most likely has to be viewed in the context of your overall strategy. Examine the extent to which resources required by you will be available in that geography. Also, consider the tangible and intangible assets that you may already have in that country; you may be able to leverage these as you start your sourcing operations from there.

Migrate Your Operations

The *migration* of tasks—along with knowledge, systems, and capabilities—is the phase when tasks that are currently being run in-house/onshore are handed over to an external vendor or moved offshore. An outsourcing/offshoring methodology and toolkit (see the following sidebar) is typically used as a guideline and checklist to ensure smooth transition. Most vendors (and clients) use broadly similar approaches, although details vary, and there is almost always a need to customize the task depending on the specific situation and needs.

In all cases, you will need to ensure that the task is well documented, as you train vendor/offshore employees to carry it out. The technology and bandwidth required to perform tasks and access each other's systems will have to be designed, procured, and deployed.

Once the task has been migrated, its operations from offshore/offsite will begin. You will need experts from technology, domain, and task areas in both organizations to oversee design and implementation of the transition process.

The Genpact Transition Toolkit

The following describes, at a high level, the outsourcing/offshoring methodology and approach being followed by Genpact—a leading BPO provider—as it helps its clients relocate business processes to a remote location.

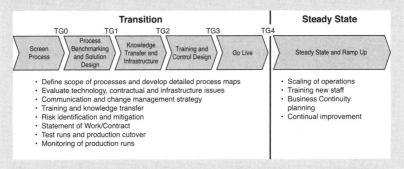

The process tracks the five phases of a Six Sigma project: *define, measure, analyze, improve,* and *control.* "Toll gates" separate various phases; they require certain conditions (such as a decision, deliverable acceptance/sign-off, etc.) to be met before the effort can move on to the next phase. Thus, at each tollgate, cross-functional teams meet and decide on the go/no go decision.

The **transition phase** consists of five subphases, and it results in transitioned processes running at the remote site in production.

The "screen process" subphase defines the scope of individual processes, and it evaluates their technological and legal requirements. A detailed premigration questionnaire is administered, risks of the individual processes evaluated, and the financial case—involving cost/benefit analysis, savings, and payback-period calculation—is developed. The output of the process-screening phase is evaluated as a part of TG0 (that is, the toll gate following the "screen process" phase).

Following this, the "process benchmarking and solution design" subphase begins. Current processes are documented and, if necessary, new processes are defined. Depending on the situation and project expectations, the processes may be redesigned or left as such prior to transitioning them offsite. Various elements of the project plan—such as detailed risk analysis, identifying technology requirements, change management, communication methodology, and the training plan—are developed, and detailed process maps are also created. These maps identify hand-offs, upstream and downstream linkages, and IT infrastructure needs for the processes.

The "knowledge transfer and infrastructure preparation" phase comprises activities intended to ensure that the necessary knowledge transfer needs are identified in detail, training requirements are identified, new sites for the business processes are prepared to receive the necessary supporting infrastructure, and any legal issues (such as existing licenses and contracts that impact processes being transitioned) are managed.

The "training and control design" phase involves the training of Genpact employees, final validation of the performance baseline, implementation of controls for the production, and creation of a "statement of work." The remote site is readied for the run of the production process (both in terms of the human capital and the supporting infrastructure), and the commercial contract is finalized.

Finally, the processes are carried out from the remote site as a part of the "go live" phase. Processes being executed remotely are tracked and monitored, and results are analyzed for performance and risk. Necessary change requirements are identified and implemented.

Once the kinks and issues that may have been faced in the "go live" phase have been resolved, the operations enter the **steady state phase**. Processes continue to be tracked, and various data about their performance are collected. Disaster recovery and business continuity plans are firmed up and tested. The team is ramped up as the process delivery scales up, and new staff is continually trained. The statement of work is revised, renewed, or—as necessary—terminated.

Integrate Your Operations

As companies move beyond migrating merely transactional tasks and start to offshore more knowledge-intensive and complex processes, they need to ensure a seamless functioning across the extended organization. Even as processes move outside a firm's boundaries, companies need to ensure control of overall cost, risk, and quality. This can be achieved by ensuring continued operations integration.

As the complexity of moving a process—across a firm or geographic border—increases, the importance of maintaining deep integration also rises. Different platforms—across organizations and geographies—must remain synchronized. You are aiming for seamless process integration, because the (unacceptable) alternative is silos as well as ever-increasing IT and handover costs between organizations and processes.

Let's explore this conceptually. As shown in Figure 3.10, different tasks in an organization have linkages, and they share data, information, and logic. Once your organization decides to move a particular task, such as Task-Z, this task will no longer be run within the organization. However, this particular task will continue to have linkages with other tasks (Task-A, Task-C, and Task-D). On top of this, there may be some information in Task-Z that may be required later by your organization.

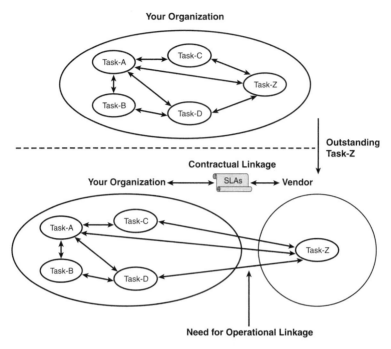

Figure 3.10 Moving a task across a border creates the need for operational linkages.

In addition to operational linkages, Task-Z may produce information that the organization would like to access later. For example, a call center may collect detailed information on which types of customers call at what times. Following an advertising campaign or a coupon promotion, product managers may want to rummage around in this data looking for patterns. But if the data is trapped in another geography or firm, this kind of rummaging won't be easy.

Upon outsourcing, there is a risk that the information infrastructure connecting you to the outsourced tasks may deteriorate or be severed. Getting data and ad hoc information from the vendor may not be easy—or cheap. (Vendors typically charge companies substantial amounts to provide out-of-scope services, including nonstandard kinds of information analysis.) The data that you get from your vendor may not be readily usable (different structure, application platform, etc.), or may not be at the level of detail you need.

For these and other reasons, it is important to take steps to ensure operational linkage and integration, even as various tasks and task infrastructure (data centers, applications, etc.) are moved out of the firm. Although a contract and the various SLAs can ensure legal coverage, only operational linkage can ensure you have access to the kinds of assets and resources you previously owned when you need them. Planning for this becomes even more important as you begin to work with multiple vendors, and as assets you previously owned are now distributed across multiple geographies and legal entities. You will need willing collaborators in the "extended enterprise" as you explore various ways to optimize and innovate.

You can take help from various tools available in the market, such as Janeeva Assurance, to ensure that key operational linkages remain in place. These tools provide for a common infrastructure, and they put standards in place that promote effective communication between in-house capacity and outsourced/offshored operations.

Summary: Making It Real

In this long chapter and its appendixes, we've covered a lot of territory. We've described the three distinctive goals that your organization can pursue through offshoring. We've distinguished between *tasks* and *processes* and illustrated the "power of processes." Finally, we've presented an eight-step roadmap for successful service offshoring. Collectively—we hope—this has served as a useful exercise in "making real" the realities of outsourcing and offshoring.

Any "how-to" chapter about this enormous topic is necessarily incomplete. (Whole books have been written about topics to which we've devoted only a few short pages.) What we've tried to do is give you a flavor of the implementation challenges you're likely to face as you venture into this new world—and of the kinds of resources that are out there to help you.

In the next chapter, we dig deeper into one of the topics introduced in this one: *who's out there, and what might they do for you?*

Endnotes

[1] Linda Cohen and Allie Young, *Multisourcing*, (Boston: Harvard Business School Press, 2005).

[2] J. Peter Donlon, "How Improved Billing Can Help Offset Rising Costs," API Outsourcing, Inc., 2005, www.apifao.com/company/news25_best_practices.html (accessed on May 18, 2008).

[3] J. Peter Donlon, "How Improved Billing Can Help Offset Rising Costs," API Outsourcing, Inc., 2005, www.apifao.com/company/news25_best_practices.html (accessed on May 18, 2008).

[4] Dana Stiffler and Christa Degnan Manning, "When Outsourcing Isn't the Answer: Diageo's 'Virtual' HR Shared Service Center," AMR Research.

[5] "IBM's outsourcing services in Asia Pacific: beyond managed services to business transformation deals," Forrester, 2007.

[6] www.wachovia.com/inside/page/0,,134_307%5E1280,00.html (accessed August 4, 2008).

[7] www.eds.com/services/contactcentertransformation/.

[8] Author interview. The vendor and client wish to remain anonymous.

[9] "Assessing the Role of Information Technology (IT) & Enterprise Software in BPO," EquaTerra, 2007.

[10] www.banktech.com/rdelivery/showArticle.jhtml?articleID=163700514.

[11] www.washingtonpost.com/wp-dyn/content/article/2005/06/17/AR2005061701031.html.

[12] www.usatoday.com/money/companies/management/2004-04-25-conseco_x.htm.

[13] www.businessweek.com/smallbiz/content/mar2004/sb20040311_4465_sb014.htm.

[14] www.theregister.co.uk/2003/12/18/lehman_moves_help_desk_out/.

[15] http://news.bbc.co.uk/2/hi/uk_news/england/3421385.stm.

[16] www.marketwatch.com/News/Story/Story.aspx?guid=%7BFE2A01C5%2D387A%2D445C%2DB9CF%2DD13B4CEB8170%7D&source=blq%2Fyhoo&dist=yhoo&siteid=yhoo.

Appendixes for Chapter 3

Appendix 3A

Locating a Task on the Process Decomposition Compass

To consider whether a given process is efficiency focused or effectiveness focused, ask the following kinds of questions:

Key Questions	Efficiency/ Scale	Response		Expertise/ Effectiveness
1. How easily can the activity be specified and documented?	Easy	Moderate	Difficult; only some aspects	Not possible
2. Do existing service levels/performance indicators for this activity focus internally (how work is performed) or externally (impact on business drivers)?	Internally focused	Mostly internally focused	Strongly influence KPIs of business served	Direct linkage with KPIs of businesses served
3. How long does it take for a new employee / transferee to become proficient in the role?	< 3 Months	3-6 Months	6-12 Months	> 2 Years
4. Are your best performers distinguishing themselves on consistency and speed or on creativity and business impact?	Productivity & accuracy	Proficiency and consistency	Creativity	Business impact
5. Are mistakes that may occur today typically caused by clerical error and failure to follow standard procedures or because of faulty analysis or failure to understand complexity of situation?	Keystroke/ clerical	Procedural	Lack knowledge	Analytical thinking

To consider whether a given process is standardized or customized, ask the following kinds of questions:

	Generic/ Standardized			Localized/ Customized
1. Are there process interdependencies that prevent physically separating this work from groups/individuals who receive services?	Connected thru phone, email, workflow	Requires monthly face-to-Face	Requires daily working sessions	Requires daily working sessions
2. Are the policies and processes used (or envisioned) the same or similar across the business units?	Highly standardized	Very similar	Somewhat customized	Highly customized
3. Is the technology used (or envisioned) the same or similar across the business units?	Same ERP & enabling tools	Some common tools	Mostly different	Completely different
4. Are internal and external sources of information and/or direction the same or very similar across the business units?	Highly standardized	Very similar	Somewhat customized	Highly customized
5. Is signficant third party cost/involvement part of this activity? If so, are common 3rd parties used across the business?	Common 3rd parties	Some overlap	No third party usage	Third parties used, but not common

Appendix 3B

Assessing the Feasibility, Value, and Risk of Potential Outsourcing Efforts

Feasibility

To consider whether a given process is feasible, ask the following kinds of questions:

	Very Feasible			Not Possible
1. How easily can the activity be specified and documented?	Easy; rules-based processes	Moderate; some judgment required	Difficult; only some aspects	Not possible
2. Are there interdependencies that make separation of work between an outsource and in-source service delivery difficult?	No, easily segmented	Limited interdependencies on some transactions	Moderate interdependencies	Highly integrated tasks with irregular data flows
3. Can successful outcomes be defined for each activity in measurable terms?	Yes, key metrics known; easy to measure	Metrics exist for some activity	Few outcomes; subjective measures	No outcomes; highly subjective measures
4. Do external providers exist for each activity?	Yes, mature marketplace	Significant, qualified providers to ensure competitiveness	Few qualified providers	Untested
5. Are market solutions proven or experimental?	Commodity service	Some proven solutions exist	Limited solution maturity	Highly customized solutions
6. To what extent is internal company knowledge essential to performing the activity?	No internal knowledge required or easily obtained and documented	Some basic, documentable knowledge required	Detailed knowledge, not formally captured, is required	Intimate company knowledge and history required
7. What is the nature of the change required? Can we make that change?	Minimal or manageable change impact	Limited change; limited stakeholders	Moderate change to stakeholders	Large impact to many/key stakeholders; low ability to impact

Value and Risk

To consider whether a given process has high or low risks/rewards, ask the following kinds of questions:

	High Reward/ High Risk			Low Reward/ High Risk
1. Will the outsourcing process allow increasing management focus on core activities?	Yes, burden from management lifted	Most distractions eliminated	Moderate impact on management	No impact
2. How do current quality & cost compare to best practices and external providers?	Far superior to internal results	Somewhat better than current cost and quality	On par with current cost and quality	Worse than current cost and quality
3. Will costs go down . . . or become more predictable . . . or variabilized by outsourcing?	Lower cost, full unit pricing	Slightly lower cost, some variability	Level costs, some variable	Highly negotiated price changes
4. Is an outsourcer better able or more likely to invest and bring improvements to market faster?	Yes, provider process/tools far better than internal	Some improvement in process possible	Provider on par with internal process and tools	Provider process / tools worse than current
5. What is the confidence in achieving the desired business case through outsourcing vs. internal transformation?	Much more likely through outsourcing / contracted savings via predictable pricing	Believe there is benefit via outsourcing, but difficult to predict due to pricing uncertainty	Unknown or somewhat more comfortable with internal transformation estimates	Believe results through outsourcing will be worse than internal transformation
6. What is outsourcing's impact on business continuity planning?	Reduced risk through redundant provider sites and/or robust disaster recovery approach	Limited ability to restore some processes	Backup possible but with degraded service or lengthy interruption	Outsourcers ability to provide redundancy / disaster recovery worse than current solution
7. What would outsourcing's impact be on morale?	Little risk or manageable impact via change management program	Some risk; concerns with effectiveness of change management program	Potential regional / business unit impact	Wide morale impact to organization; likely business disruption
8. Is there any market perception risk to outsourcing?	Little or manageable risk	Some risk; some external visibility	Moderate risk; external visibility of outsourcing	Highly visible externally; locations in sensitive areas

Appendix 3C

Assessing the "Offshoreability" of Potential Tasks and Processes

Ask the following kinds of questions to assess the "offshoreability" of various processes:

	High			Low
1. How labor intensive is the process?	High labor / all manual processes	Moderate labor / some enabling technology	Low labor / highly automated	
2. How specialized are the skills required to perform the job requirements?	None; entry level / generic skills only	Some; advanced level; can be obtained fairly quickly	Some; takes a fair amount of time to master	Having skill level is 1st hurdle for job
3. How documented is the process?	Very documented; up to date desk top procedures	Documented to desk level / needs updating	Documented with flow charts for SOX compliance	Little to no documentation
4. How simple are the business rules that are applied in the process?	Very simple; Yes or No with no gray area	Simple; very little interpretation required	Moderately complex; at least 50% judgement	Very complex; 100% judgement
5. How stable are the business rules used and the application of those business rules in the process?	Highly stable; business rules / application never change	Stable; business rules and / or application change time to time	Some unstability; business rules / application could change based on business needs	Unstable; business rules constantly changing
6. How critical is having local domain knowledge of the business	Not critical	Somewhat critical	Highly critical	
7. Are there process interdependencies that make segregation of work between an offshore / onshore service delivery model difficult?	No; process is self contained	Some but would be manageable	Yes; large amount throughout process	
8. Can the process be configured such that sensitive data can be protected independent of the location where the work is performed?	Process does not have sensitive data	Sensitive data but workarounds can be developed for protection	Data is so integrated in the process it cannot be segragated from where it is performed	
9. Are their physical barriers or constraints between a provider of information and the processessor of information in an offshore locations?	No constraints (e.g. receive data via phone, email, or web)	Some physical constraints but able to workaround (e.g fax to location)	Highly constrained - must pass physicall pass information	

10. Can documents utilized in the process be easily managed through imaging / workflow / file sharing website?

Yes - standard documents flow through process	Would need to use a combination of workflow & file sharing	Iterative process; can utilize file sharing website	Would be very difficult; process uses one-off documents

11. What is the percentage of customer contact within the process?

a Voice within Organization (Internal Client)

> 50%	25% to 50%	10% to 24%	< 10%

b Voice outside Organization (External Customer / Vendor)

> 50%	25% to 50%	10% to 24%	< 10%

c Email within Organization (Internal Client)

> 50%	25% to 50%	10% to 24%	< 10%

d Email outside Organization (External Customer / Vendor)

> 50%	25% to 50%	10% to 24%	< 10%

12. How easily to use are the systems utilized in the process for completion of normal work?

Easy; screen Driven / All data resides in one place	Fairly Easy; data resides in a few managable places	Moderate; requires some manipulation of system to retrieve data	Complex; constant manipulation of system to retrieve data

Appendix 3D

What's Typically Covered in an SLA?

Every service level agreement is different, but most share some version of the following eight kinds of information:

- **Service level name, category, and type**—This service name should be used in the reporting of the service level. You can categorize service levels into different groups, such as cost, quality, and so on. Service level type is used to indicate the relative importance of the service level—for example, they could be "key" or "critical." Typically, "critical" service levels are associated with financial incentives and penalties.

- **Definition**—Measures for service levels must be defined in the agreement, because any misunderstandings are likely to lead to reporting of inaccurate data by the vendor. Be as *specific* and *exhaustive* as possible. For example, include formulas, if required. Include the data source (for example, from where will the call time be picked up?). Include details on how data will be aggregated. Be careful not to aggregate too much data, because a large project with good results may obscure poor performance in several small projects. If you must aggregate data into one measure, ensure it's weighted appropriately and data doesn't get skewed. Specify any other measures—such as those required to calculate primary measures and measure defects—that would be useful in the reporting.

- **A "reporting commences date"**—This may be used to indicate exactly when the service provider should begin to report measurement data on a service level. The beginning of the contract may include a honeymoon period before reporting begins.

- **A "measurement reporting frequency"**—This may be used to specify a frequency for data reporting. Over time, you should be able to discern trends in the data.

- **Target**—Setting targets for various service levels is a critical component that requires careful thought. It should be based on baseline data or some way of arriving at the benchmark. There may be some areas where you may want to negotiate better targets than those arrived at using the baseline data. You can also set "sliding targets" for the vendor—that is, setting a higher target as the volume of service increases. For example, for fixing defects, you can set different targets based on the number of defects fixed in an assessment period. If you have a higher-than-expected number of maintenance requests, your target can be set at a particular level; if you get fewer than that many requests, your target can be lowered a bit.

- **Continuous improvement**—Many contracts include a provision for continuous improvement of service levels on an annual basis. Identify service levels in which you would like to see (and where there is scope for) continuous improvement. Many service levels could be included, but you may conclude that some are already at a level where it might not make business sense to improve. You may specify targeted percentage improvements for different service levels. These may vary based on the service level, improvement potential, and your business need.

- **Performance review period**— This is the time period after which the vendor's performance on the service levels will be assessed against the target, and incentives/penalty clauses may be invoked. (This period normally would be different from the regular reporting period of the measures.) Identify this period after considering the specific service and its inherent variability, your business focus, and your need to influence vendor behavior. For example, you may assess the system availability on a yearly basis, delivery of system enhancements on a quarterly basis, and quality issues and business impact on a monthly basis.

- **Earn-back windows**—You can provide incentives to the vendor to recover from performances that fall below your expectations—for example, by providing them with an "earn-back window," which is a period during which a vendor can perform at or above the targeted service level to earn back any penalty that they have previously incurred. These windows can be set to different time periods: one month, three months, six months, or even longer. The longer the window, the longer the vendor must sustain the improved performance to prevent penalties from being applied.

4

The Supply Side

Let's assume that you understand *why* you might want to offshore some of your business activities (Chapter 2, "The Economics and Drivers of Offshoring") and that you have a better idea about *how* that might be done (Chapter 3, "Making It Real"). Now let's look at *who* is out there.

We look first at a topic we introduced in earlier chapters: How big is the offshoring universe? The answer, as you'll see, is that the universe of activities, geographies, and potential partners is large and growing.

Second, we look at the history of the supply side. In business, memories tend to be brief (today and tomorrow is what counts). But to some extent, we do steer by our wake, and it's helpful to understand, for example, that the earliest Indian players entered the offshoring game in the early 1970s, and that they've been at it—and getting better at it—for more than three decades. We in the United States tend to think that our role is to lead change, and the role of the rest of the world is to follow our lead. In offshoring, this has long since stopped being the case. Many of the most innovative firms are located in developing countries.

History also helps us understand *how* and *why* this field changes. Put simply, underlying dynamics have characterized offshoring throughout its history. Companies that understand those dynamics tend, over the longer term, to be the winners.

We also take a systematic look at who's out there, and what they're good at. We survey the landscape of offshoring and describe the alternative business models you're likely to come across within that landscape. We present a way to think systematically about your offshoring options ("navigating the offshoring shoals"). Finally, we look at the realities and potential of geographic expansion—a subject that we extend in the Appendixes for Chapter 4.

Collectively, these resources should help you understand and think through your offshoring options.

The Dimensions of the Supply Side

As you have seen, many factors have converged over the past few decades—including technological advancements, policy liberalization, a growing demand for IT and business process services, and new entrepreneurial opportunities, among others—to fuel the phenomenon of offshoring. This is particularly true for the global delivery of information technology (IT) and business process outsourcing (BPO) services from offshore. According to recent estimates from McKinsey & Company, the combined potential market for global offshoring of IT and BPO was around $300 billion in 2005, and was more or less equally split between IT and BPO. It's important to note that the *actual* offshore exports of IT and BPO amounted to only $18.4 billion and $11.4 billion (11.1 percent and 8.4 percent of the estimated potential markets, respectively), but each sector was projected to grow to $55 billion by 2010.[1]

Other observers, including NASSCOM and Gartner, generally confirm McKinsey's analysis and projections, as summarized in Table 4.1.

TABLE 4.1   Software (IT) and BPO Offshoring

Software (IT) Offshoring (Billions)*

Year	2003	2004	2005	2006	2007	2008	2009	2010
IT Offshoring	9.8	12.3	15.2	18.4	22.1	26.3	31.6	38.2
IT Services (Global)		418.0	444.0	470.0	498.0	528.0	558.0	598.0
% of Potential Market		2.9	3.4	3.9	4.4	5.0	5.7	6.5

BPO Offshoring (Billions)**

IT Offshoring		3.0	6.4	12.6	20.1	30.2	42.9	
IT Services (Global)		111.3	121.1	131.6	144.4	157.5	172.0	
% of Potential Market		2.7	5.3	9.6	13.9	19.2	24.9	

*Source: NASSCOM Strategic Report 2006 (p. 34) and NASSCOM Strategic Report 2007.
**Source: Gartner Article: "'Offshore BPO Becomes Irrelevant as Service Providers Go Global."

Note, too, that these estimates were limited to the offshoring of *existing* business processes. Obviously, the introduction of newer off-shore-only products and service offerings—for example, those aimed at preventing revenue "leaks," enhancing analytics support for decision making, and increasing monitoring and quality—will further increase this potential.

We've recently seen a broad-based move to offshore not only peripheral activities, such as software development, but to also off-shore "core" processes, such as R&D and engineering in the automotive industry and product design in telecommunications. As shown in Figure 4.1, the growth rates for offshore provision in some of these core areas is higher than in the more traditional IT, call-center, and back-office functions.

And finally, we should note that the base of companies that are ready, willing, and able to offshore is growing rapidly (see Figure 4.2). It's not surprising that the largest companies are leading the way, given 1) their overwhelming need to cut costs and grow profits, and 2) their deep financial and organizational resources. Somewhat more

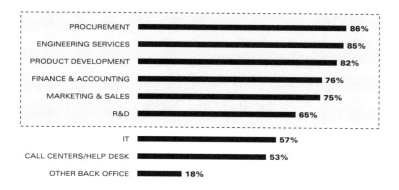

Figure 4.1   Planned growth in offshoring, by function, in the next 18–36 months[2]

surprising is the fact that smaller companies are outpacing medium-sized companies in their embrace of offshoring. We can conjecture that this represents the willingness of small and innovative firms to take risks, and perhaps their determination to "change the game" to their own advantage.

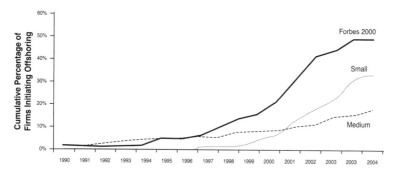

Figure 4.2   Cumulative percentage of firms initiating offshoring by size[3]

As noted earlier, India has emerged as a global leader in offshoring. In 2005, it accounted for 65 percent of global IT exports and 45 percent of global BPO exports. The 50 largest IT global services suppliers had 430,000 of their total workforce of 1.7 million employees (that is, more than 25 percent) located in India.[4] The Indian market has grown more than tenfold since the late 1990s (see Figure 4.3). In 2006, it exported $31.3 billion worth of IT and IT-enabled (or BPO) services.[5]

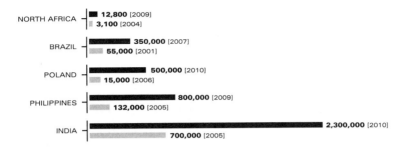

Figure 4.3   Employment in the IT/BPO industry

But that's only part of a much bigger picture. Despite India's growth and leadership position, many other countries have been positioning themselves to grab a piece of the growing IT and BPO services pie. In the Philippines, for example, the number of employees working in the IT/BPO sector is projected to grow from 132,000 in 2005 to 800,000 in 2009—a six-fold increase in four years. Similarly, the number of people employed in the contact centers in Brazil has increased by more than six times from 55,000 in 2001. Although we expect India to maintain its leadership position, its share of offshore services provision will likely decline as other countries grow this sector aggressively.

The global offshoring "pie" continues to expand as overall demand for these types of services grows. Most notably, demand from Europe for offshored services is on the rise. Multinationals based in France, Germany, Spain, Japan, and Australia (and in the Western Hemisphere, Canada) were happy to let U.S.- and U.K.-based multinationals take the initial leap of faith; today, they are making a concerted effort to catch up with those pioneers.[6]

Partners in Perspective: A Quick History of Offshoring

To understand and distinguish among today's cast of characters in the drama of offshoring, it's helpful to understand where they came from and what they've been through. We can consider the history of offshoring in six phases, the first two of which overlap significantly.

Phase I: Indian Software Gets an Onshore Foothold (1973–1988)

Any starting date we might choose for this complicated story would be somewhat arbitrary, but we'll pick 1973: the year that Tata Consultancy Services (TCS) reached a milestone agreement with the U.S.-based Burroughs Corporation. Under that agreement, Burroughs agreed to secure programming contracts for TCS in the United States, and TCS would act as Burroughs's sales agent in India.

TCS—a small service bureau under the wing of the sprawling and powerful Tata Group—had been founded in 1968 to serve as an internal management-consulting group, with a focus on shared IT services. When the internal workflow proved insufficient to sustain the business, TCS began soliciting outside clients. A successful engagement with the Central India Bank led to other work in both the Indian public and private sectors.

One problem facing TCS was that India had strict foreign exchange requirements, making it difficult for TCS to import the hardware required for its projects. But if TCS could generate hard currency through export earnings on its own, the approval for imports would be much quicker. This led to its deal with Burroughs, then the world's second-largest computer hardware manufacturer.

The Burroughs alliance worked out well. In 1974, a Burroughs reference led to TCS's first large U.S. software project, for the Detroit Police Department. TCS split the development work between Bombay and Detroit. The project was completed quickly and under budget. Over the next several years, TCS completed additional projects for the State University of New York, several U.S. banks, and the City of Detroit. On most of these projects, TCS provided services such as coding/testing and acceptance testing/implementation. Projects were jointly delivered, with TCS providing low-cost qualified programmers who worked closely with and under the direction of Burroughs project managers. This "rent-a-programmer" business was generally referred to as "body-shopping."

By 1977, Burroughs-related business accounted for more than 90 percent of TCS's exports, and a growing portion of its domestic business was developed on Burroughs machines. When IBM abruptly left India in 1977 because of changes in the laws regulating foreign ownership, Burroughs approached TCS to form a joint venture to manufacture its computers in India. TCS declined—wary of permanently allying itself with a single hardware platform—and the four-year-old partnership collapsed.

The end of the Burroughs relationship led to a fundamental rethinking of TCS's strategy. The firm shifted its focus to IBM hardware and software and opened a New York sales office. TCS's breakthrough project came from the Institutional Group and Information Company (IGIC), a data center for ten banks in the U.S. Northeast, which hired TCS to migrate its systems from Burroughs hardware to IBM mainframes. The work launched a substantial migration business, in which TCS was compensated for its specific competencies, not just for low-cost generic programming services.

After the success of the IGIC project, both the custom programming and migration businesses grew quickly. As TCS's skills developed, the company took on more and more project management responsibility, gradually shifting from time-and-materials billing toward fixed-price contracts. By the late 1980s, TCS had firmly established itself and, as the firm built its reputation, competed less and less on price.

Meanwhile, the mix of business in India was also shifting. When the government lowered tariffs on hardware, large firms began to acquire their own computers and TCS moved away from the service-bureau business and toward application development. Overall firm revenues grew steadily in the 1980s—from $8 million to $38 million in 1990—and employment grew from 430 to 2,300.

During this period, nearly all export work was done at a client's facilities. Supporting a programmer in the United States was significantly more expensive than one in India, but telecommunications bottlenecks and client concerns about control and quality necessitated onsite work. As TCS grew and began sending hundreds of employees abroad, however, dollar costs surged and it became increasingly difficult to obtain enough work visas. At the same time, advances in software engineering and telecommunications were changing the cost-benefit calculus in favor of "offshore" work—that is, programming services performed in India for foreign clients.

For all of these reasons, TCS made an aggressive move to a new business model in 1988. The company purchased an IBM 3090 mainframe—the first in India—and had it installed in its new development center in Chennai (Madras).

Of course, TCS was not alone in the invention and evolution of the onshore-to-offshore era. Infosys was founded in Pune, India, in 1981. The firm signed its first U.S. client (New York–based Data Basics Corp.) that same year and opened its first U.S. office (in Boston) in 1987. Infosys initially offered mainly onshore software services. By the late 1980s, it, too, was investing in offshore staffing and infrastructure. Wipro Technologies, founded in 1980, was established as the domestic information-services arm of Wipro Limited, a highly diversified manufacturer. Like TCS and Infosys, Wipro quickly began offering "onshore" services in the United States and Europe and, by the late 1980s, was pursuing offshore provision.

Phase II: Early Experiments in the United States and Ireland (1981–1990)

Now we shift to concurrent activities in the developed world. More than 40 years ago, firms in the United States began relocating their call center operations from expensive cities to smaller towns. At that point in time, "going international" was not a realistic option, due to high telecom costs, lack of skilled suppliers abroad, and the high barriers to investment in services. But even within the United States's continental boundaries, the urban/rural cost differentials allowed businesses to achieve cost savings in the range of 20 to 30 percent simply by shifting the location of their back-office functions.[7] As a result, places such as South Dakota began to appear as the return address on credit-card statements.

Gradually, the costs for rural employees and infrastructure in the United States rose toward those of more urbanized areas, and companies once again began chasing lower costs by moving business activities across national borders. In the 1980s, U.S. companies relocated some of their routine information and data processing work to places such as Mexico and the Caribbean. There were three compelling reasons: 1) wages that were a fraction of those in the United States, 2) a generally cooperative (and in many cases, English-speaking) labor force, and 3) much cheaper office space. Advances in telecommunication and satellite communication also helped stimulate and sustain early offshoring activities. Although these efforts represented only a very small percentage of business activity, they helped establish the idea that service activities could be performed remotely.

We should note that this initial wave of relocation went well beyond low-end clerical activities. Countries such as Ireland invested in the necessary infrastructure and actively promoted themselves as offshore destinations. In the 1980s, for example, Ireland developed a digital-based telephone network, which (after Germany's) was the second-most advanced in Europe. Ireland attracted leading global software companies such as Microsoft, Oracle, and Corel, all of which established software-manufacturing centers there in the mid-1980s.

Phase III: India-Based Software Exports (1990–1995)

The next phase began when GE's Jack Welch decided to take a chance on "true" offshoring to India. In 1989, Welch was in India selling airplane engines and plastics to the government when the conversation turned to software. Welch liked what he heard and sent ten people from his staff to check out Indian software capabilities. GE soon signed several software sourcing agreements, totaling $10 million. This boosted Indian credibility at a time when the country was still regarded by many as a risky backwater.[8] Emboldened by GE's move—and attracted by the large pool of English speakers and the abundance of technically proficient employees— American Express, Citicorp, HSBC, and others began offshoring development work to India. The assignments consisted largely of software-application maintenance, application development, and platform migration activities in software—that is, basic development activities.

Meanwhile, large businesses were moving away from legacy systems and toward industry-standard platforms (that is, away from mainframes to workstations and PCs, and away from custom mainframe applications to industry-standard packages such as SAP and PeopleSoft). This meant that provider firms could afford to make *software-specific* investments, rather than investments in client-specific capabilities. This helped create a trained workforce with portable skills, able to serve multiple clients.

Phase IV: Growth of Business Process Offshoring (1995–2002)

Over time, businesses began to use offshoring for an increasing number of other business service areas, including data entry, call centers, payments processing, and accounts receivable management. The trailblazers of this new direction were primarily "captives" of multinational firms. American Express established the first business-process captive operation in India in 1993, through the consolidation of its JAPAC (Japan and Asia Pacific) back-office operations. British Airways founded a wholly owned subsidiary in November 1996 with 200 accountants. General Electric set up its Indian subsidiary, GECIS, in 1997; it started with low-end data-entry tasks, but rapidly moved into insurance underwriting and other higher-value activities.

The growing offshore sector in India successfully lobbied the government to adopt industry-friendly policies and initiatives, such as the liberalization of telecommunications, accomplished through the New Telecom Policy of 1999, which introduced IP telephony and ended the state monopoly on international traffic. As international connections opened up, independent third-party providers began to enter the market, lowering costs and catalyzing the growth of call centers and data-processing centers.

The growth of captives created a cadre of Indian managers who gained experience working for world-class organizations. Many of these managers ultimately used their knowledge to launch their own companies. In 2000, for example, Raman Roy and several senior executives left GECIS and—securing venture capitalist funding from Chrysalis Capital (now ChrysCapital)—started Spectramind, which was sold to Wipro in 2002.

By 2002, all major Indian IT companies had begun offering BPO services. In addition, global outsourcing players such as Convergys and Sitel had set up operations in India. Within the BPO market, medical transcription was one of the first activities to go offshore. Data processing, medical billing, and customer support soon followed. Call centers also took root in countries such as the Philippines and South Africa; however, India continued to be the leading offshore destination, thanks to a critical mass of software firms and technically qualified workers.

Phase V: Geographic Expansion and Acquisition (2003–2006)

By the early 2000s, both the IT (that is, software) industry and the IT-enabled services (that is, BPO) industry had put down strong roots in India. But several challenges were emerging. For one thing, the growing demand for talent led to substantial wage inflation, with average wages in this space growing at more than 30 percent annually in the late 1990s.[9]

At the same time, corporations that were offshoring to India began to be concerned about the risks inherent in concentrating their services in a single geography. These concerns intensified in 1998, as tensions with neighboring Pakistan increased, and both countries detonated nuclear devices. This geopolitical uncertainty, coupled with wage inflation, persuaded many firms to diversify geographically.

Many multinational providers with a presence in India already had a small presence in other countries, and it was relatively easy for them to take their learnings from India and open additional offshore centers. For example, during this period, Accenture opened centers in Hungary and China, while Capgemini established a center in Poland.

Many of the Indian providers were growing rapidly and, to service global multinationals more effectively, also expanded geographically to be closer to their key customers. During this period, Infosys opened centers in both the Czech Republic and China, Wipro went to the Philippines, and the always-aggressive TCS expanded its international base in multiple directions.

During this phase, moreover, numerous other countries set out to emulate India's success. They developed national knowledge-sector policies and began positioning and marketing themselves as attractive nodes in the emerging global knowledge-work marketplace. It soon became clear that the globalization of business process service delivery no longer would be limited to India. China, Southeast Asia, Central and Eastern Europe, and Latin America all emerged as viable exporters. During this period, A.T. Kearney expanded its annual location attractiveness index from 25 countries in 2004 to 40 countries in 2005, reflecting the growing number of credible service providers (see Appendix 4A).

As companies added service capacity in new locations, "India sourcing" evolved into *global* sourcing. Savvy providers offered to divide projects into components and process them simultaneously from multiple locations. This type of global network reduced location risks, provided flexibility, and hedged against wage pressures or skills shortages that might occur in a specific geography.

As experience with offshoring accumulated, firms began to move beyond simple labor arbitrage, investing in process competencies and quality methodologies such as Lean and Six Sigma. Standardized service level agreements and operational metrics were developed, thus allowing more and more activities to migrate offshore, and for third-party providers to close the gap with captive operations.

The other major offshoring trend to emerge in this period was *acquisition*—with global firms acquiring leading local firms (see Table 4.2), and Indian providers acquiring assets in North America and Europe (see Table 4.3).

TABLE 4.2   Notable Acquisitions by Global Firms

Global Supplier	Acquired Company	Date of Purchase	Value
CSC, USA	Covansys, USA*	April 2007	$1.4 billion
EDS, USA	RelQ, India	Feb 2007	$65 million
Capgemini, EU	Kanbay, India	Oct 2006	$1.3 billion
EDS	mPhasis, India	Oct 2006	$380 million
Capgemini	Unilever India Shared Services	Sep 2006	N/A
CA, USA	XoSoft, India	July 2006	N/A
R. R. Donnelley	Office Tiger, USA*	March 2006	$250 million

*Firm had substantial offshore presence in India

TABLE 4.3   International Acquisitions by Indian Firms

Offshore Vendor	Acquired Company	Geography	Date of Purchase	Value
Genpact	ICE Enterprise Solutions	Netherlands	March 2007	N/A
TCS	TKS-Teknosoft	Europe	Oct 2006	$81 million
Cognizant	Almnet Solutions	USA	Sep 2006	$15 million
I-flex	Mantas	USA	Aug 2006	$123 million
Wipro	Enabler	Portugal	June 2006	$52 million

The trend can be traced back to 2004, when IBM acquired Daksh, an Indian BPO provider. Several U.S. and European multinationals subsequently followed IBM's lead. The developed country acquisitions were made to increase Indian companies' onshore/nearshore presence, and also to achieve a more balanced onsite and offshore resource mix, especially for higher-value activities such as R&D, engineering services, and equity research.

Phase VI: Global Talent-Seeking (2007 to the Present)

As developed-country firms improved their offshore capabilities and became more comfortable managing service delivery from offshore, they began to look globally for unique skills. For example, within an integrated circuits firm (for example, Intel or Texas Instruments), product engineers in China and Taiwan might work to customize standard products for specific clients, thus freeing up their U.S. counterparts to focus on designing the next leading-edge chip.[10] Firms have started using offshore resources to invent new products, extract greater value from existing business processes through reengineering, service higher-value knowledge processes such as patenting, and develop new capabilities and offerings.

The nature of R&D—formerly internal and domestic—has started to change.[11] R&D strategies have moved toward decentralized systems and cross-border knowledge flows.[12] Networked R&D has become a key priority on management agendas, adding to an increased involvement of low-cost sites and partners in core product lines.[13] The need for cost savings and access to talent has caused firms to rapidly increase R&D spending in developing economies.[14]

One example in India is the $120 million John F. Welch Technology Centre, opened by GE in India in September 2000. The center conducts research and development for GE businesses worldwide. Microsoft has a similar facility in China, where more than 300 researchers and engineers carry out fundamental, "curiosity-driven" research.

In some cases, offshore R&D operations have taken the lead. Broadcom's Bangalore operation, for example, is responsible for semiconductor design and manages the company's teams in the United States, Singapore, and Israel.[15]

Firms have also started to offshore other knowledge-intensive, high-end processes. These activities, which have traditionally been less structured, require advanced analytical and technical skills along with domain expertise. Emerging areas include data-search management, biotech, pharmaceutical research, remote tutoring, educational development, publishing, animation, and simulation. Several global players (such as McKinsey, Goldman Sachs, and A.C. Nielsen) have established significant high-value operations in India. Evalueserve has projected that global knowledge process outsourcing (or KPO) will grow from $1.3 billion in 2003 to $17 billion by 2010.

Firms have also started exploring ways to use cost-effective skill sets offshore to improve their capabilities and offerings. These fall into three broad categories:

- Enhancing existing activities through rigor (that is, defect elimination, better measurement, reduction in process variation, etc.)
- Ensuring greater output quality
- Pursuing smaller opportunities that were previously not viable

This last point deserves scrutiny. A more flexible cost structure has enabled firms to chase smaller opportunities, which tend to fall into one of two categories. The first is *preventing value leaks*. A leading U.S. bank has claimed that shutting down these value leaks (mainly through better fraud detection) has saved $100 million.[16] The second is *cultivating new sources of value*, such as differentiated services, cross-selling within existing markets, and introducing cost-effective service offerings for underserved customers and markets. A survey by A.T. Kearney found that a quarter of firms reported that they have enhanced their revenue performance through offshoring.[17]

This brings our historical survey up to the present day. Perhaps the key lesson we should take away from this history of a seemingly exotic sector is that on the most fundamental level, *it's not exotic at all*—a point we revisit in subsequent sections. Companies (whether buyers or sellers of offshoring services) encounter constraints, in response to which they innovate. A successful innovation creates a temporary advantage, which leads to higher performance and growth. Then come imitation, increased competition, declining margins, and new constraints. Once again, the company that is buying or selling offshored services must find a new edge to succeed.

Understanding the Vendor Landscape

Now that you've seen how offshoring has developed, we can take a snapshot of the global sourcing landscape today. As suggested in the preceding pages, offshoring follows the fundamental rules of economics and incorporates most of the lessons learned in the fast-growing universe of global trade. These include the following:

- **The need to strike appropriate balances**—Firms must balance cost savings against the investment required to achieve those savings. (Refer back to the earlier discussion of transaction cost economics, or TCE, for clarification.) At the same time, they must weigh the risks inherent in offshoring (including loss of control, exposure to macroeconomic risks, public perception, the distribution of sensitive data and intellectual property, and so on) against the likely benefits.

- **The need to achieve scale**—For many basic operations, the key is gaining sufficient scale to minimize costs. Large firms can achieve this internally. (GE and American Express, for example, have tens of thousands of potentially offshoreable positions.) Smaller firms generally go to outside vendors, who gain scale by aggregating across many customers.

- **The need to build and control an expertise**—Scale isn't always the most important consideration. Some businesses involve specific skills—for example, in fields such as radiology, genomics research, and so on. This creates the need to gain access to specific people, who by and large tend to have bargaining power and mobility (that is, lots of career options). In some cases, multinational corporations—for example, large pharmaceutical firms—can successfully hire and retain these people. In others, the talent bands together and acts as a group (for example, ITTIAM, paralegals, and radiologists) that offers its services as independent vendors.

- **The need to create or embrace appropriate business structures**—We've already introduced the notion of controlling risks. Higher perceived risks (to business processes, intellectual property, outsiders, or data) make it more likely that a particular process or task will be kept in-house. In some cases, this implies an advantage for large firms who can afford captives for scale processes because the incremental cost of adding on additional processes is low.

Many types of vendors and corporations are delivering global IT and IT-enabled services from offshore. These organizations employ a variety of business models for providing offshore services, which can be grouped into four categories:

- Captives of multinationals
- Offshore IT vendors
- Multinational outsourcing firms
- Offshore BPO-specific firms

As we briefly look at these four types of vendors, keep in mind the 2×2 first introduced in Chapter 2. As we make references in subsequent pages to "moving down" or "moving to the right" in the 2×2 shown in Figure 4.4, this is the grid to which we'll be referring.

Captives of Multinationals

As you have seen, firms don't have to outsource their activities in order to leverage offshore advantages; they can keep the work inside the firm, but procure it from remote locations. So-called "captives" are wholly owned subsidiaries of multinationals, and this business model is used by many prominent companies today, including American

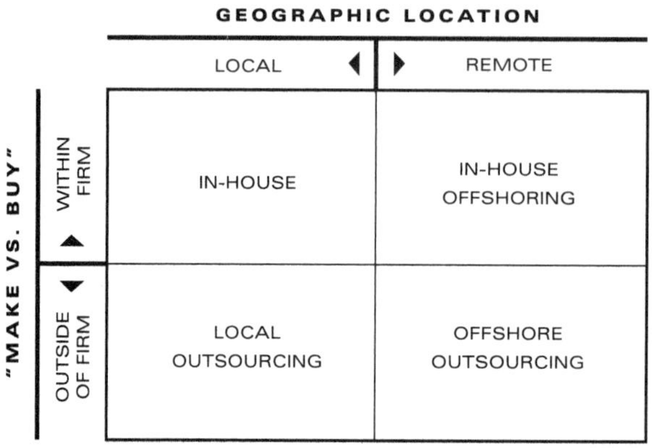

GEOGRAPHIC LOCATION

	LOCAL ◀	▶ REMOTE
WITHIN FIRM ▲	IN-HOUSE	IN-HOUSE OFFSHORING
OUTSIDE OF FIRM ▼	LOCAL OUTSOURCING	OFFSHORE OUTSOURCING

"MAKE VS. BUY"

Figure 4.4   The outsourcing and offshoring decisions lead to four potential arrangements.

Express, Microsoft, Oracle, and Motorola. Companies that set up captives in offshore locations move from the upper left to the upper right of our grid.

According to Infosys, about 56 percent of these captives started as wholly-owned subsidiaries, and about 13 percent were founded as joint ventures. To generalize, this business form was prevalent when there were few local providers, and transactions costs were perceived to be high (that is, few local suppliers, high search and negotiating costs, and high perceived likelihood of holdup). Initially, only large corporations found it made sense to set up captives, due to the high startup costs and the focus on low-value-added activities. This meant, in turn, that large scale was important to earn back the setup investments.

American Express established the first business process captive operation in India in 1993, and British Airways started its wholly owned subsidiary in November 1996. Business process operations for General Electric—set up as GECIS in 1997—scaled rapidly and reached 12,000 employees by 2003. (British Airways and General Electric divested control in their captive operations in 2002 and 2004, respectively.)

The stampede of multinationals setting up offshore captives started around 2000. At that time, firms with an existing offshore presence (such as HP, HSBC, and JPMorgan Chase) started expanding rapidly. Many firms that had no prior offshore experience (for example, Dell, AOL, and SAP) observed the first movers' success and moved to establish their own operations. Most of them expanded rapidly. Dell, for example, launched its captive in June 2001 and employed 10,000 people by April 2005. The activities within the captives have followed the shift in services—early captive centers such as Oracle and SAP were IT- and software-focused, whereas more recent captives have targeted both back-office processing and higher-value business processes.

As Figure 4.5 indicates, there has been a steady growth of both U.S.- and European-based captives.

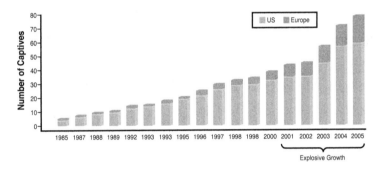

Figure 4.5   Growth of captives in India[18]

As of 2006, the average size of a captive in India was around 1,000 people, with a median of 375. Fewer than ten companies employed more than 5,000 people.

Captives in India today account for $9 billion of exports—or 30 percent of the Indian total—and EquaTerra estimates that the number of captive centers in India will grow by approximately 30 percent over the next several years. In addition to new captive formation, existing captives are expected to grow their headcounts at a 50-percent annual rate. Taking the next logical step, some captives are leveraging their capabilities to provide services to other companies. ABN Amro, for example, provides trade finance back-office processing for other banks from its facility in India.

Captives are pursuing a range of different strategies to develop scale, including hosting vendor employees within their facilities, pressuring their parent organizations to in-source work previously outsourced to third-party vendors, and building capacity in hopes that they will attract demand.

Note how the past, present, and likely future of captives follows the "script" laid out earlier in the form of economic principles and imperatives. At first, the only viable model was captives established by large global firms. As procedures became established and learning occurred, some managers struck out on their own and established third-party vendors. As the range of services available through third-party providers expands, the advantages of captives diminish. Slowing growth limits career opportunities; attrition becomes a major challenge. Divestitures by early movers, such as GE and British Airways, have already signaled a maturing of the market, especially for commodity and industry-standard business processes. These trends will only accelerate and intensify in the future.

Offshore IT Vendors

Offshore-based IT service providers such as TCS, Infosys, Wipro, Satyam, and Mphasis—in the lower-right corner of our 2×2—have both grown aggressively and matured substantially in recent years. Most of these service providers started out by providing technical resources onsite to clients located in the United States and Europe (the service model referred to previously as "body shopping," and the lower-left quadrant in our 2×2). Over time, they built the necessary supplier relationships and capabilities to manage and deliver software projects from offshore. They have since won increasingly large outsourcing contracts and migrated larger systems-development projects offshore.

As higher-value work started moving offshore, some of these vendors set up centers dedicated to individual clients, which were isolated from the rest of the vendor operations by firewalls and access restrictions to ensure security and privacy of client data and intellectual property. In addition to providing several service offerings with IT services, these vendors have invested in domain capabilities and now offer several business process services. The logic was, and is, "If you trust us to *build* your systems, why not let us *run* them as well?"

IT vendors have followed several different approaches to building capabilities in business process services. TCS, introduced earlier, got into BPO through a series of joint ventures—with Singapore Airlines to establish an operation serving the travel industry and with HDFC to target the UK financial services industry. In 2003, TCS moved to consolidate its BPO operations—acquiring stakes from Singapore Airlines and Swiss Air, and divesting its financial services stake to HDFC.

More recently, TCS has emphasized organic growth, particularly in geographic information systems and engineering services, which the firm sees as providing opportunities for differentiation. TCS also stayed in the acquisitions game. Several purchases helped the company expand internationally in business process services.

There were many paths to success. Infosys established a wholly owned subsidiary, Progeon, to offer BPO services—generally in the commodity areas such as call centers and payments processing—for the systems it built for customers. Progeon was later reintegrated into the parent firm when Infosys reorganized along industry lines. Wipro acquired Spectramind in 2002 and grew it rapidly into India's largest call-center services provider.

There are some important differences between software and business process services, including the composition of the two workforces. Whereas software is primarily driven by high-skill engineers, BPO operations are much more varied. They require several layers of managers who can interact with customers. In many cases, however, the actual work is more low end—for example, payments authorization, help-desk support, or responses to email inquiries.

The amount of front-office and call-center activity carried out by these software vendors varies quite a bit. Most of them, though, have attempted to limit their exposure to call-center work because of its commodity nature, and some decline to take on any call-center work unless it is part of a larger process they will be servicing. Today, some are moving their call centers to other locations, such as the Philippines, both for cost and geographic-diversification reasons.

The software firms have been expanding abroad aggressively. TCS, for example, now operates in 41 countries, spanning the globe. Infosys (23 countries) and Wipro (also 23) are not far behind.

Multinational Outsourcing Firms

As the offshore delivery model gained prominence, several global outsourcing firm—including companies such as IBM and Accenture—established and aggressively expanded operations in India and other locations. Their move (in our 2×2, from the upper left to the upper right from their perspective, and from the lower left to lower right from their customers' perspective) was largely a defensive move in response to 1) the increasing competition from offshore vendors, and 2) customer pressure for lower costs. Leading multinational service firms (such as IBM, HP, and EDS in data systems; Convergys and Sitel in call centers; and Accenture and Siemens in business services consulting) now have a sizeable offshore presence. Many of these firms long have had international operations that were established to follow their existing customers abroad. But the move to global sourcing (tapping into low-cost talent to serve remote customers) was new.

These firms are growing very aggressively offshore. As noted previously, IBM reentered India in 1992 after leaving the country in 1978 following a dispute with the government. IBM employed 38,000 in 2005, 60,000 in 2006, and is projected to grow to more than 100,000 by 2010. At the end of its 2007 fiscal year, Accenture's Indian workforce outnumbered its domestic U.S. payroll. "Twenty years ago, when we first came to India [as Arthur Anderson], this was an outpost. Today, it is the flagship of our global delivery network,"

CEO William Green told reporters during his first visit to India in January 2007.[19]

Some of these firms have built capacity offshore through acquisitions. For example, EDS acquired Mphasis in 2006. Following this acquisition, Capgemini paid $1.25 billion to acquire Kanbay (in October 2006), and thereby added 5,000 employees in India. It seems clear that EDS and Capgemini plunged into these acquisitions in part to keep pace with IBM and Accenture's growing access to global talent. At the same time, they are protecting their own customer bases from incursions by the larger Indian firms, such as TCS and Infosys.

Offshore BPO-Specific Firms

Along with the increase in volumes and value being delivered from offshore, there has been an expansion in the types of activities being offered, resulting in more and more processes in a greater number of industries being serviced from offshore. This has led to increased fragmentation and specialization, and the emergence of different types of offshore BPO-specific firms.

One category of firms focuses on a broad set of processes that are common across various industries: payments processing, call-center support, and procurement. These firms include broadline providers such as Genpact and WNS, which formerly were captive operations. They tend to be large, providing expertise in a range of business process services as well as reengineering solutions.

Others—such as Spectramind, founded in 2000, and later acquired by Wipro—grew as independent third-party BPO vendors. Spectramind, as noted, was started by industry veteran Raman Roy, who had previously led both American Express and GECIS operations in India. These firms deliver a broad set of services, leveraging the scale of their operations and their sophisticated process disciplines.

In addition to these large firms, numerous smaller niche firms provide focused services in areas such as tax preparation, business analytics, animation, product design, equity research, and so on.

These firms first focus on building domain-specific knowledge and capabilities. In many cases, they start with low-end services, but the domain focus allows them to move on to deliver higher-end services. For example, a publishing firm that at first only prepared drawings for chemistry texts now offers a full range of back-office services, including copyediting, XML formatting, and technical support. It has even expanded into the highly specialized realm of academic journals.

A limited number of firms, such as Evalueserve and Office Tiger (acquired by R. R. Donnelley), provide high-end knowledge-process services, such as equity analysis, legal research, and business analytics. This is often referred to as knowledge process outsourcing (KPO) and has seen rapid growth, averaging more than 25 percent annually since 2004.[20] These firms focus on domain knowledge and therefore hire selectively for talent. Instead of growing volume and trying to capture scale advantages, these firms focus on building a differentiated knowledge base and skills. Some companies, such as ITTIAM Systems, focus on specific technologies such as Digital Signal Processing (DSP) Systems, and in many cases license their intellectual property. Focusing on wireless, wireline, speech, audio, imaging, and video segments, ITTIAM Systems provides "off-the-shelf" components that can be plugged into its customers' systems.

Navigating the Offshoring Shoals

So far, we've looked at the history of, and significant players in, the offshoring world. Now let's revisit the concepts of transaction costs economics (TCE)—first introduced in Chapter 2—to help you think more systematically about your offshoring options.

For the sake of the discussion, let's first set up an outsourcing/offshoring spectrum (see Figure 4.6), at one end of which you find a company that probably doesn't exist anymore: the company that performs all tasks within the firm, at headquarters. At the other end of the spectrum is a company that is willing and able to have any task performed anywhere, inside or outside the firm (another organization form that probably doesn't exist in the real world today).

Figure 4.6   Navigating between two extremes

How do you position yourself on this spectrum? First of all, let's assume you are motivated to think about this question in some meaningful way—most likely, a competitive shove. But changes in technology or regulation, at home or abroad, may also push you toward a move into offshoring. In the real world, you probably take a baby step first: a call center in India, for example. When you take that small but significant step, you start moving "eastward" on the spectrum. Note that the arrow points in both directions: Companies can and do retrench in situations where it appears they've gone a "bridge too far." For our purposes here, though, we'll focus on eastward movement.

Almost immediately, however, you can see that the spectrum is too one-dimensional a construct to capture the complexity of moving offshore. So let's take a second slice. Figure 4.7 puts your company at the heart of the matter: in the middle of the diagram. The tighter the circle is drawn around your company, the less offshoring you do (and the farther "west" you reside in Figure 4.6). But look at the three arrows projecting out from that center: the *task type,* the *organization type,* and the universe of *locations.*

You can go out from the center—headquarters—along any or all of these axes. You will do so based on the intersection of the *opportunity* you perceive and the *transaction costs* associated with that opportunity. Over time, as demonstrated earlier in the chapter, both the

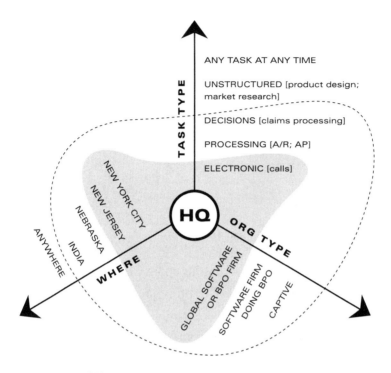

Figure 4.7   Offshoring involves decisions along at least three dimensions.

opportunities and transaction costs associated with offshoring tend to evolve—sometimes slowly, but sometimes quickly and dramatically.

Where should you perform a specific task? Look to the relevant infrastructure and human resources (as well as the regulatory and political climate). Are the people with talent in place? Are there companies with the scale and competencies required to meet your needs? Has a recent technology change made it possible for you to move farther out along this axis (for example, IP telephony that lowers communications costs and allows a move from Nebraska to India)? Have the Indians who worked for your company or in your industry moved back home to take advantage of the Indian boom, and if so, are they available to provide services to your company?

Which tasks should you move offshore? Again, a changing technology may make more things possible. A strengthened telecom infrastructure, for example, makes it as easy to route calls around the world as across the street. Going farther out this axis, you find tasks that are labor intensive and rules based (for example, accounts receivable), which are transferable with sufficient documentation and supervision. Still farther out on this axis, you find tasks that require more judgment (claims processing) or may even be largely unstructured (market research). Your assessment of the level of the local talent (*where*) now intersects with your understanding of what's moveable and what's not in your organization. Perhaps most important, as you gain experience with low-risk offshoring, your comfort level with and ability to manage offshore processes will rise. As you gain confidence, tasks further and further along the task dimension become feasible.

Along this dimension, too, you also have to consider the risks associated with customer perception and public perception. If sentiment in your home country (or home government) is running high against a particular nation, that nation may be disqualified as a provider, at least in the short term.

Finally, we once again encounter *organization type*. Does the information absolutely have to stay in the building? Can it go across the street? If it can go across the street, it can probably go to a captive organization elsewhere in the world (assuming adequate local talent and infrastructure). If it can go to a captive, there's a good chance it can go to a "liberated" captive—a company that has spun off from its original parent to provide specific offshored services to companies like yours.

To summarize: As you consider your offshoring options, think about how location, task, and organization type can be made to intersect to your advantage. At the same time, scrutinize the likely transaction costs associated with your options. What's the cost of bargaining and agreeing to a contract in Country A versus Country B? What will be the cost of monitoring and enforcing that contract? Will you be subject to "holdup"? Will there be a remedy in the case of nonperformance?

Geographic Spread in a Dynamic Landscape

Ten years ago, offshoring was largely an India-centric phenomenon. Today, more than 30 countries are involved in offshoring in more or less significant ways. As you've seen, this expansion has been fueled by numerous parallel forces.

Looking first at the customers' perspective, a broader geographic base is a good thing. Companies purchasing offshored services can reduce country-related risks and other "X-factors" by broadening the geographic base of those purchased services. Although India continues to have the enormous advantage of a large pool of (reasonably good) English speakers, many countries offer enough people to serve as a second or third node in the global supply network. It is also clear that in the globalizing economy, business can and will be done in other languages. Many firms have opened delivery centers to service various language groups—Mexico and Argentina for Spanish language, northeast China for Japanese, North Africa for French, and so on. Other factors beyond language matter as well. China is strong in technical areas such as engineering and scientific research. The Philippines has many English speakers with a cultural affinity for the U.S. Jordan serves as a back-office hub for many global firms' mid-East operations.

Looking at the "producers'" perspective, we see a complementary set of incentives to broaden the geographic base. For example, India-based firms have grown outward from their home country, in part to reduce their own costs, hedge geographic risks, and serve their multinational customers more efficiently and effectively.

At the same time, other countries in the developing world—understandably envious of India's success and convinced that they can compete in at least some aspects of the offshoring phenomenon—have systematically studied India's example and have taken steps to emulate it.

Like who, and like how? The Appendixes for Chapter 4 help you start answering these questions.

The first (Appendix 4A) is A. T. Kearney's "country attractiveness" survey, which that firm has kindly given us permission to reproduce here. As you will see, this annual survey presents data on the top 50 offshoring destinations around the world. For many managers, it's a very useful starting point.

How do you dig deeper? Look at Appendix 4B, which provides a more in-depth look at 24 countries and includes a helpful "SWOT" (strengths, weaknesses, opportunities, and threats) analysis for each. This appendix draws heavily on analyses by EquaTerra, and we thank that company for giving us access to this resource.

Of course, before you make significant investments in offshoring, you'll have to dig far deeper. How do you think about that challenge? Appendix 4C presents a series of nine country profiles, which are mainly intended to help you get a better feel for the key differentiators across the key established and emerging offshoring players. We look at a number of consistent criteria across countries, including the following:

- **The key triggering moment**—That is, what precipitated the growth of offshoring in this locale?
- **The important sector characteristics**—These include size, composition, growth rate, employment, key corporations involved, and major issues and challenges
- **Resources for additional research**—These are provided so that you can explore your opportunities more or less in real time.

A caution: These kinds of profiles become dated almost from the moment they are created. The offshore market is nothing if not *dynamic*. Companies are constantly changing their organization types. (As the offshore industry matures, substantial merger and acquisition activity is already going on, and more can be anticipated.) New companies—indeed, entire new countries—are getting into the game. Next year's offshoring "snapshots" will necessarily be different from this year's.

Let's assume you now feel you have a reasonably good feel for the landscape of offshoring: which players are good at what, and what the trend lines look like. In the next chapter, we take a different slice. We look at the implications of offshoring for *your* company. What will have to change, within your organization, to increase your odds of succeeding at the services shift?

Endnotes

[1] "Extending India's Leadership of the Global IT and BPO Industries," NASSCOM-McKinsey report, December 2005, p. 28.

[2] Duke University and Booz Allen, "Next Generation Offshoring: The Globalization of Innovation," 2007, www.naaahr.org/downloads/OffshoringKeyIssuesFacing Service.pdf (slide #9, accessed on May 18, 2008).

[3] Duke University and Booz Allen, "Next Generation Offshoring," 2007, www. naaahr.org/downloads/OffshoringKeyIssuesFacingService.pdf (slide #8, accessed on May 18, 2008).

[4] Nick Mayes, "Top 50 Vendors Look Beyond India," *Computer Business Review* (May 14, 2007), www.cbronline.com/article_news.asp?guid=A055CF97-AA07-422D-9B3A-32C3A3850FF1.

[5] "Strategic Review: Annual Review of the Indian IT-BPO Sectors," NASCCOM, February 2007, p. 8.

[6] A. T. Kearney, "Execution Is Everything: The Keys To Offshore Success," 2007, p. 7.

[7] R. Dossani and M. Kenney, "The Next Wave Of Globalization: Relocating Service Provision To India," *World Development*, Vol. 35, No. 5, 2007.

[8] "Sam Pitroda: Father of Modern Indian Telecom," The Cook Report on Internet, 2004, pp. 13–17.

[9] Suma S. Athreya, "The Indian Software Industry and Its Evolving Service Capability," *Industrial and Corporate Change*, Vol. 14, No. 3, 2005, pp. 393–418.

[10] J. Halgel III, "Offshoring Goes on the Offensive," *McKinsey Quarterly*, Issue 2, 2004, pp. 82–91.

[11] A. Bardhan and D. Jaffee, "Innovation, R&D, and Offshoring," University of California at Berkeley, Paper No. 1005, 2005.

[12] M. Zanatta and S. Queiroz, "The Role of National Policies on the Attraction and Promotion of MNE's R&D Activities in Developing Countries," *International Review of Applied Economics*, Vol. 21, Issue 3, 2007, pp. 419–435.

[13] H. Andrews, "Making Networked Research And Development Pay," *Engineering Management Journal*, Vol. 17, Issue 2, 2007, pp. 20–23.

[14] Booz Allen Hamilton & INSEAD, "Innovation: Is global the way forward?" 2006.

[15] R. Dossani and M. Kenney, "The Next Wave Of Globalization: Relocating Service Provision To India," *World Development*, Vol. 35, No. 5, 2007.

[16] "Extending India's Leadership in the Global IT and BPO Industries," NASSCOM-McKinsey Report, 2005, p. 38.

[17] A. T. Kearney, "Execution Is Everything: The Keys To Offshore Success," 2007, p. 7.

[18] Manish Subramanian and Bhuwan Atri, "Captives in India: A Research Study," Infosys, February 2006, p. 3, www.infosys.com/global-sourcing/white-papers/captives-research-v2.pdf.

[19] Kalpana Shah, "Accenture shifts growth to India," Red Herring, 2007, www.redherring.com/Home/20989.

[20] "Strategic Review: The IT-BPO Sector in India," NASSCOM, 2008, p. 58.

5

Shifting Skill Sets

In the past few chapters, we have highlighted the opportunities created when a firm undertakes global sourcing. These can include significant cost savings, the ability to access new talent pools, and the opportunity to tap into industry best-practice delivery platforms.

But while the services shift creates many new possibilities to create value in your organization, it also requires the development of new and different skills sets in your management team. Simply put, instead of directly managing people and outcomes, the global sourcing manager generally exerts influence indirectly, through negotiations, mutually agreed-upon goals, and the intelligent design of incentive systems for vendors.

These new functions require global managers to draw on a very different toolkit. Some of these skills are obvious—for example, analytical skills, IT solutions, and structured root-cause analysis all play an important role in managing offshore operations. But some of the changes are less obvious. As you'll see, the global operations manager has to step up his game on both the analytical and the soft-skills end of the spectrum. In the traditional developed-country back office, middle managers generally possessed vast context-specific expertise, often spending the bulk of their careers moving upward within one organization, and enjoying clear and visible status symbols.

In a flat, process-oriented, global-sourcing-focused organization, however, few if any of these characteristics are present. And the transition from one kind of organization to another, as you will see, is not always seamless or painless.

This chapter is organized into three parts. The first part orients you by presenting a simplified but useful model of what managers *actually do* in the generic process of management. The second contrasts the skills needed in a traditional back-office operation (think, for example, of a claims operation at a Midwestern insurance company) with the skill sets needed in an organization that has embraced global sourcing.

In our third and final section, we present lessons drawn directly from the experiences of several dozen firms that have embraced global sourcing. You will note that throughout this chapter, we draw heavily on the first-hand experience of people on the front lines of the services shift.

What Do Managers Do?

The act of management is both complex and situationally driven. Nevertheless, certain broad generalizations hold true across the spectrum of general management. In broad terms, a manager's job is to *analyze what's possible, set goals,* and *coordinate the organization's resources* to reach those goals. More succinctly, in the words of pioneering management scholar Mary Parker Follett, "A manager is a person who gets things done through other people."

For our purpose—exploring how offshoring alters the skill set required for managers—these definitions are somewhat too general. For this discussion, therefore, we will focus on six distinct activities that most managers perform:

- **Analyze the environment and set organizational goals—** One of the primary responsibilities for senior managers involves assessing the business environment, setting reasonable organizational goals, and creating plans for achieving those goals.
- **Communicate goals and objectives—**Once overall goals have been determined, it is critical to break these activities

down into pieces that can be easily digested by the manager's organization. This involves taking large goals and translating them into deliverables that correspond to each piece of the organization. It also involves moving these goals from the boardroom to the shop floor.

- **Organize resources and motivate team members—** Organizing involves undertaking preparations necessary for implementing plans. The manager needs to decide what jobs need to be performed to realize the plan, and then allocate the right people and adequate resources to those tasks. With jobs divided, it is important for managers to ensure coordination of the efforts. Managers typically break down and clarify the goals that each team or individual has to perform and assigns them work schedules and deliverables. Ensuring effective time management and economical resource usage becomes a key priority.

This last step begins to move the manager out of the realm of business concepts and into the realm of psychology and sociology. *Who works well with whom? Which team members need a pat on the back, and which need a kick to the backside?* More broadly, how does the manager balance the short-term imperative of optimizing performance with the long-term goal of cross training, career planning, and building for the long run?

- **Monitor and analyze organizational performance—**Once the plan is in place, the manager must monitor and analyze the performance of the organization against the plan. Structured monitoring is one key to continued performance improvement. It generates data on performance, which is the critical input to the perform-analyze-improve cycle.

- **Reward good performance and penalize underperformance—**After analyzing the organization's performance (which is a fairly conceptual/analytical activity), a manager must translate this back into the realm of personnel management. The simplest level involves annual raises and periodic promotions/separations. But on a day-to-day level, the manager must know which buttons to push for every direct report. Again, does an employee respond to a pat on the back or a kick in the pants? Does the employee desire structure from above, or prefer a well-specified goal with the flexibility to achieve it as he or she best sees fit?

- **Report on performance**—Once a cycle of performance has occurred, a manager must compile performance and personnel data and then report these results up the hierarchy and to peer units. When executed intelligently, accurate reporting spurs the start of another perform-analyze-improve cycle.

The relative importance of—and the time dedicated to—these various managerial functions varies widely based on the organizational level and function of the manager. For example, the roles of strategist, communicator, and resource allocator are central to the jobs of a company's top managers, reflecting top management's responsibilities for planning, organizing, and controlling the strategic direction of the firm. In addition, monitoring the external environment takes on more importance for top managers because they must scan the organization's environment for pertinent information.

Senior executives expend a lot of effort scoping out "the business environment." This requires an increased awareness of business, economic, and social trends. Executives devote substantial time to managing relationships with key customers, identifying new business opportunities, monitoring corporate performance, and gathering market data and other trends outside the organization.

For middle managers, core roles include motivating, monitoring, and allocating resources. These roles are in keeping with middle management's job of organizing, leading, and controlling the functional or divisional units of the firm. In addition, because middle management is responsible for disseminating, explaining, and implementing the strategic plans designed by the top management, the role of communicator is crucial for middle managers.

Mid-level managers also focus on linking various groups. Coordinating interdependent groups is a key activity. Managers review the plans and work of different groups and help them set priorities and integrate activities. As managers move up toward middle management, "managing group performance" becomes most important.

For frontline managers/supervisors, the role of interpersonal leader is the most important. They spend most of their time directing nonsupervisory personnel. They also act as spokespersons, disseminating information to their groups and serving as liaisons between their groups and the rest of the organization. In addition, they acquire and distribute the resources their groups need to do their jobs.

First-level managers are more "one-to-one" with their subordinates. They are primarily concerned with managing the performance of individuals on their teams. Their tasks include motivating and disciplining subordinates; keeping track of performance and providing feedback; training, coaching, and instructing employees in how to do their jobs; and improving communications and individual productivity.

In essence, managers at all levels have a crucial representative function—a role referred to by management and business strategy scholar Henry Mintzberg as *spokesperson.* This includes representing the work group to others, communicating the needs of one's work group to others, and helping subordinates interact with other groups.

Contrasting the Old with the New

Now that we've reviewed the activities involved in the classic definition of "management," let's contrast the old with the new. How do skill sets change when we move from the traditional back office operation to the new global sourcing operation?

Let's start with the traditional firm. The typical middle manager in most traditional firms starts at the bottom and works his way up. The path to success involves a tremendous amount of *context-specific* knowledge. In these environments, the person who gets promoted is generally the one with the most detailed knowledge of specific forms, customers, and history. Career paths generally reside within one function, and within one organization. The best payables clerk, for example, becomes the payables supervisor. The best payables supervisor becomes the accounting manager. In the traditional model, the best administrative director becomes the CFO.

The staff overseen by the manager is likely to come, overwhelmingly, from the local area. They share a culture, a common history, and in many cases similar hobbies. To a large extent, the staff has been to high school or college together, root for the same sports teams, and belong to the same clubs and churches.

This environment puts a premium on certain kinds of skills. Most interactions are face-to-face, so reading people and knowing which buttons to push are very important. A huge percentage of management is accomplished by "walking around," which helps the manager judge performance through body language, the height of the pile in people's inbox, and the general buzz from the organization.

Some automation may occur, but this is generally driven by the IT organization, and in many cases, the manager represents the needs of operations versus the needs of IT. (IT, in other words, tends to be the "other.") Few traditional managers have strong analytical, IT, or systems analysis skills. Most resources, including IT resources, are controlled administratively within the organization—either by the manager directly or by appeals for directives from managers higher in the organization. In other words, if someone isn't getting what he or she needs from the organization, he or she may be able to get the higher-ups in the hierarchy to make it happen.

In the traditional back-office environment, the signs of success and status are very visible. First-line employees work in cubicles, supervisors have larger workspaces, and each level of management has increasingly larger offices. A manager's status can easily be inferred from the dimensions and window-count of her office, the number of her direct reports, and the size of her budget—all of which tend to progress in rough lockstep.

Now consider a vendor manager in an organization that has moved to global sourcing. In this "New World," the skill sets needed for high performance tend to be very different from those in the traditional organization described previously. For example, context-specific knowledge about one company's history, policies, and procedures is much less important than in the "Old World" organization. Instead, managers need strong process skills—capabilities that allow them to map, analyze, and perform root-cause analysis on operational processes. It is vitally important that managers in these settings are comfortable with IT issues (databases, security issues, control points, etc.).

Instead of having a large staff that can be managed by walking around, global sourcing managers are likely to be managing vendors with their own staff in various remote locations. The primary interaction is via daily, weekly, and monthly performance scorecards from the vendor or a third-party monitoring organization. In the Old World, intuition and deep local knowledge are important; in the New World, numeracy and a feel for statistics matter much more than intuition.[1]

These are "generic" skills—not in the sense that everyone possesses them, but in the sense that those who do can move easily across functions and even organizations. Deep contextual knowledge of specific forms, customers, or employees' quirks become a distraction from the key task at hand—that is, standardizing and "routinizing" the firm's processes.

In the offshore world, the headcounts and budget directly controlled by managers are reduced dramatically. The global manager's resources are spread around the globe, which generally means that personal charisma and face-to-face emotional intelligence become less important, whereas cross-cultural sensitivity and the ability to set clear, objective, measurable goals becomes more important. Because the sourcing manager rarely controls front-line workers directly, he or she must manage the *process*, tweak the incentives, and generally depend on persuasion and logic—rather than commands—to get the job done.

Finally, status symbols in the new networked organization are far less visible. In one large pharma company with significant offshore activities, we have worked with a manager of vendors. He sits in a cubicle that's pretty far from the windows, and he has no direct reports. People don't walk up to his desk looking for guidance, and the people around the water cooler don't lower their voices when he walks by. In other words, the traditional visible symbols of success, power, and prestige are largely absent from his work environment. And yet, he personally controls more than $1 billion of spend, and makes in excess of $300,000 a year.

This is a different world.

What This Means for Your Company

This shift in management roles has broad implications for your company, assuming you seek to capitalize on the opportunities offered by global sourcing. First, you will need to seek new skill sets in middle-management positions, with an emphasis on both analytical and soft skills. Second, you will need to revisit and reconceptualize basic organizational issues. (Most Old World organizations don't have the people they need for the New World, and recruiting and retaining these people means the creation of new career paths, new status markers, and new incentive systems.) Finally, you will have to communicate a new working culture to your employees. Gone are the days of "9 to 5, Monday through Friday in the Detroit office." Today's managers need to keep their passports in their desk drawer and their immunizations up to date. They need to be ready to catch an overseas flight at the drop of a hat. They need to keep their BlackBerries and cell phones charged up and on at all times—almost literally.

In the following sections, we look at each of these trends in greater depth, with insights and real-world anecdotes from those on the front lines of the services shift.

New Skill Sets: Analytical

As a firm navigates the transition from the traditional back office to a global sourcing approach, its need for individuals with superior analytical skills increases dramatically. As soon as a system moves offshore, managers must become much more deeply involved in the process flow, necessitating familiarity with statistics, process mapping, information systems, and root-cause analysis. The setting and verifying of performance metrics, process analysis, and structured thinking around contracts and metrics are essential skills that allow managers to continually improve operations. As Vinay Gupta, CEO of Janeeva—an Ann Arbor-based software firm that provides outsourcing assurance tools—explains, "The process of moving something offshore—or to a vendor in general—means that you have to specify performance metrics and what is, and is not, acceptable performance. This is a prerequisite to offshoring, and once it has been done, the opportunity to use analytics for continuous improvements increases dramatically."[2]

Once these skills are in place, managers also need to be able to use them to facilitate practical problem solving. A senior executive at a leading financial services firm (whose firm prefers not to be identified, so he is referred to as "John Smith") explains: "Once you have a solid analytical foundation, then there is a premium on common sense and problem solving. The vendor managers have to use the analytics to get a feel for what is really happening, then use their common sense to problem-solve. In the Old World, there was a tendency for lower-level managers to simply implement procedures blindly, kind of 'work to rule.' That doesn't work with global sourcing. You really have to know what is happening, why errors occur, and how all the pieces fit together."

Jim Enzor of Delphi Corporation concurs: "In this global environment, you must think systematically. If an error occurs, you don't just fix it. It's important to analyze the situation, track critical issues upstream, determine the source of the error, and keep everyone on board to fix the process." In essence, vendor managers have to move beyond procedures to anticipate and solve problems. Rather than simply follow instructions from top management, they have to develop a new understanding of the data and then tease out the patterns that are concealed within the statistics.

This can be especially challenging given that many of the processes managed by vendor managers are not fully understood by the senior management in most companies. As Enzor explains, "Top management generally tends to minimize this effort. Whether it's outsourced or offshored, they don't often think about the IT platform, necessary controls, and required skills that are needed to manage a globally diverse workforce. But if you're going to do this right, somebody has to tackle all that." In addition, the minute an administrative process is outsourced, expectations rise. Frank Cocuzza, senior vice president and CFO at Penske Truck Leasing, notes that "when our administrative processes were internal, people thought of them as a cost center. We underinvested and tolerated marginal performance. The expectations for outsourced operations are much higher."

Danny Ertel of Vantage Partners, a Boston-based consulting firm that has worked with many offshoring firms, explains the difference between the Old and New World management styles further: "The days of 'management by walking around' are gone. Offshoring requires a shift from managing people and their activities directly to managing a third-party relationship, its outputs, and their enablers. To the extent that people try to hang on to the old ways, they're missing the boat and will be left behind."

In fact, the failure of many managers to make the transition Ertel describes is a common enough phenomenon that we will examine it more fully in the subsequent section on organizational issues.

New Skill Sets: Negotiation and Soft Skills

Managers in an offshoring organization also need vastly improved negotiation and soft skills. Why? Because, as noted, they no longer *directly* control the resources they are responsible for. Instead of managing people and outcomes through formal authority, managers need to be able to influence resources controlled by others through negotiation, effective contracts, and simple persuasion. As Mark Hodges, chairman of the board of EquaTerra, explains, "People in these virtual, multinational teams have to be highly personable. They achieve results through influence, so people must like them and want to work with them. Interactions are collaborative, so you need some charisma. It's important to lead the team through personality, because these managers have little formal authority." "James Jones," a senior executive at a leading commercial bank who wishes to remain unnamed, concurs. "When you go to offshoring, managers have to transition from a directive style to an influence style."

Janeeva's Vinay Gupta elaborates on the transition from directive to influencing styles of management he has observed with his customers: "Clients discover that their managers have shifted from managing people and outcomes directly, to managing a contract. They can only influence outcomes indirectly—through the vendor. Many firms thought they could hand all the personnel issues off to the vendor, but that's not the case. We see that vendor managers are still deeply involved in training, retention, and incentives issues. But it is now an arms-length influence, not a hierarchical, boss-subordinate, relationship."

This new style of management requires a level of cross-cultural comfort that was largely irrelevant in the Old World—to be able to work with people from different cultures and contexts, as well as to be able to explain this new culture and context to the client organization. "James Jones" explains how this new emphasis created difficulties for his firm as the organization transitioned to offshoring: "Firms move either across firm boundaries or geographic boundaries, and the highest risk is generally moving across cultural and geographic boundaries. In [our bank], we found that managers were more comfortable managing across organizations than across geography." Or, in our vocabulary, the bank's managers proved more comfortable with outsourcing than with offshoring.

The new style of management also requires strong communication skills. As "John Smith" explains, "The vendor manager has to know his company really well, and he also has to know the other company really well. He has to present the vendor internally all across the organization. And he has to communicate his company's goals to the vendor."

The new model also requires individuals who don't need constant or visible support systems around them. As "Smith" observes, "In the New World, the vendor manager acts almost like an outsider—to both organizations. He has to know who to contact, who can get things done, and how to work the system in both companies. This requires a high level of business acumen and numeracy." Often, the skills required in the offshore organization are completely different from those required in the traditional back office. N.V. "Tiger" Tyagarajan, executive vice president of Genpact, elaborates: "In many cases, the best managers in the Old World are the worst managers in the New World. The Old World involved a lot of walking around, context-specific knowledge, one-to-one interactions, but not much data. In the New World, the processes and systems generate much better data, but the job involves managing peers within your company and at the vendor."

New Organizational Challenges

The new skill sets described by our interview subjects create a series of organizational issues that companies must address. First, companies have to devise new methods of developing, recruiting, and retaining talent to address their new needs. If the organization is committed to retaining employees who may not be ready to make the transition to the New World, it has to consider cross-training and repurposing.

In addition, the old model of vertical career paths no longer applies because talent is much more transferable. Because of this, retaining talent has emerged as one of the most difficult challenges for an offshoring organization; this is compounded by the fact that, as noted earlier, many of the "status markers" traditionally used to retain valuable employees no longer apply.

Career paths, for example, vary dramatically from the old organization to the new. Take a traditional managerial path: an individual excelled as a clerk, moved on to be a successful supervisor, then a manager, and eventually a director and vice president. In most cases, this climb took place within one function, and within one organization. In a global sourcing organization, movement is more often lateral—between different functions, and even across different organizations. As Vinay Gupta explains, "It is common to see a talented person move from a vendor to a customer, then back to another vendor. The demand for these people is high, and their skills transfer easily across organizations."

Status is less clearly defined in an offshoring organization, as well. As Genpact's Tiger Tyagarajan notes, in some cases managers no longer have control over the people whose work they are responsible for. Jim Enzor agrees, adding that a manager may have few direct reports within the company: "Instead, he's now managing a vendor. In some cases, it's awkward, because the vendor manager is overseeing a relationship with someone who appears to be more senior than the internal manager." Although many managers may approach an organization with the traditional "pyramid" model in mind, this shape no longer holds in an offshoring organization. EquaTerra's Mark Hodges notes, "In the offshore model, everything is the opposite. In the offshore world, managers are rewarded on outcomes, not the number of people who report to them. They have an influence over operations, but not direct authority to make things happen. Two thirds of the budget and people they are used to are now likely gone—located at a vendor site in another country."

Because many of these visible status symbols are gone, other incentives have become more crucial in recruiting and retaining good managers. Pay, for example, becomes more important, with market rates being the prime determinants. In the Old World organization, people tend to put a high value on comfort and security, in return for which (consciously or unconsciously) they sacrifice a certain amount of "hard" compensation. In the New World organization, by contrast, improved data and metrics make clear just how much value is being created, and by whom. And because effective vendor managers are in such short supply, they know they can get the market rate. If you don't pay them that rate, someone else will.

Because their skills are so transferable and job switches so common, vendor managers tend to be more project-focused than career-focused. In the Old World, the typical manager is career-focused. Not so (or not as much so) for the New World manager, who looks for well-defined projects, works diligently to achieve the specified objectives, and expects to be well rewarded for success. And when the final milestones are reached, they are likely to feel that it's time to strike a new deal—either with your firm or someone else's.

Offshoring can dramatically change the basic organization of the office, as well, both by reducing the number of people involved and shifting the emphasis away from the physical office space. Brad Rubin, who directed outsourcing and offshoring for TransUnion Interactive (which grew at more than 30 percent per year in his tenure), notes that "Offshore outsourcing allowed us to dramatically reduce overhead while simultaneously positioning the business for rapid growth. We had three well-compensated, highly-skilled managers who performed the work of twelve people in a traditional back-office or call center environment. These vendor managers knew our operations, our vendor operations, and how to effectively use technology to collaborate and execute projects offshore. It was a huge paradigm shift from a traditional operations' mindset."

Jim Enzor adds that, after offshoring, "instead of an office environment where you manage dozens or hundreds of people right outside your door, you now need a networked office. You might work out of your house, or any other virtual office environment. All you need is a cell phone, a laptop, and access to performance databases."

Other Issues and Needs

Although managers in the New World of offshoring are not necessarily expected to be sitting at their desks 24/7, there is an expectation of near constant availability that many Old World managers find difficult to sustain. As Vinay Gupta explains, "The amount of travel required has increased tremendously. We generally tell people to expect at least one week a month of international travel, and several shorter—typically domestic—trips per month, as well. People also work much longer hours. It's not that you have to be at the office all the time. But you are expected to be available by phone or email 12 to 16 hours a day to deal with stuff that might pop up on the other side of the world."

Because the expectations are so different, it's hard to transition internal people to these new roles. "John Smith" explains that at his firm, "We didn't tend to find these people internally. They were either working for vendors or doing some type of process consulting. You need people who are willing to buck the system, and you generally don't find those in the existing organization." Mark Hodges agrees, noting that EquaTerra works with its clients to recruit new managers from suppliers and consultancies in India. "Our customers need these people inside their organizations," he explains, "and they have found it very difficult to grow them on their own."

According to Tiger Tyagarajan, "A lot of the people who are best at these jobs come from the IT and sourcing worlds where they have managed large projects. These projects had clear outcomes and metrics, and they depended on other groups to deliver." Brad Rubin agrees, noting that he looks for people "who are experienced in software operations or have performed software sales. We look to MBAs, industrial engineers, software engineers—basically we target highly analytical people with strong communication and interpersonal skills. Candidates who have been Sales Engineers are ideal for the role." Age and mental flexibility can be important factors, as well. Hodges volunteers that "many middle managers are Luddites. To manage global sourcing effectively, you must be familiar with WebX, Skype, Microsoft Office, mobile phones, and various ways of accessing information, knowledge, and the Internet. All of this comes naturally to those under 35, but it's a mystery to many people over 50."

A Case-in-Point: Penske Truck Leasing

Penske Truck Leasing is a transportation and logistics organization of high complexity. (It owns, leases, and provides maintenance for over 220,000 trucks out of 750 locations and provides logistics management services on a global basis.) In 1999, Penske began a small outsourcing relationship with Genpact in Mexico; in 2001, they outsourced some operations to Genpact's India operations.

Following the outset of an economic slowdown and in the midst of a major post-acquisition shakedown, Penske decided in 2002 to significantly expand its outsourcing of back office operations, but decided on an alternative approach to the standard model—an experimental "virtual captive[SM] [3]" operation in partnership with Genpact. By 2001, Frank Cocuzza, senior vice president and CFO, became convinced that "Genpact could do many of these processes better than we could. They had built a world-class approach to back-office processes, while we had focused on our front end and treated our back office as a cost center. Over the years, we had underinvested in the back office."

The company consolidated six administrative support centers and transitioned the work to three centers: one in Reading, Pennsylvania; one in Juarez, Mexico; and a third in Hyderabad, India. In total, Penske has migrated 28 processes to India and 16 to Mexico. Today, Penske's global administrative platform consists of just over 1,200 people, with 395 of these positions located in the United States in finance, 404 in offshore finance, and 410 in offshore field support.

In fundamental ways, this services shift has transformed the way the company does business. According to Cocuzza, "Before we off-shored, we were reactive—primarily to volumes and complaints. We had not invested in good metrics or creating any for quality control 'inside the process.' The concept of a first-pass yield, while standard in manufacturing, was foreign in ours and in most back office operations. Going offshore changed all that. Genpact insisted that we *define success* in terms of metrics that they could be held responsible for. In effect, they helped us move from a cost-cutting mode to a service mode."

The company used the offshore move to bring about much-needed changes in its administrative processes. The move allowed the company to identify areas that weren't working, map out every process, apply appropriate checks, and restructure the workflow to improve results. It was a difficult transition, but Genpact's expertise made it easier. According to Cocuzza, "Genpact had the infrastruc-ture, the hiring machine, the process management orientation, and the focus on quality that were required to make this a success."

Nevertheless, the transition proved impossible for some of Penske's managers. Cocuzza explains that "in terms of managing remotely, we had quite a few managers who couldn't step up to the table. Something like half had to transition out. The new managers had to think of the workers in India and Mexico as their team, and for some, this proved impossible."

In a roundtable discussion with first-line managers, the authors gained a clearer sense of the changes required on the ground at Penske as the company moved to offshoring. "In the Old World," one manager explained, "there was a lot of management by walking around. You knew all your workers very well, socialized with them, had coffee with them, and generally had lots of informal interactions. In the new model, 90 percent of my workers are over 1,000 miles away. We manage through process metrics and by the numbers. I am less concerned if they've had a good week or bad weekend. I just want to know if the work was done on time, and to standard."

Another first-line manager offered a concrete example of the differences in process management before and after offshoring. "In the old system," he noted, "it was largely batch processing. The key questions were, 'Did you get all the work done today?' and 'Were there any problems?' Moving the processes offshore pushed the operation toward a more process orientation. We now know exactly which transactions were not completed, whose desk they're sitting on, and if we discover errors, we generally know who when and where they occurred."

Yet another first-line manager noted that while setting goals hadn't changed dramatically, the *monitoring* aspect of his job had changed completely: "We have much more hard data now, which leads to more formal feedback. It occurs on scheduled calls, and it revolves around numbers." Because this can make the relationships feel impersonal, he noted, "it's really important to work to build those relationships when you visit, because if you don't you can end up talking past each other. Although most of my 'staff' are in Juarez (Mexico) and India, I'm on the phone with the line supervisors every day. We visit at least quarterly. Technically, the workers are employed by Genpact. But we treat them like they are Penske resources—which of course they are."

The first-line managers also noted how important it was to create a sense of identification with Penske among the vendor employees. "One thing we were surprised at," explained one manager, "was that it was important for the offshore workers to feel a sense of belonging to the U.S. operation. Everyone in India and Mexico is a Genpact employee, but they really want to identify with Penske. We've designed a series of reward and recognition events to help build this connection."

Mid-level managers—that is, the supervisors of the first-level managers quoted previously—also noted similar changes. "In terms of the Old World versus New World model," one mid-level manager explained, "we used to manage based on experience and intuition, but generally did not have much data to support our decisions. Going offshore forced us to rip apart our processes."

Several also mentioned how difficult it was for first-level managers to make the transition to the offshoring model. "For some people," a mid-level manager noted, "this felt like ripping apart their whole world. There was resentment, things like, 'I've been here for 15 years and know how this works; why do I have to fill out the stupid report?' Among the first-line supervisors, the failure rate was probably 50 percent."

Why was the failure rate so high? Mid-level managers cited several factors: deficient skill sets, an inability to adjust to new expectations, and a refusal to cooperate. This last factor was referred to as the "patriot response." According to one mid-level manager, some first-line managers simply felt that offshoring was "un-American." More frequently, the managers found that individuals who had excelled at Penske before the shift were simply not equipped for these new responsibilities. Before the transition, one mid-level manager noted, "their authority came from knowing all of the details of all of the processes. They just couldn't get their head around the idea of managing through metrics, root-cause analysis, and controls. It was a shift from supervising and controlling to truly managing, and many people couldn't make it." The focus on relationships shifted as well. "We moved from a *people-dependent* process," one manager explained, "where people were key—hiring them, motivating them, developing or reprimanding them—to a *true process*, where the focus was on timeliness and errors, not people."

In addition, the amount of travel required in the new model proved too much for some Penske first-line managers. As one mid-level manager noted, many individuals he supervised suffered from "travel anxiety." They may have been comfortable with periodic trips to Philadelphia or Chicago, but became very nervous when their travel involved another language, chronic jet lag, and unfamiliar food.

Finding new people to fill gaps in the organization proved more difficult than many of the mid-level managers expected. "Not even one out of 100 resumes has it," one mid-level manager noted. "It's easy to identify people for the Old World. They're good at routines and are task-oriented. For the New World, you need people who are good at troubleshooting, who can act as detectives to chase down root causes, and can think one step ahead and prevent errors before they happen. Perhaps most important, there is a real premium on flexibility. The old model was strictly hierarchical. In the new model, feedback keeps bubbling up from below. This isn't a sign of disrespect, it's smart people pushing to do better—but many managers aren't comfortable with this."

In terms of their own responsibilities, the mid-level managers noted many dramatic changes. "The pace of change is much faster," one manager explained. "We used to have to pull ideas out of the front-line workers. Now they come flowing in." The transition also called for reworked processes and detailed process mapping. "It's much more difficult to make the transition than most people think," another manager noted. "All those things that used to be off the grid—like informal phone calls and emails to sort out nonstandard items—those activities now have to be documented, moved into the flow, and accounted for. At the end of the day, it strengthens the process. But it's a huge amount of effort to get from here to there."

Senior management at Penske confirmed the importance of the new process mapping. "When everyone was co-located," Frank Cocuzza explains, "there was a tremendous amount of informal collaboration. People would talk to each other over the cubicle walls, at the water cooler, and at lunch. When you move the process offshore, it's important to formalize these interactions." In addition, Cocuzza noted that the organization needed to reexamine how it thought about communication. "One of the big challenges," he explains, "was moving beyond just verbal communication. Developing a sense of empathy with the Mexicans and the Indians was important. You have to understand their body language, and how they think about work relationships. We spend a lot of time on building those connections.

The metrics are vital, but you need to complement them with a strong connection between the workers and the organization."

Change in a Changing World

The Penske experience is typical of other firms interviewed in our work. In most cases, there was tremendous anxiety among first-line supervisors about moving to the New World, and whether there would be a role for them after the transition.

And the truth is that for many, there was *not* such a role. At Penske, as at almost every other firm we spoke with, the desire was that everyone would make the transition. But in fact, typically between half and two-thirds of these lower-level managers *don't* make it—whether because they lack the skill sets, don't want to travel, or are concerned about the "patriotism factor."

Although we will continue in this book to sidestep the political aspects of outsourcing and offshoring—not because we lack opinions, but because we think the *economics* of global sourcing march on independent of those politics—it may be worth noting at this point that recent developments have tended to muddy the patriotism factor even further. In some cases, it turns out, the only way to "save American jobs" is for a company to engage in aggressive offshoring. A recent *BusinessWeek* article told the story of a Green Bay, Wisconsin–based paper machinery manufacturer that, after being acquired by a St. Louis–based holding company, moved its design center to Chennai, India—and thereby gained enough additional engineering capacity to improve its record of on-time deliveries.

BusinessWeek called this an example of "transformational outsourcing," and noted that "many executives are discovering offshoring is really about corporate growth, making better use of skilled U.S. staff, and even job creation in the United States, not just cheap wages abroad."[4] And although this is a somewhat mixed example—combining as it does manufacturing with manufacturing-related services—

we argue that the underlying dynamics are likely to be even *more* relevant to the services sector. On a going-forward basis, the easy gains from labor arbitrage will be available to most firms. Once that happens, the source of advantage will shift to accessing talent and tapping into global resources to facilitate transformation.

And as we've tried to emphasize in this chapter, that transformation has to extend to individuals and individual jobs. Even in transformational success stories, it's still all about change, and changing work environments, and changing skill sets, and who is best able to adapt to all this change. Among middle managers, it seems, the success rate is somewhat higher—but we should reiterate that in the process of succeeding, their work lives change dramatically. They go from being local stalwarts to road warriors. Instead of spending their time coordinating work teams and motivating people face-to-face, they live in the world of SLAs, intercontinental travel, and root-cause analysis.

What about senior managers? We hope and assume that many of the readers of this book are senior managers. If that's true for you, congratulations; you may be in the best possible position to take advantage of the kinds of organizational transitions described in this chapter. If you chart the right course, and invest wisely in your people—and yes, disinvest when necessary—you are likely to see productivity increase as costs decrease. You are likely to know *more* about your organization—thanks to improved reporting—even as your resources become more dispersed geographically. And perhaps most rewarding of all, you're likely to get the benefit of great business ideas, bubbling up from the virtual trenches.

Endnotes

[1] Throughout this chapter, we'll use "Old World" and "New World" as shorthand for two different business environments within which skill sets are exercised. Obviously, the two worlds exist simultaneously and are likely to do so indefinitely.

[2] Unless otherwise noted, all quotes in this chapter are from the authors' conversations with the quoted individual. We are grateful to these sources, and others who aren't named here, for sharing their insights with us.

[3] The term "virtual captive" has been service marked by Genpact.

[4] "The future of outsourcing," in *BusinessWeek*'s January 30, 2006 online "special report."

6

The Services Shift: Policy Implications

In most countries today, services account for the largest share of economic activity. In the United States, for example, services account for 67 percent of both GDP and employment if we exclude government from our definition of "service," and fully *80 percent of GDP and 83 percent of employment* if we include government. These are staggering figures, from almost any perspective. And because the manufacturing sector itself has a steadily growing component of services—such as R&D, design, logistics, marketing, and servicing—even these huge percentages tend to understate the importance of services.

So the policy implications that grow out of the expanding globalization of services are both far ranging and complex. In recent decades, many restrictions to trade in manufacturing have been removed via trade agreements and the World Trade Organization process. The demand for a corresponding liberalization in the services sector has become more and more insistent—and as you've seen, is already well underway.

Two factors distinguish trade in services from manufacturing. First, taking the economist's perspective, services typically involve a larger share of labor in overall costs. So developing countries' advantage in services is often larger than it is in manufacturing. Second, services impact a much broader share of the workforce. From a political standpoint, therefore, trade dislocations are much more broadly felt.

As demonstrated in earlier chapters, the global trade in business services is increasing at a rapid pace. At the same time, the *nature* of this trade is changing. Global production networks are emerging in services, and even high-end white-collar activities and processes have proven to be amenable to offshoring. This increase in the quantity and value of business services traded, along with the associated dislocation impacts for professionals and skilled labor, has put the services shift into the national spotlight in developed countries around the world.

International trade theory, largely based on the comparative-advantage arguments discussed earlier, argues that increased trade between two countries tends to be beneficial to both. Many economists contend that trade in services is no different from trade in goods, and that it should have similar consequences. Even developed countries such as the United States and Germany, they argue, would benefit overall from the reallocation of white-collar work to those best able to perform it. But some economists, including Nobel Prize winners, are not so sanguine. (We'll return to them shortly.) They argue that current trends may change the fundamental rules of the game, leading to unexpected and negative consequences.

Given this significant difference of opinion, how should policy-makers respond?

One of the challenges in analyzing the impacts of increased trade in services, and responding on a policy level, has been the lack of reliable and useful data. Unlike manufactured goods, services don't have to physically cross borders—only ideas and information, often in the form of electronic files, actually move from place to place—so it is much harder to collect trade data for services that compares to manufacturing-related data. Even at aggregate levels, services-related data is scarce when compared to merchandise data. Censuses of service businesses are done much less frequently, and less information is collected.

Designing effective policy measures in this environment can be quite challenging. Consider the perspective of the countries in the developing world. Generally speaking, their economic policies are aimed at encouraging the accumulation of productive resources and their productive use. The conventional prescription to promote services is to invest in human capital and business infrastructure to stimulate broader economic growth. But that is a very broad prescription, indeed. Should they be investing in upgrading their education systems? Should they deregulate or subsidize their telecommunications system? Should they be offering incentives to companies to set up operations there? What would such incentives look like?

And what about the perspective of the developed world? Should developed countries adopt a laissez-faire approach to the services shift, or should they intervene in some way? In *what* way? If there is an appropriate short-term response and a different long-term strategy, how are they different? How should policymakers prepare their economies for the long term?

Let's explore these questions, starting with the developing world, and then moving to the developed world. In both cases, we'll look at the same sequence of issues: first the opportunities inherent in services offshoring, then the challenges, and finally, some of the policy approaches indicated by those opportunities and challenges.

We should reiterate here at the outset of this chapter that we intend to sidestep the mainly emotional elements of this policy debate. Just as it makes little sense to command the waves—they're going to do what they want, anyway—we think that arguing over the inevitable aspects of offshoring isn't a very productive exercise. From our point of view, it's far better to understand the phenomenon, and then *act* on that understanding.

A Developing-Economy Perspective

First, let's review the potential benefits of a policy "tilt" toward strengthening the services sector in developing economies. Then we'll look at the challenges inherent in such a tilt, and explore some of the mechanics of creating and sustaining it.

The Potential Benefits

The globalization of services, as we've seen, presents a unique opportunity for developing economies.

First, and most important, there is a huge global market for services. (NASSCOM'S most recent estimate is in excess of $300 billion.) Willie Sutton once explained that he robbed banks because that's where the money is. Developing nations go after services for the same reason.

Second, services tap into what developing countries have—a large and low-wage labor pool—and don't demand what these countries don't have: capital. A call center, for example, requires something between $7,000 and $10,000 of invested capital per job created, or roughly 100 jobs per $1 million invested. Even a small and relatively uncomplicated manufacturing facility requires far more capital per job, as well as far more investment up front, before the first job is created.

In addition, exports of services can scale rapidly and earn significant foreign exchange for developing countries. For example, growth of Indian IT services exports from tens of millions of dollars in 1990–91 to more than $31 billion in 2007 has contributed to impressive growth in India's foreign exchange reserves: from $5.8 billion in FY 1990–91 to $272 billion in 2007. The industry's contribution to India's GDP increased from virtually zero to more than 5 percent during the same period.

Growth in the services sector leads to job creation and increased employment. The Indian IT services sector, largely powered by exports, directly employed more than 1.6 million in 2007. Most services jobs focused on exports are better paying, and provide better benefits, than equivalent domestic-sector jobs.

In addition, growth of the services sector can help create indirect employment in other areas of the economy. According to NASS-COM, the sector has helped create an additional 4 million jobs through "indirect" and "induced" employment. *Indirect* employment includes expenditures on vendors, including telecom, power, construction, facility management, IT, transportation, catering, and other services. *Induced* employment is driven by employees' spending on food, clothing, utilities, recreation, health, and other services. Greater access and better quality of producer or intermediate services also can stimulate the growth of, and employment in, downstream and related industries.

As you will see, policymakers can grow the services sector in two basic ways: 1) encouraging domestic entrepreneurs, and 2) encouraging foreign investments by multinationals. Although domestic organic growth is certainly important, most of the attention today focuses on foreign investors. These investments can help jumpstart an industry— for example, the BPO industry in India—as they inject financial resources into the local economy (see the upcoming sidebar). Once established in their new "homes," multinationals can raise additional capital in both domestic and international markets, thereby creating new infusions locally.

Foreign investments are not only about securing capital; they also are about instilling locally some of the competitive advantages of multinationals, including technology, organizational and managerial skills, and entrepreneurship. Done right, this diffusion of knowledge and technology into the local economy leads to increased competitiveness. Local employees of multinationals acquire these new skills and knowledge; when some move to local competitors or start their own firms, they carry and spread these learnings. One notable example is Raman Roy, who helped GE Capital set up GECIS in 1997, and then left to start India's largest independent outsourcer, Spectramind, which he sold to tech giant Wipro Technologies in 2002. It was his former parent company, Roy readily admits, that taught him how to seize opportunities, take risks, and make mistakes. "GE," he says, "is among the best incubators of talent and has a great culture of encouraging entrepreneurship."[1]

"Spillovers" from FDI are the result of linkages between multinationals and local suppliers and customers. They occur when local firms benefit from a multinational's superior knowledge of product, process, technology, or markets. For instance, local Turkish banks adopted modern planning, budgeting, and electronic banking techniques from the multinationals.[2] These linkages can be backward (relationships with suppliers) or forward (contacts with customers).

Although diffusion is generally a good thing, its quantity and quality can vary a great deal depending on the "absorptive" capacity of the local economy. Many factors—such as intensity of competition, quality of local human capital, and strength of linkages between multinationals and local economy—can affect this process of diffusion.

Rapidly growing and more efficient services sectors can have an impact on the effectiveness of other related sectors of the economy as well. As intermediate services improve to global standards, they can help other sectors of the economy that consume these services get more competitive in the global marketplace. (One example is IT that is "consumed" by the manufacturing sector.) A policy focus on growing information technology and IT-enabled services can be a stimulus for upgrading critical infrastructure and initiating regulatory reforms—and these improvements are essential if the country aspires to be a serious contender in the emerging global services marketplace.

The Challenges

So growing the services sector presents multiple benefits to developing countries. But this is almost always easier said than done. Developing economies face multiple challenges as they seek to attract and grow global services industries. These can be considered in four "buckets":

- Infrastructure
- Human capital
- The regulatory environment
- Social repercussions

Foreign Investment Jumpstarts the Indian BPO Industry

The Indian IT industry grew largely through the efforts of local entrepreneurs. The Indian BPO industry, by contrast, took a very different path. Why was it difficult for independent vendors to start and scale BPO? We can point to three basic reasons:

- The real-time and business-critical nature of BPO was perceived to carry greater risk than IT projects, which could be batched up and only brought online after testing.

- Potential customers initially were reluctant to outsource their business processes.

- Indian IT services companies were then busy scaling up delivery of their IT services, and did not want to get into seemingly "low-end" business processes.

As a result, the Indian BPO industry arose mainly through multinational involvement and foreign direct investment (see Figure 6.1).

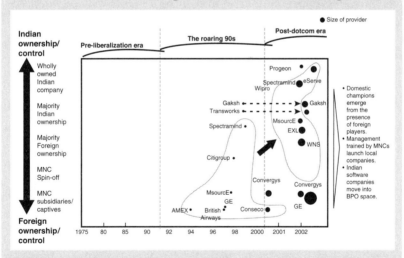

Figure 6.1   The evolution of the Indian BPO sector

Source: McKinsey Global Institute

The multinationals, including American Express, GE, and British Airways—clustered at the base of the middle column—identified the initial BPO opportunity and then provided the necessary capital, technology, training and business to pursue that opportunity. The decision by these reputable companies to offshore business processes to India gave greater credibility to the industry, and increased the comfort level of other organizations to procure business services from there.

The BPO industry needed stronger infrastructure, in part because its real-time nature demanded a reliable power and connectivity infrastructure, especially when compared, for example, to project-oriented IT services. Powerful multinational companies, including GE, lobbied the government for improvements in telecom and other key infrastructures. Meanwhile, these companies could invest in captive operations in India, because those centers—once up and running—had the huge benefit of a guaranteed demand from the parent.

Of course, once the BPO industry was established and companies became comfortable with sending business processes to India, the leading IT services companies and entrepreneurs took the leap.

Infrastructure

Obviously, a robust telecom system is an indispensable building block when a nation is attempting to build its IT and BPO sectors. Maybe less obvious, but equally important, are the roads and bridges needed to get workers to and from their jobs. Many older cities in the developing world, whose road networks were created before cars and buses became ubiquitous, are already terribly congested. Today, it can take two hours to drive the ten miles from downtown Bangalore to the outlying Electronics City.

Bringing in services jobs from the developed world usually translates into welcoming high-level visitors from overseas, which puts new demands on transportation systems and upsets the status quo. For example, India has run into trouble as it has tried to upgrade its airports, with the airport-based unions asserting (probably with some justification) that a more efficient airport translates into fewer jobs.

When you think of a country such as Haiti—which although it has plenty of low-wage workers, has almost no business-oriented infrastructure—it becomes clear how critical a role infrastructure plays in a country's competitive position.

Human Capital

We've been using the phrase "low-wage workers" as a convenient shorthand. The truth is, of course, that not all inexpensive workers are equally valuable in the global services economy. The first hurdle, most easily cleared by Indians and other former subjects of the British Empire, is passable English. Indian call centers spend large sums on what is called "accent neutralization," helping their workers conform to (mostly) American expectations.

But developing human capital goes far beyond verbal cosmetics. General education levels are critically important: Is the worker literate? Does he or she possess at least minimal computational skills? And the need to function in a business environment adds new layers of complexity. In many cases, local workers need to be educated in the basics of how offices work. (How is conflict handled?) To the extent that they have contact with overseas colleagues, they need to understand cultural norms behind the business interactions. ("Americans like to get right to the point. Americans don't tend to talk casually about their families at work.") These are things that may be taken for granted back in America, but may be largely alien to a local workforce.

The Regulatory Environment

Developing countries tend be short on the expertise that is required to establish and sustain an effective regulatory apparatus. For example, countries need to define the new rules of the game when they open up sectors such as telecom that were previously government monopolies, but many countries simply aren't competent to deal with the complex technical and legal issues that accompany such fundamental policy changes.

A principal concern as companies look to shift services to the developing world is the safety of their intellectual property. This is to some extent a cultural issue—the Chinese, for example, have a deep-seated notion dating back to Confucius and beyond that good ideas need to be shared—but it is also a question of appropriate laws that are adequately enforced.

We've already alluded to the importance of generating foreign direct investments (FDI). Effective FDI promotion requires a capacity to assess national strengths, global investment trends, and the known strategies of potential investors—and then effectively bring together all three in the regulatory context.

At the same time, it's not enough simply to attract foreign investments. Those investments have to be made in a way that—from the host country's perspective—maximizes domestic benefits and minimizes (and mitigates) domestic costs. Obviously, a longer-term goal in opening up sectors to foreign investment and competition is to absorb global best practices, and thereby increase local capability and competitiveness. But these benefits don't materialize automatically. For example, multinationals may employ locals primarily in low-level jobs and decline to upgrade them over time. Their use of expatriate managers and professionals can hold back local skills development and the diffusion of knowledge into the local economy. Similarly, their use of foreign suppliers can limit the development of local enterprise. For all these reasons, developing economies need to set up their regulatory environments in ways that ensure the effective diffusion of skills into the local economy.

It almost goes without saying that companies are inherently conservative; they invest where their funds are safe and generate an adequate rate of return. Almost every law passed and regulation imposed has some impact, direct or indirect, on a country's profile on the world stage: business friendly or business unfriendly? Many of the sidebars in this chapter enumerate the ways that countries attempt to present themselves to potential investors as stable and reliable partners.

Tax policy is a particularly important component of the regulatory environment. Does the local tax structure provide adequate incentives for the scale of investments that are needed? Will the taxes imposed be low enough to allow businesses to flourish, and at the same time, high enough to provide the kinds of expanded services that these new neighbors will require? The perception of "freeloading" outsiders—even outsiders who are providing jobs—can lead to political and economic instability.

Social Repercussions

This brings us to our fourth and final "bucket": social repercussions. Although efficient multinationals can bring the benefits of increased competitiveness and higher-quality services, they can also crowd out existing domestic firms. This can lead to dislocation of the domestic labor pool, which can lead in turn to social and political unrest. Meanwhile, overemphasizing exports-based services sectors can negatively impact other sectors of the economy, by draining off scarce and badly needed resources. It can lead to an increase in economic disparities, and bring local customs into conflict with global (that is, "Western") norms. Aljazeera.com pointed to this fundamental issue:

> The call centers create new forms of social division, separating these reconstructed young adults from the rest of society. The easy mixing doesn't extend to the lower castes, the poor, or the majority who speaks only *Kannada* [the local language] and have no knowledge of English. It reinforces social gulfs, alienating people from their traditions, without offering them any place in the values they have to simulate in order to ease the lives of distant consumers they will never meet. India, according to the prophets of globalism, is to become the back office of the world. The economic benefits are only too clear, but these entail social costs. The loss of jobs to rich countries is small compared to the cultural hybridization of hundreds of thousands of young Indians.[3]

In short, there are both great benefits and significant costs on the table when developing countries set out to build their services sector.

Success on this front can bring new challenges and exacerbate existing challenges, such as traffic congestion; it can also create secondary challenges. (Before, we didn't need business-class hotels; now we do.) Failure to cope with these existing and secondary challenges can be frustrating, demoralizing, or even politically calamitous.

So how should developing countries proceed on the policy front?

Policy Measures

Today, a number of developing countries are implementing regulations specifically aimed at attracting and growing foreign investment in services. Their collective experience suggests that it is important to calibrate the scope, speed, and nature of liberalization, and to build a strong and effective regulatory framework that encourages competition and local capability-building.

The investment promotion agencies (IPAs) of the developing countries are increasingly targeting service sectors. In a 2004 survey conducted by the U.N. Center on Trade and Development (UNCTAD), 59 national investment-promotion agencies reported putting higher priority on services that could generate export revenues (see Table 6.1).

This interesting but somewhat confusing table calls for some decoding. It summarizes responses from eight developed nations, eight Central and Eastern Europe (CEE) nations, and 43 developing nations. (Developing-nation responses are further broken out in the three right-hand columns.) The only absolute numbers in this figure are the bottom row; all the rest of the numbers are percentages. As you can see, IT and call-center services were the most sought-after service functions in all regions. (More than half of the countries in Africa were actively seeking FDI in these areas.) At the other end of the spectrum, Latin American countries aren't betting heavily on R&D, and Asian-Pacific countries are shying away from offshore banking.

TABLE 6.1   Service Functions Targeted by Investment Promotion Agencies (2004)

Service Function	All Countries (%)	Developed Countries (%)	CEE (%)	Developing Countries (%)	Africa (%)	Latin America (%)	Asia-Pacific (%)
IT services	75	100	80	70	63	77	73
Call centers	61	75	70	56	53	62	55
Shared services centers	43	63	60	35	26	38	45
Regional headquarters	38	63	50	30	21	38	36
R&D	33	75	60	19	26	8	18
Offshore banking	15	-	-	21	26	23	9
Others	21	25	30	19	26	8	18
No. of responses	59	8	8	43	19	13	11

Source: UNCTAD Survey of IPAs, conducted January–April 2004

Countries have implemented a wide variety of policy measures to promote themselves as attractive destinations for business services. These are detailed in the following subsections.

Financial Incentives

Many countries use fiscal and financial incentives to attract foreign investors. Both developed and developing countries apply a wide range of subsidies to attract and retain the production of services. Several countries allow duty-free inputs and also provide subsidies linked to special zones of various kinds. Developed countries rely more on direct grants, whereas developing countries tend to favor tax incentives.

For example, in 2001 the government of Mauritius offered a tax holiday until 2008, and a 15-percent corporate tax thereafter; alternatively, companies investing in call-center and back-office services could opt for a uniform corporate tax rate of five percent. The Mauritian government also provides for duty-free imports of specified equipment, accelerated depreciation, electricity tariffs at competitive rates, a 50-percent reduction in personal income tax for foreign IT specialists, and fast-track processing of work visas and residence permits for expats.

Croatia grants about $2,100 for each new employee recruited. Malaysia's Multimedia Super Corridor seeks to attract call centers, whereas Ghana offers call-center companies a corporate tax holiday for ten years, a maximum corporate tax rate of 8 percent, and also duty-free imports. Gambia provides a variety of tax and investment incentives to attract IT services (see sidebar).

Some have disputed the effectiveness of incentives, especially after a service sector has established a foothold in the country. They argue that tax breaks, import duty exemptions, land and power subsidies, and similar incentives can be costly and unnecessary. By waiving the 35 percent tax on corporate profits for companies that moved back-office processing and IT jobs, for example, India offered concessions worth roughly $6,000 annually per employee. It has been argued that these funds could have been spent more productively in upgrading the relevant Indian infrastructure.

McKinsey's survey of 30 executives found that financial incentives were the least important factor in their decision to move services to India. Factors such as local infrastructure, availability of trained workers, regulatory environment, and accessibility by air were rated as more important.[5] Incentives increase the risk of competition between different locations and a resulting "race to the top," especially when it comes to export-oriented FDI. Resource-constrained developing countries should use incentives judiciously, and only after concluding that they are the best use of resources in the economy.

Gambia Attracts IT Services[4]

Gambia provides a variety of tax incentives to attract foreign direct investment in priority sectors such as IT services and financial services. To take advantage of these benefits, a corporation registered in Gambia must invest at least $100,000 in the country, and that investment must contribute to one or more of the following objectives:

- Foreign exchange generation through exports or import substitution
- Local sourcing of materials, suppliers, and services
- Employment generation
- Introduction of new technologies
- Contribution to local socioeconomic development

Free trade zone incentives—in the form of tax and duty concessions or exemptions—apply to investments that generate employment and develop human capital. These cover activities such as packaging, labeling, warehousing, transportation, energy, telecom, financial services, information technology, and health services. A substantial portion of the company's output (currently 70 percent) also needs to be exported in order for the company to take advantage of these incentives.

Export-Processing Zones (EPZs)

These are traditionally used to attract FDI in export-oriented goods production, and are now gaining importance in services. These zones seek to attract services by providing high-quality infrastructure—telecom, power, and technology support—and financial incentives. They are also home to an educated and skilled workforce.

More than 90 of the 116 countries in International Labor Organization's EPZ database promote a range of service activities. Services within these zones have rapidly grown to include call centers, medical diagnoses, as well as architectural, business, engineering, and financial services.

In India, for example, many of the offshored services have been attracted to various dedicated software technology parks (STPs) set up by individual states to promote exports. The first ones were established in 1991 in Bangalore, Pune, and Bhubaneshwar. In addition to providing modern computing and telecom infrastructure, these parks provide a "single window clearance" mechanism to simplify bureaucratic hurdles, permission for 100-percent foreign ownership, a greatly simplified process to obtain a five-year tax holiday, duty-free imports, and permission to subcontract software development activity.

Mauritius provides a state-of-the-art office and telecom infrastructure through its "Cyber City" project. Its computing-on-demand facilities provide disaster-recovery services. The Government of Dubai created an Internet City[6] in the 1990s to serve as a hub for regional headquarters. Jamaica provides export-free zones and duty-free imports, as well as special capital allowances such as accelerated depreciation, to attract IT services to the country.

Attractive Infrastructure and Skills

As you've seen, quality infrastructural services are essential for the production and delivery of various information technology–enabled services. The lack of a quality telecom infrastructure, for example, effectively prevents a country from participating in the global services revolution. Liberalization and competition may be necessary to ensure a strong and globally competitive telecom network and Internet connectivity.

The upgrade of the telecom infrastructure in India has been a key driver of that country's growth in offshoring. Various policy reforms since 1994—when the National Telecom Policy opened up the sector to competition—have contributed significantly to the rapid expansion of the Indian telecom network.

Besides telecom, international connectivity—both in terms of air links to facilitate passenger travel and broadband data connectivity— is also important. In India, Mumbai and the southern states that were

Jamaica Attracts IT and Services[7]

The Jamaican government has developed several incentives for growth of information technology and the knowledge-services industry in the country. These include the following:

- **Export-free zones**—These allow for tax exemptions, duty-free imports, repatriation of earnings, and minimized customs procedures for companies operating within specified export-processing zones in the country.

- **Duty-free imports**—These include capital goods, raw materials, components, or articles used in the manufacturing process, as well as specified articles for the construction, alteration, extension, repair, or equipping of premises in the free zone.

- **Exemption from taxes on income and profits in perpetuity**

- **Freedom from import/export licensing or quantitative restrictions**

- **Free repatriation of profits and dividends**

- **The Export Industry Encouragement Act**—This provides duty-free importation of raw materials and capital goods, and a tax holiday on profits for ten years.

- **Moratorium on duties**—This allows investors without free-zone status to pay their import duties over an average two-year period.

- **Telecommunications licenses**—Companies in the ICT sector with single-entity free-zone status can apply for licenses to provide their own telecommunications.

- **Accelerated Depreciation/Special Capital Allowance**—Qualified businesses (based on amount of exports) are granted a special allowance of capital expenditure for 50 percent of the full cost of any new machinery in the year of purchase, and a further 50 percent in the second year.

in close proximity to the landfalls of fiber optic cables have been most successful in attracting offshore services. (Fiber optics are generally cheaper and more efficient than satellite links.) In the Philippines, expansion of the multimedia infrastructure and reregulation of telecommunications have led to better services and more stable and reliable fiber-optic links; this, in turn, has facilitated the growth of the call-center industry there. Good and low-cost telecommunications suited to data and voice transmission have been an important factor in the location of shared service centers in Chile. The industry there was privatized and liberalized in the 1980s, and the telephone network was digitized in the 1990s. Tax reforms in 2002 helped bring a number of highly skilled competitors into the Chilean marketplace, and today the country has 15 fixed telephony operators, 33 long-distance carriers, and 54 ISPs.[8]

Human Capital and Skills Development

These also constitute an important policy area. Although some of the skills needed for offshored services are generic in nature, others are specific to a technology or domain area, and countries need to ensure that there is a sufficient talent pool and skills base available for the services it is trying to attract. India's software export performance is largely based on its large pool of English-speaking and technically trained manpower. Within India, most software companies are in areas with a high concentration of technical institutions and private training institutions. The rapid growth there, however, is exposing a skills deficit, and it is estimated that the industry will face a shortage of about half a million workers by 2010. Even less sophisticated services such as call centers require specialized skills, including customer support and telesales.

In short, countries need to take steps to ensure an adequate supply of the required skills. In that spirit, the Industrial Vocational Training Board of Mauritius provides training to call-center and other services agents. Hungary is developing specialized vocational training programs for both shared services and customer services. In the Philippines, the government has reaffirmed the use of English as a medium of instruction, and has partnered with industry and large universities to develop training and bridging programs to meet the needs of the contact-center industry.

Some countries encourage private-sector training through the provision of grants and tax incentives. In Jamaica, for example, employers are eligible for a reimbursable training grant, which is administered by the agency responsible for vocational training. Companies may access training grants up to a maximum of $20,000 (Jamaican) per employee. Croatia offers incentives (of up to 50% of related costs) for vocational training or retraining of employees.[9]

Strengthening Data Protection and the Intellectual Property Rights Regime

Ensuring data security, privacy, and intellectual property protection has become key to attracting knowledge-intensive services. As global sourcing moves into more complex (and strategic) services, this only increases in importance, so policies and regulations that strengthen these protections and ensure adherence to global best practices in these areas are becoming critical.

Some developed countries prohibit the exchange of data with countries that do not have adequate data-protection legislation; European firms, for example, are restricted under the Data Protection Directive of 1995 as to what data can be transferred or stored in countries without equivalent rules and enforcement procedures. Some companies have cancelled offshore contracts upon discovering weak procedures in these areas.

Strong regulatory frameworks and governance structures are emerging as a competitive advantage. For example, Singapore— which is no longer a low-cost location for export-oriented services— attracts investments in services based on the strength of its regulatory framework. Its free trade agreement with the United States sets high standards of protection and enforcement of intellectual property; it has also signed a memorandum of understanding to the same end with the European Union.

Attracting FDI: Services Differ from Manufacturing

To attract FDI in services, countries generally have to come up with different forms of financial assistance than they did to promote manufacturing. For example, the investment-promotion agency in the Czech Republic found that its incentive scheme from 2000—which had been designed principally for the relatively high fixed capital investments needed for manufacturing—was not well suited to business-support services investments.

Accordingly, the country's policymakers came out with a new program that focused more on human capital than on money. Qualifying investors were given a subsidy of up to 50 percent of eligible business expenses (that is, wages or capital expenditures on tangible and intangible assets), along with a subsidy covering 35 percent of special training and 60 percent of general training.[10]

An effective combination of policy measures can help motivate a sector. Let's look again at the case of India. While the IT sector took off on the efforts of entrepreneurs, the government stepped in with a variety of measures to promote and strengthen the sector. First, the government set up software technology parks in 1991.[11] By 1995, IT as a sector was well established in India, and the potential of software development was better understood. At that point, however, infrastructural issues were beginning to inhibit the growth of the industry, and the government of India took steps to address this problem.

In August 1995, for example, Internet connections were made available commercially to the public. In 1997, the import duty on computer software was abolished. Telecom reforms brought in a large cohort of inbound/outbound call centers and data-processing units, particularly because the government allowed 100-percent foreign ownership in the sector.

In a major 1998 initiative, the government formed a national task force on information technology and software development.[12] The group developed the Information Technology Action Plan, a report containing 108 recommendations covering both bottleneck areas and broad promotional measures that were crucial for developing a stronger IT industry in India. The recommendations of the group were ultimately accepted by the government. Concurrently, the New Telecom Policy of 1999 introduced Internet Protocol telephony, and brought an end to the state monopoly in international calling.

The IT industry's growth, both in terms of the scale and the value of activities being performed, also led to increased client concerns around risks—operational, strategic, and geopolitical. To address security and privacy concerns, and to provide a legal recourse, the government implemented the Information Technology Act of 2000, which provided legal recognition to electronic records and digital signatures, established Cyber Appellate Tribunals, and provided for penalties and adjudication of cyber crimes. Significantly, the government also provided tax exemptions for the industry until 2008. This tax-exempt status ensured that firms could reinvest profits toward scaling up their operations and building new capabilities.

A Developed-Economy Perspective

Over the long term, the increasing globalization of services is beneficial to the developed economies. Benefits include reduced costs, gains in productivity, the creation of newer jobs, and faster growth in developing countries, which leads to increased exports to those countries. Research undertaken by the McKinsey Global Institute found that offshoring creates a net additional value for the U.S. economy,[13] as shown in Figure 6.2. This value—estimated to be as much as $1.14 for every dollar spent offshore in India in 2002—comes from reduced costs, increased exports, repatriated earnings, and the redeployment of labor into higher value activities.

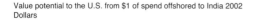

Value potential to the U.S. from $1 of spend offshored to India 2002
Dollars

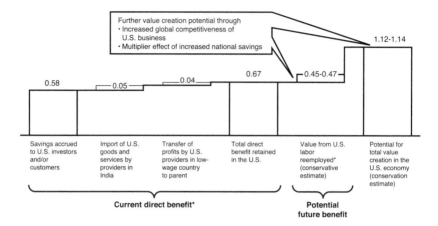

Figure 6.2   Value potential accrued to the United States

* Estimate based on historical reemployment trends from job loss through trade in the U.S. economy.

Source: McKinsey Global Institute.

Economic Benefits and Newer Possibilities

Corporations can save substantially when they offshore certain business services, and cost savings still constitute the largest form of economic value capture through offshoring. According to MGI, for every dollar offshored, 58 cents were captured through net cost reduction to businesses, even while they got services at similar or better service levels. These cost savings are driven primarily by differences in unit cost of labor between developed and developing countries. In many cases, reengineering has led to increased productivity as well.

Developed countries need new markets. As emerging economies develop and grow, they also become a new source of revenues for goods and services from developed economies. MGI estimates that for every dollar spent offshore, offshore service providers buy an additional five cents worth of goods and services from the U.S. providers in low-wage countries and obtain their hardware, software, and network infrastructure mainly from developed economies. As they grow and become more sophisticated, they tend to buy more high-end business services, including legal and financial services.

Many global services firms are based in the United States. These companies repatriate profits from their operations offshore back into the United States, which adds up to an additional four cents per dollar spent offshore.

Sourcing of low value-added services from abroad gives workers in developed countries an opportunity to move on to other potentially higher-value new jobs. According to MGI, if redeployment happens at the rate it has over the past two decades, then for every dollar spent offshore by the United States, the economy captures an additional 45 to 47 cents per dollar from new-jobs creation. There is empirical evidence to suggest, moreover, that services workers who are displaced by trade suffer smaller earnings declines and find employment more quickly than displaced manufacturing workers. According to the U.S. Department of Labor, the typical manufacturing-sector worker displaced through offshoring and other trade-related dislocations experiences 14.1 weeks of unemployment as a result of that displacement, whereas the average services-sector worker goes 11.9 weeks between jobs.[14]

Increasing Productivity

By its nature, the globalization of services expands trade into sectors of the economy that were previously insulated from foreign competitions. In February 2004, N. Gregory Mankiw, a Harvard professor then serving as chairman of the White House Council of Economic Advisers, caused a national uproar when he suggested that offshoring is only "the latest manifestation of the gains from trade that economists have talked about at least since Adam Smith.... More things are tradable than were tradable in the past, and that's a good thing."[15]

Controversial or not, Mankiw makes an important point. Although it often generates friction, trade almost always leads to increases in productivity. Why? First, increased competition from abroad creates pressures for greater efficiency at home. This causes less productive firms to exit the market, and ensures that the firms that remain in the market step up their games.

Second, offshore outsourcing enables developed-economy firms to focus on those core functions where they add the greatest value. (Think back to Porter's value-chain framework, introduced earlier.) As firms reallocate resources toward higher-value activities, the developed economy overall realizes productivity gains.

Third, trade enhances productivity by promoting reductions in the costs of technology and other inputs that improve the efficiency of business processes. For example, offshoring of IT services tends to reduce the cost of these services, making IT-enabled products and services more affordable, and ultimately leading to the increased diffusion of productivity-enhancing technology throughout the entire economy. For instance, the lower cost of offshored health-record transcription services encourages more health-care providers to keep digitized medical records, thereby improving the efficiency and productivity of the health-care industry.[16]

In a study of global sourcing of IT hardware between 1995 and 2002, researcher Catherine Mann found that global sourcing contributed between 10 and 30 percent of overall price declines (that is, beyond the strong parallel contributions made by advances in technology and innovation). Lower prices for IT hardware led to better deployment, which led to the faster transformation of business processes through more efficient work practices and new products. All these contributed to increased productivity across the economy.

This increase in productivity, cost savings, and efficiency enables firms in developed economies to remain more competitive, create greater value for their stakeholders. and increase investments. Furthermore, these benefits can translate directly into lower prices for consumers, increased access to goods and services, and a positive impact to the quality of life.

Although it is tempting to compare the costs born by the directly displaced with the direct savings realized by those firms that choose to offshore, this dramatically underestimates how productivity growth works its way through the economy over time. Trade is simply one mechanism that facilitates productivity growth. Others include new technologies, process innovation, and the entry and exit of firms.

It is important to remember that *everyone* in a country benefits from productivity increases—not just those who become more productive. Consider the cases of bartenders and barbers. In the United States, people in these professions make 50 to 100 times as much as their counterparts in India, and about 20 times as much as their counterparts in China. But why *is* that? Certainly U.S. bartenders and barbers are not 20 to 50 times as productive as their counterparts overseas, nor is the quality of their work 20 to 50 times as high. Simply put, they make more because the United States overall is a productive and wealthy country. Much of this wealth flows to everyone in society—even if they do not work in a trade-exposed sector. So nearly everyone in the United States (teachers, artists, auto mechanics, barbers, etc.) benefits from the processes that continually push productivity higher. When toting up the gains and losses from trade, it is easy to forget these secondary and tertiary effects—even though in the long run, they are larger than the direct effects.

A Bridge Across the Emerging Demographic Deficit?

Offshoring may also prove crucial to addressing the emerging demographic deficit in Europe, Japan, and the United States. The population of these developed economies is aging, and their fertility rates are projected to continue to remain low. These trends will almost certainly lead to workforce shortages in the future, and associated societal challenges. According to one estimate, the shortfall in the developed economies will be in the range of 32 to 39 million workers by 2020.[17]

Let's consider the case of Europe. Recent U.N. projections estimate that the population of Europe will drop from 728 million in 2005 to 653 million in 2050—a decline of more than ten percent—mainly as the result of falling fertility rates.[18] Decreasing fertility will lead inevitably to a decline in the number of young people, and by extension, the amount of workers (human capital) available to the European economy. Current estimates project that the working-age population (15–64) will decline 20 percent between 2005 and 2035, and a further 15 percent by 2050.[19] Unless increases in productivity offset these declines, Europe will see reduced per-capita income growth, savings, and investment, leading in turn to a long-term decline in real GDP.[20]

The lack of new births, coupled with increased life expectancies, will cause a steady aging of European society. By 2050, the median age of Europeans will increase from 39 in 2005 to 47, with the number of individuals over 65 increasing 57% to 180 million.[21] Furthermore, the population of individuals over 80 years of age is expected to more than double in size to 62.7 million in 2050.[22] This will greatly increase the costs of public health care, and the growing population of elderly will place increasing pressure on the shrinking numbers of wage earners for support. Without policy reforms or tax increases, governments will be unable to meet even their current obligations.

Japan and the United States are following the same path as the EU, although the situation is a bit worse in Japan and a bit better in the United States. The emerging demographic deficit creates a dilemma for developed countries. If the work is to get done, the countries must either import workers via immigration, or send the work to the populous countries via offshoring.

Developed countries can take a range of policy steps as they face up to the emerging demographic deficit. These range from rationing services to increasing workforce participation/productivity to importing workers or services.

The Challenges

Increasing services globalization carries some inherent challenges and risks for developed economies. In recent years, a number of highly visible pundits have argued that this can lead to a loss of domestic employment, downward pressure on wages, a declining average living standard, and risks to national security and consumer privacy. For example, Lou Dobbs—the CNN business news anchor, and author of *Exporting America: Why Corporate Greed Is Shipping American Jobs Overseas*—has taken strong position against the "offshoring of American jobs" in the popular media. According to Dobbs, "We have put our middle class directly in competition with third-world labor.... One doesn't have to be an economist to understand that the middle-class dream is under assault by our trade policies."[23]

The consulting industry, too, has fanned the flames. The public debate about offshoring and job losses in the United States can be traced back to widespread media coverage of a report published by Forrester Research in November 2002, which concluded that 3.3 million jobs would be lost in the United States by 2015 as a result of offshoring. Since then, there have been a variety of estimates of this potential impact (see Table 6.2). Within the United States, service industries account for around 80 percent of employment, so it is only natural for people to worry about job losses due to offshoring.

TABLE 6.2 Offshoring Impact on U.S. Jobs and Wages

Source	Measure	Number of Workers Affected
Job Losses		
Wired magazine (Pink 2004)	U.S. service jobs leaving the United States each year for the foreseeable future	200,000
Prism (2004) metaanalysis	Percentage of IT job losses from the United States over the next five years	7%–8%

TABLE 6.2   Offshoring Impact on U.S. Jobs and Wages

	Source	Measure	Number of Workers Affected
	Deloitte Research (2003)	Financial services jobs that may move offshore	850,000 (15% of employment)
	Forrester (2002)	U.S. service jobs lost by 2015	3.3 million
	Evalueserve (2003)	All jobs lost (2003–2010): worst case	1.3 million
	Evalueserve (2004)	Total jobs offshored in IT and BPO in 2010	775,000 IT jobs 1.4 million BPO jobs
	Shaw quoted in McDougall (2005)	IT jobs moving offshore in 30 years	30% of total IT jobs
Wages			
	Bardhan and Kroll (2003)	U.S. workers in service jobs vulnerable to offshoring	14 million
	Progressive Policy Institute (2004)	U.S. IT jobs vulnerable to offshoring	12 million

It's not only pundits and consultants with national platforms who raise cautions about the globalization of services. Paul Samuelson, the Nobel Prize-winning MIT economist, published a paper in 2004[24] in which he observed that under certain hypothetical circumstances—two goods being traded between a high-wage and a low-wage country—free trade could actually *hurt* the developed country, and leave it worse off than before. We won't go into the specifics of his argument here; suffice it to say that he sketches out a scenario whereby the low-wage country with a huge and reasonably skilled workforce might hurt the higher-wage country by increasing its productivity in a particular high-value good formerly made by the higher-wage country.

But a McKinsey study later concluded that the Samuelson scenario—while perhaps possible in theory—bore little relation to what was actually happening, and therefore posed a minimal threat.

Low-wage companies lack sufficient numbers of skilled workers, McKinsey argued. Offshoring in the services sector, moreover, typically involves moving lower-value-added activities offshore, which "reinforces, rather than erodes, the productivity advantage of high-wage countries."[25]

Most informed observers agree on at least three key points:

- First, service globalization is not likely to affect aggregate U.S. employment in the long run. (That is, displaced workers are redeployed to other sectors.)
- Second, the relocation of service "production" abroad does lead to job losses in some sectors and shifts to other sectors in the short term.
- Third, even if one adopts the most aggressive estimates, those job-loss numbers remain small when compared to the overall labor pool and the average annual churn of jobs in the U.S. labor market.

On this last point: Employment is around 140 million in the United States, with around 35 million annual job switches—the vast majority of which are voluntary. If we take ten-year averages, around 3.5 million new positions are created each year, and 2.1 million positions eliminated—through firm creation and growth, and decline and failure, respectively. By comparison, the high-end estimates of jobs lost due to offshoring are around 250,000—approximately 0.2% of total jobs, or 0.7% of annual job switches.

Still, part of the larger calculation is political, and the political repercussions of services offshoring could be significant if these job losses are concentrated either in just a few industries or a concentrated geographic area. (When Reuters announced its intention to move 20 editorial jobs from the United States and Europe to a facility in Bangalore, for example, a disproportionate howl arose among the media.[26]) Similarly, political pressures are likely to increase as services-offshoring moves to higher-value activities. A majority of the services jobs being offshored today are low-value jobs that are structured, well defined, and not business critical. Over time, that is likely to change (see Figure 6.3).

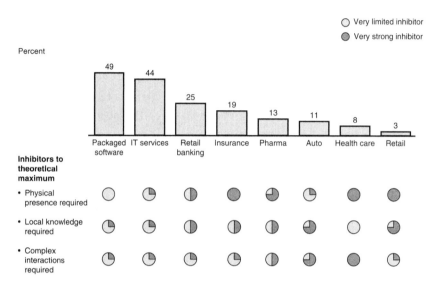

Figure 6.3 Portion of jobs that can theoretically go offshore

Source: McKinsey Global Institute analysis.

In addition to straight-out job losses, there are also fears that some of the sectors exposed to offshoring will experience downward wage pressure, even if positions are not lost. This needs to be examined in a larger context. Since the 2001 recession, wages have not moved up in parallel with productivity growth, and total labor compensation as a share of national income has declined slightly (from 66 percent in 2001 to 64 percent in 2004). During that same period, wages and salaries as a share of national income declined from 55 percent in 2001 to 52 percent in 2004, and median family income in the United States declined by 3.6 percent between 2000 and 2004.

It is extremely difficult to determine, however, how much of this economic backsliding can be attributed to globalization. Economist

Richard Freeman argues that the virtual doubling of the world labor force has cut the capital/labor ratio:

> The capital/labor ratio is a critical determinant of the wages paid to workers and of the rewards to capital. The more capital each worker has, the higher will be their productivity and pay. A decline in the global capital/labor ratio shifts the balance of power in markets toward capital, as more workers compete for working with that capital.[27]

Freeman estimates that the ratio has declined by 55 to 60 percent of what it would have been without globalization.

Other authorities, including Dani Rodrik, have argued that as globalization makes the services of large numbers of workers more easily "substitutable" across national boundaries, the bargaining power of immobile labor vis-à-vis mobile capital erodes.

Some have argued that offshoring may contribute to a decline in strength of some U.S. industries, and may even threaten U.S. leadership in innovation and technological development. "We fear the abruptness with which a lead in science and technology can be lost," the National Academies wrote in 2007, "and the difficulty of recovering a lead once lost, if indeed it can be regained at all."[28] Such a decline, along with the pressure on wages, may negatively impact the average living standards in the country.

Experts also express varying degrees of concern that offshoring could pose security risks, including increased risks to national security, critical infrastructure, and personal privacy. For example, offshoring development of software used in defense systems could set up a scenario whereby foreign workers with hostile intentions could obtain highly sensitive information, or introduce malicious code into software products that could interfere with defense or infrastructure systems. There is also the fear that offshoring could expose corporations to data, network, and information security risks, while posing greater privacy and identity-theft risks to individuals.

Policy Measures for the Short and Long Term

How should the short-term challenges outlined previously be managed through policy measures? Basically, there are two possible approaches: 1) attempting to slow or stop the progress of services offshoring, and 2) attempting to soften the adjustment costs that result from job dislocation.

Looking to the first of these two strategies, governments in developed economies can adopt what might be called a "sand in the gears" approach. Proponents of this view believe that government should do all it can to slow the globalization process when it imposes costs on citizens. For example, this approach would suggest that government contracts should prohibit any portion of the work being performed to be done overseas.

Further, they suggest that government should withdraw research and tax subsidies from corporations that perform or move work abroad. They argue that professional licensing requirements should be extended to cover all public and private work performed offshore, and that government should not offer temporary visas to workers who manage offshore operations—thereby making it more difficult to move work abroad.

Reflecting the security and privacy concerns that have been raised about performing work offshore, it has been suggested that personally identifiable information about American citizens should be transferred to only those nations that meet high standards of privacy protection and enforcement. Proponents of this strategy further suggest that transmission of personally identifiable information about American citizens outside of the United States should require approval from the concerned individual.

Although such policies may sound attractive, particularly to those affected by foreign competition, they are extremely difficult to implement, because global services networks operate in large part outside the regulatory reach of governments. It is hard to measure and monitor the exact amount of trade in services because, unlike manufactured goods, intangible data and information flows can't be regulated at national borders. If GM moves an auto-parts plant to Mexico, the products of that plant can be identified and embargoed from import into the United States, either by stopping the trucks at the border or by impounding the containers coming into Long Beach. Not so with data streams, where you can't track the jobs, and you can't track the work.

Even if global data and information flows *could* be monitored, it would be extremely difficult to enforce any restrictions or regulations that were applied to those flows. (Think of the difficulties that even authoritarian countries face when they attempt to limit their citizens' access to the Internet.[29]) Overall, in a globalized era when ideas, capital, and investments can easily cross national boundaries, protectionist policies only aggravate the challenges that grow out of offshoring.

Protectionism is also expensive. It may cost a great deal to save jobs—and these costs to the national or state treasury often greatly exceed the benefits of retaining jobs for a few. A New Jersey state government effort to prevent a call center for unemployment services from relocating to India resulted in that state's taxpayers paying—on top of the original contract cost—an additional $900,000 to save *12 jobs.* "Saving" 1,400 such jobs in the future would cost the state an extra $100 million—or $71,000 per job. In another famous case, TCS won a contract from the state of Indiana to perform software development work. When state legislators found out that much of the work was to be done from India, the contract was cancelled and re-bid— with a provision that the work be done in the United States. TCS won the re-bid—performing the work out of its Phoenix Development Center. The new contract delivered exactly the same services, but for an extra $8 million.[30]

What's the alternative policy approach? It might be summarized as "lessen the impact and minimize the pain"—or, more colloquially, "grease in the gears." This strategy acknowledges the downside of the services shift, and seeks to provide help and support to impacted workers. Some of the workers who lose their jobs to trade will be unemployed for a period of time before they find new jobs; this calls for new approaches to unemployment benefits. Some will end up with pay cuts at their new jobs, which may argue for some type of temporary wage insurance or for unemployment benefits to be paid on a sliding scale that requires moving out of depressed areas after some period of time. The pace at which job-specific skills lose value in the global marketplace is accelerating; therefore, workers require continual training and skills upgrades. In many cases, people need support—psychological as well as financial—while between jobs, and as they learn to cope with the turmoil associated with job change.

Collectively, these policies are aimed at easing the transition of workers displaced by trade, and providing them with incentives and support to train and prepare them for newer jobs. They are aimed at ensuring the current livelihoods of American workers, while preserving the benefits of an open and innovative economy.

Globalization and rapid changes in technology require companies to field a more flexible and adaptable workforce. Arguably, however, employees should not have to bear all of the costs associated with this change in the business environment. In recognition of this fact, some developed countries have policies in place to help their displaced workers absorb the pains of unemployment and prepare for reemployment. For example, trade adjustment assistance (TAA) and alternate trade adjustment assistance (ATAA) programs in the United States are targeted specifically at displacements resulting from trade. These are hardly new ideas. The TAA concept was introduced in the Kennedy administration in 1962 to compensate workers who lost their jobs due to trade liberalization that was assumed to benefit the economy as a whole. It extends unemployment benefits for an extra year, and provides training and health care for those whose job loss is associated with shifts in trade. Alternative trade adjustment assistance (ATAA) provides several types of support, including the following:

- Wage insurance for workers who find work but at a lower wage
- Funds to help in relocation to more vibrant geographies
- Training credits to encourage lifelong learning and redeployment to new sectors

Unfortunately, the results of these initiatives have been disappointing. Participation has been low, and benefits have being denied to three-quarters of the workers who have been certified by the government as eligible. TAA has extended assistance only to some 71,000 new workers a year[31] (see Table 6.3). Note that displaced workers in services sectors experience shorter periods out of work and smaller declines in earnings than displaced manufacturing works.

TABLE 6.3   Earnings Impact on Displaced Workers (2001–2003 Averages)

	Full-Time Workers Displaced (Thousands)	Average Earnings on Lost Job	Change in Earnings in New Job	Average Weeks without Work
Trade displaced (TAA)*	71,000	$32,505	-21%	80**
Total displaced	2,068,000	$42,687	-16%	11.9
Manufacturing displaced	693,000	$40,154	-20%	14.1
Services displaced	953,000	$45,479	-13%	10.5
Services potentially affected by offshoring	205,000	$60,535	-14%	13.1
Telecommunications	77,674	$52,830	-26%	14.7
ISP, data processing, and other info services	9,000	$62,366	-24%	
Architectural, engineering, and related services	41,000	$61,058	-16%	18.7
Computer systems, design, and related services	75,000	$65,921	-6%	14.5

Note: Table refers to full-time workers with at least 2-year tenure.
*TAA displaced workers estimate based on entire TAA population. Earnings estimates of TAA displaced workers based on those that completed the program.
**Author's calculation based on TAA data

The basic problem the United States faces in this difficult realm is that the existing solutions are piecemeal, fragmented, and internally inconsistent. Over the past half-century, the federal government has implemented a series of programs in isolation, responding to the crisis of the moment. When a tariff deal caused dislocations in a particular sector (agriculture, textiles, etc.), the government moved to address that. When NAFTA cost people in certain industries or geographies their jobs, programs to minimize that pain were implemented. Some programs extend benefits; others offer retraining credits; still others provide wage insurance of one kind or another. Some encourage relocation; some discourage relocation (at least implicitly); and some don't address relocation at all.

A thoughtful paper from three Brookings Institution researchers—Lael Brainard, Robert E. Litan, and Nicholas Warren—suggests some remedies for this hodge-podge of policies and programs.[32] They argue that we need a *broader* program, aimed at helping more displaced workers, and a *more comprehensive* program, which would comprise, for example, the following:

- **Unemployment insurance**—This would continue to serve as a safety net for families and individuals.
- **Basic-skills training programs**—This includes training in writing, problem-analysis, and so on, rather than sector-specific training (which often trains for jobs that don't exist).
- **Incentives for employers to hire unemployed workers**—This includes tax credits, training credits, and so on, to entice employers from simply "poaching" employees from competitors.
- **Incentives for workers to relocate**—This is meant to achieve the politically unpalatable but economically crucial goal of moving workers out of pockets of depression (such as one-industry towns built around a failing industry).

- **Wage insurance**—This is the most ambitious part of the proposed program, which would guarantee that for a stated period of time—say, two years—the wages of displaced workers would not be allowed to go below a stated percentage of their predisplacement wage (although this benefit would have a dollar cap imposed). The program would be funded by a minimal tax on existing worker payrolls, and might amount to something like $25 per worker per year.

Of course, even such a sweeping proposal would only be the first step toward a truly comprehensive policy approach. Additional steps might include, for example, portable health benefits and portable pensions (such as are enjoyed by many teachers and other public employees).

All of this would cost money, of course. Each country's political leadership needs to decide what level of assistance it wants to extend to those whose lives are disrupted as a result of increased trade. Currently, spending varies dramatically by country. In the United States, for example, it constitutes only 0.5 percent of GDP on unemployment support, as compared to 3.1 percent in Germany and 3.7 percent in Denmark.[33] Only after such a consensus is reached can the necessary resources be found and applied.

For the Long Term

To conclude this chapter, let's put on our economist hats once more. From the economist's perspective, there are basically three ways to drive higher standards of living. The first, simplest, and most basic is to *accumulate resources*. Sometimes that is achieved through population growth, or through a larger percentage of people joining the workforce, or through higher savings rates, or through a smarter workforce.

The second is to *reallocate resources*. We've just looked at this option, in the form of the Brookings proposal just outlined. You move workers out of low-productivity or declining sectors, into high-productivity or growing sectors. The same dynamic applies to capital reallocation.

The third way to drive higher standards of living is through *innovation:* inventing new things, or new ways of doing business.

Although different nations are good at different things, there is no reason why a nation that is lagging behind in one of these realms can't try to do better. For example, the United States is relatively good at reallocating resources and extremely good at innovating—but demonstrably *terrible* at accumulating resources. Women have already entered our workforce; our population is aging, rather than growing; our savings rates are the lowest in the world.

For the long term, therefore, the United States should put policies in place that will 1) promote savings over consumption, and 2) create a smarter workforce. The tools needed to achieve the former goal include reduced taxes on dividends and capital gains, and increased taxes on consumption (either through sales taxes or value-added taxes, or VATs). It seems clear that programs such as Medicare and Social Security will have to shift from their current funding model—which is essentially an *unfunded* model (the famous "lock box" is filled with IOUs from your children)—to a forward-funding model, in which the money taxed from an individual in his or her lifetime is used to provide benefits to that individual. The alternative is grim: huge, unfunded drains on the long-term savings of the country.

Revising the tax code and the Medicare and Social Security systems in these directions will be politically difficult, but achieving the second objective—a smarter workforce—will be orders of magnitude harder. It will require a dramatic, far-ranging overhaul of our K–12 education system, into which we pour more money per student than nearly every other country in the world, and out of which we receive well below-average performance. We, the authors, don't present ourselves as experts in K–12 education. (In fact, despite having advanced degrees and experience teaching at some of the world's top universities, we would be *barred* from teaching in many public school systems today, because our degrees are not in education.) But we don't hesitate to raise our voices in favor of a spirited debate, and a *resolution* of that debate.

Do we need charter schools, pilot schools, or their equivalent? Probably.

Should more effective teachers be paid more, and less effective teachers be paid less? Almost certainly.

Should gifted teachers with unconventional credentials be allowed to teach? Absolutely.

In short, our schools absolutely have to be come less *producer* focused (that is, focused on the needs of the teacher) and more *user* focused. Schools must become less bureaucratic and precedent driven, and more *output* oriented: Are our children getting what they need?

And as long as we're tackling every controversial issue on the political landscape, we shouldn't overlook the immigration debate. Currently, legal immigration into the United States favors family members of existing U.S. residents. From a resource-accumulation perspective, this is exactly backward. We should be following Canada's lead and Europe's lead by favoring immigrants who promise to be most valuable to our economy: scientists, engineers, computer programmers, and so on.

By focusing on what we in the United States are bad at—resource accumulation—we don't mean to slight what we're good at. Despite the concerns mentioned earlier, the United States continues to be an engine for innovation. This trait results from a multitude of factors—for example, an emphasis on independent thinking, a steady in-migration of new minds, a risk-taking culture with no stigma attached to trying and failing, a (reasonably) noncorrupt bureaucracy, and financial markets and a venture capital system that are unrivaled at taking new ideas and turning them into global products.[34] It's a remarkable "virtuous circle." The quality of life and relative openness to external cultures and ideas in the United States attracts talented and ambitious people from around the world—and these workers tend to be the kind of people who bring with them the knowledge and skills needed to further contribute to growth and innovation.

In the United States, therefore, long-term policy measures should strengthen those institutions that nurture that spirit of innovation. Investment in innovation and education is a must—not just at the K–12 levels, as advocated earlier, but at *all* levels—if the United States hopes to remain at the forefront of the global economy. That education should prepare workers to thrive in a world of rapid globalization and disruptive technology changes. Technical knowledge and skills won't be enough; in tomorrow's world, a broader set of skills and creativity will be required. Industry association, unions, companies, and academia can together help workers anticipate changes and prepare for them. By monitoring changes in employment demand and elaborating skill sets required in those areas, they can help workers better prepare for career shifts.

The National Academies' "Committee on Prospering in the Global Economy of the 21st Century"—which consisted of 20 individuals with diverse backgrounds, including university presidents, CEOs, Nobel laureates, and former presidential appointees—came up with four key recommendations along these lines:

- Reforming the K–12 education system to increase America's talent pool in science, math, and technology. They suggested increasing recruitment of science and math teachers each year through competitive scholarships.
- Reforming higher education to offer more scholarships for science, mathematics, engineering, and technology. They also endorsed tax credits for continuing education; fostering skill-based, preferential immigration; and expediting residence and extending visas to foreign scholars who stay in the United States.
- Stimulating the U.S. research base by increasing government investment in research.
- Using incentives to spur innovation in the private sector.

What about other developed economies? For a number of reasons, Europe and Japan are in a far more difficult position than the United States. Although they are better at resource accumulation, they are far worse at resource allocation. Their labor regulations, for example, are highly restrictive, preventing the easy hiring (and firing) of workers. Cultural issues also come into play. Much has been made recently of the more casual approach to work in Europe: shorter workdays and workweeks, longer and more frequent holidays, and so on. Japan still suffers from the widespread exclusion of women and minorities from positions of authority in the workplace. To maximize opportunities in the globalizing world, these nations will need to embrace greater labor market liberalization and increase their cultural openness.

That, in turn, will enhance their ability to innovate. For Europe, this is not a "nice-to-have," but a necessity. Already, the relative attractiveness of the United States as the destination of choice for would-be innovators is globally recognized. Here's how Nandan Nilekani, the CEO of Infosys, perceives Europe's challenge:

> You [in the United States] have this whole ecosystem [that constitutes] a unique crucible for innovation. I was in Europe the other day, and they were commiserating about the 400,000 [European] knowledge workers who have gone to live in the United States because of the innovative environment there. The whole process where people get an idea and put together a team, raise the capital, create a product and mainstream it—that can only be done in the United States.[35]

To remain competitive in the global services economy over the long term, Europe will first have to attend to its near-term challenges, including rising health-care costs and a weaker telecommunication infrastructure (as compared to other developed economies). Then the European nations—individually and collectively—will have to do some creative thinking and make some hard choices.

Policy in Perspective

Globalization has come to the service sector. In some ways, it's the same old story: For many individuals, trade is disruptive and inconvenient. But in the long run, and taken in the aggregate, it is a vital element of growing productivity and living standards. Over time, many clever approaches have been proposed to mitigate or stop trade flows, but history shows that countries that embrace trade prosper, and those that don't, don't.

But trade in services differs in some important ways from what we have traditionally seen in manufacturing and/or natural resources. It affects huge new areas of the economy. Many of the tasks and processes that move are not "low end," but rather affect people "like us." As the old economist's joke puts it, "A recession is when your neighbor loses his job. A depression is when you lose yours." There is more than a grain of truth to this.

The good news is that the policies that made sense to deal with globalization in manufacturing largely apply to the services shift. Think long term, invest in accumulation, allow reallocation, and promote innovation. And most of all, *don't throw sand in the wheels of commerce.* It's expensive, and it doesn't work. Instead, look for the lubricant.

Endnotes

[1] "Offshoring: Spreading the Gospel," *BusinessWeek* (March 6, 2006), www.businessweek.com/magazine/content/06_10/b3974074.htm.

[2] C. Denizer, "Foreign Entry in Turkey's Banking Sector, 1980–97," *The World Bank Group Policy Research Working Papers*, No. 2462 (2000), p. 18–20, http://econ.worldbank.org/external/default/main?pagePK=64165259&theSitePK=469372&piPK=64165421&menuPK=64166093&entityID=000094946_00110805385813.

[3] J.P. Pradhan and V. Abraham, "Social and Cultural Impact of Outsourcing: Emerging Issues from Indian Call Centers," *Harvard Asia Quarterly*, Volume IX, No. 3, Summer 2005, www.asiaquarterly.com/content/view/155/40/.

[4] "World Investment Report 2004, The shift towards services." United Nations conference on trade and development, www.unctad.org/en/docs/wir2004_en.pdf.

[5] D. Farrell, J.K. Remes, and H. Schulz, "The truth about foreign direct investment in emerging markets," *The McKinsey Quarterly* (2004) www.mckinseyquarterly.com/The_truth_about_foreign_direct_investment_in_emerging_markets_1386_abstract.

[6] Dubai Internet City, 2008, www.dubaiinternetcity.com.

[7] "ICT and Knowledge Services," Jamaica Trade & Invest, 2008, www.jamaicatradeandinvest.org/index.php?action=investment&id=3&oppage=4&optyp=mm&menu=incentive.

[8] "Chile: Latin America's rising star?" SharedXpertise Forums website, www.sharedxpertise.org/file/3073/chile-ideal-for-shared-services.html.

[9] "World Investment Report 2004, The shift towards services," United Nations conference on Trade and Development, July 2004, p. 208, www.unctad.org/en/docs/wir2004_en.pdf.

[10] "World Investment Report 2004, The shift towards services," United Nations conference on Trade and Development, July 2004, p. 201, www.unctad.org/en/docs/wir2004_en.pdf.

[11] "Software Technology Parks of India," DIT Ministry of Communications and Information Technology, 2008, www.stpp.soft.net.

[12] "National Taskforce on Information Technology & Software Development," National Taskforce on Information Technology and Software Development, 2008, http://it-taskforce.nic.in/.

[13] "Offshoring: Is It a Win-Win Game?" McKinsey Global Institute, August 2003, www.mckinsey.com/mgi/reports/pdfs/offshore/Offshoring_MGI_Perspective.pdf.

[14] Based on Department of Labor statistics contained in Brainard, Litan, and Warren's "Insuring America's Workers in a New Era of Offshoring," The Brookings Institution, Policy Brief No. 143, July 2005, p. 3, www.brookings.edu/papers/2005/07macroeconomics_brainard.aspx.

[15] A. S. Blinder, "Offshoring: The Next Industrial Revolution?" *Foreign Affairs* (March/April 2006), p. 1, www.foreignaffairs.org/20060301faessay85209/alan-s-blinder/offshoring-the-next-industrial-revolution.html.

[16] "Offshoring of Services: An Overview of Issues," United States Government Accountability Office report to Congressional committees, November 2005, www.gao.gov/new.items/d065.pdf.

[17] "India's New opportunity—2020," All India Management Association, 2003, www.ibef.org/download/IndiaNewOpportunity.pdf.

[18] "World Population Prospects: The 2004 Revision—Population Database," United Nations Publications, 2005, http://esa.un.org/unpp/ (accessed October 6, 2005).

[19] "Old Europe; Demographic Change; The trouble with ageing," *The Economist* (September 30, 2004) www.religiousconsultation.org/News_Tracker/old_Europe_demographic_change_trouble_with_ageing.htm.

[20] "World Economic Outlook," International Monetary Fund, September 2004, p. 40, www.imf.org/external/pubs/ft/weo/2004/02/.

[21] "World Population Prospects: The 2004 Revision—Population Database," United Nations Publications, 2005, http://esa.un.org/unpp/ (accessed October 6, 2005).

[22] "World Population Prospects: The 2004 Revision—Population Database," United Nations Publications, 2005, http://esa.un.org/unpp/ (accessed October 6, 2005).

[23] "Dobbs Speaks Downtown Against Offshoring," *The Enquirer* (September 23, 2004), www.enquirer.com/editions/2004/09/23/biz_dobbs23.html.

[24] Paul A. Samuelson, 2004. "Where Ricardo and Mill Rebut and Confirm Arguments of Mainstream Economists Supporting Globalization," *Journal of Economic Perspectives*, American Economic Association, 18(3), pp. 135-146.

[25] "U.S. Offshoring: Rethinking the Response," McKinsey Global Institute, December 2005, www.mckinsey.com/mgi/publications/rethinking.asp.

[26] "Reuters to move editorial jobs from U.S. and Europe to India," *Washington Post* (August 10, 2004), www.washingtonpost.com/wp-dyn/articles/A53035-2004Aug9.html.

[27] R. Freeman, "What Really Ails Europe (and America): The Doubling of the Global Workforce," *The Globalist* (June 3, 2005), www.theglobalist.com/StoryId.aspx?StoryId=4542.

[28] National Academies, *Rising Above the Gathering Storm: Energizing and Employing America for a Brighter Future*, National Academies Press (2007), http://books.nap.edu/openbook.php?record_id=11463&page=3.

[29] Iran recently tried to limit Western cultural intrusion into that country by restricting access to high-speed links—and thereby preventing 5 million Iranian web surfers from downloading Western music and videos. See the *Guardian* story at www.guardian.co.uk/technology/2006/oct/18/news.iran.

[30] S. Anderson, "Creeping Protectionism: An analysis of State and Federal global sourcing legislation," *The National Foundation for American Policy* (December 2003), www.nfap.com/researchactivities/studies/creepingProtect.pdf.

[31] L. Brainard, R.E. Litan, and N. Warren, "Insuring America's Workers in a New Era of Offshoring," The Brookings Institution; Policy Brief No. 143, July 2005, p. 3, www.brookings.edu/papers/2005/07macroeconomics_brainard.aspx.

[32] L. Brainard, R.E. Litan, and N. Warren, "A fairer deal for America's workers in a new era of offshoring," The Brookings Institution, September 14, 2005.

[33] "U.S. Offshoring: Rethinking the Response," McKinsey Global Institute, December 2005, www.mckinsey.com/mgi/publications/rethinking.asp.

[34] T. Friedman, *The World Is Flat: A Brief History of the Twenty-first Century,* Farrar, Straus, Giroux (2005).

[35] T. Friedman, "The Secret of Our Sauce," *New York Times* (March 7, 2004), http://query.nytimes.com/gst/fullpage.html?res=9F00E5DE1E3FF934A35750C0 A9629C8B63.

7

Looking Ahead

Economists like to make predictions. We assemble data, apply powerful tools of analysis to that information, look for trends, and make projections based on those extrapolations.

On the other hand, economists *don't* like to make predictions. (Responding to an economic advisor's penchant for saying "on the one hand...on the other hand," Harry Truman famously commented, "Give me a one-armed economist.") It is an extremely complex world out there. Apparent trend lines can prove to be a mirage. Good predictions can be made bad by a bolt from the blue—some X-factor that no amount of digging or analysis could have foreseen. Economists are scientists, of a sort; we don't want to be confused with fortunetellers.

That said, we want to close this book with seven predictions about the future of the services shift. Based on what we've included in the previous chapters, none of these predictions should be particularly startling—that is, they grow directly out of the past and present of outsourcing and offshoring. But collectively, they may shed useful light on the opportunities and challenges that lie ahead, as you contemplate a new or expanded involvement in the services shift.

Global Sourcing Will Continue to Grow— Rapidly

There is still plenty of room for growth in global sourcing.

According to a Forrester Research study in 2004, the vast majority of the revenues generated by Indian IT workers come from about 50 of the Fortune 1000 companies. At the other end of the offshoring spectrum, something like 25 percent of the Fortune 1000 had no involvement in global sourcing, and the remaining 700-or-so companies in the middle had mostly "dabbled" in offshoring.[1]

Although there will surely be vast growth in the number of firms that pursue offshore sourcing, that's only part of the story. Many of those firms counted as currently offshoring have only started their journey. Think back to the discussion of how firms' offshoring opportunities evolve as they learn. Recall GE's pioneering role in establishing the offshore industry in the mid-1990s. Tiger Tyagarajan, former CEO of GECIS and current Executive VP at Genpact—the largest and likely most sophisticated global offshore vendor—recently estimated that more than a dozen years into its offshore journey, GE has realized only 30 percent of its potential for global sourcing.[2] So expect to see more firms participating in the services shift as well as deeper involvement in the firms that are participating.

Of course, not all of the Fortune 1000 (or of any other grouping of companies) will find benefit in global sourcing. But it's safe to predict that as offshore companies develop new capabilities, more and more potential customers will turn into *paying* customers.

The Key Word Will Be "Global"

We've tried to make this point forcefully in previous chapters. Until recently, the "services shift" was largely an "India" phenomenon. Today, India remains the focal point, with a few rising rivals—such as the Philippines, China, South Africa, Hungary, and Russia. One recent study of firms offering innovation services found that 50 percent were based in India, 28 percent in China, and 15 percent in Russia.[3]

But no one holds a 50-percent market share in an intensely competitive industry for long, especially when barriers to entry are relatively low. Expect global sourcing to become steadily more global.

There are a number of contributing factors. First, of course, dozens of nations around the world have studied the model of India. They understand the huge scale of the global market for services—something like $300 billion, according to NASSCOM. They also understand that creating service sector jobs requires much less capital per job than creating manufacturing jobs—and developing countries generally have a surplus of workers while being relatively capital poor. (The typical call center, for example, requires only about $1 million of invested capital for 100 jobs—far less than it would take to create 100 manufacturing jobs.) They understand the benefits of the indirect and induced employment that accompanies a successful move into the offshoring game. And finally, they understand that exporting their brainpower instead of their manual labor leads to better diffusion of knowledge and technology into the local economy, which is a critical prerequisite to becoming a truly competitive economy.

In Chapter 6, "The Services Shift: Policy Implications," we detailed the efforts of countries such as Gambia, Jamaica, Mauritius, Dubai, the Philippines, Croatia, and others to jump into the global sourcing game. Of the 116 countries in the ILO's database, more than 90 are actively promoting a range of service activities, including call centers, medical diagnoses, and professional services. No, not all of those efforts will be successful, but many will. Ten years from now we won't be talking about "India and a few others." We'll be sifting through dozens of viable offshore centers, each offering different combinations of cost, talent, regulations, and macro stability.

Other factors will also broaden the base of global sourcing beyond India and today's other star players. India's creaky infrastructure, high turnover, congestion, skyrocketing real-estate costs, and rapidly rising wages are gradually making that country less of a perceived bargain. Between 2003 and 2008, moreover, the dollar declined 16 percent against the rupee, again hurting India's competitiveness. As the cost savings of doing business in India shrink, the "near-shoring" options for U.S. companies—that is, the opportunity to do business in Central and South America—will become more appealing. "If you're only going to have a 20-percent savings," as one IT consultant commented to *BusinessWeek*, "clients start to think about time zone."[4]

Global Services Sources Will Keep Moving "Up the Food Chain"

We've seen how multinational corporations took the first baby steps toward global sourcing by setting up captive operations in low-wage areas—first the Caribbean and later India. These captives—often owned and operated by financial-services companies—at first were thought of exclusively as back-office processors.

Gradually, though, the captives developed more sophisticated capabilities. As this happened, their parent organizations moved additional pieces of their operations offshore, including jobs that previously had been considered impossible to perform remotely. In 2003, for example, several Wall Street–based firms moved a small number of research jobs to Mumbai.[5] Only a few years later, literally hundreds of these jobs—previously performed by high-priced MBAs in New York, London, and Tokyo—had been offshored to India. The Indian service providers had moved out of the back office and invaded the middle office. Today, we see firms such as ITTIAM (chip design in India), Microsoft (graphics research in China), and Pfizer (genomics research in India) moving some of their most sophisticated jobs to low-income countries.

Some of these captives became global best-practice operations, came to realize that they could serve a much broader audience, and were spun out as independent operations. Inevitably, those "liberated captives" began adding new capabilities—and they were joined in the marketplace by start-up companies that commenced operations with more and more specialized service offerings.

This trend will intensify in the future, as increasingly competitive and specialized service providers move up their respective food chains. "After research," one journalist recently observed, "the next wave may include more sophisticated jobs like the creation of derivative products, quantitative trading models, and even sales jobs from the trading floors."[6]

Talent Will Become More Important Than Cost

This prediction grows out of the previous one. In our brief recounting of the history of offshoring, we argued that the pioneering consumers of offshored services were mainly looking to do the same job cheaper—a straight labor-arbitrage play. But, although they were attracted by potential labor cost savings, many of these pioneers came to realize that global sourcing also allowed them to access *better* talent, working with better systems, than they could hire at home.

To some extent, this was because their home countries—for example, the United States—simply weren't producing enough of the specialized talent needed to get certain kinds of jobs done. A recent survey of civil engineers in the United States revealed that about 20 percent of CE firms had experience with offshoring. Among those firms, 47 percent had ventured overseas in search of lower labor costs—but another 40 percent went to procure more capacity or specialized talent:

> Decreasing capacity constraints were identified as a major driver of offshore outsourcing by this group, who say the limited domestic hiring market for engineers prompted them to gain labor from other markets to complete their current workload or to enable them to take on additional work.[7]

In the early years, offshoring was about costs. But as the supplier base became increasingly sophisticated, firms were started and thrived by specializing in increasingly narrow niches (for example, matching insurance claims from physicians to thousands of different policies from insurance companies, or performing research to support patent applications). These firms built scale by servicing multiple clients and by investing to build best-practice processing platforms. They soon found that they could perform their specialties better than almost any potential client—and each step forward made them attractive to yet another set of clients.

One example is General Motors, which has outsourced (and mostly offshored) 100 percent of its call centers and code development. True, much of that work went to EDS, which was formerly owned by GM; nevertheless, the automaker is convinced that the call-center and IT-related work that it buys offshore is not only cheaper, but better. According to Tony Scott, chief technology officer for GM's Information Systems and Services organization, the quality is better, the services are more flexible, and it's far easier to figure out exactly what these services cost. The expiration of contracts, he adds, naturally precipitates discussions about quality and pricing, which leads to a steady upward movement of baselines.[8]

This trend is almost certain to continue in the future.

Scale Will Decline Dramatically

Maybe this prediction sounds like it runs counter to the story told in previous chapters. Aren't companies such as Tata Consultancy Services, Infosys, Wipro, and Genpact growing at astounding rates? Aren't most or all of them likely to exceed 100,000 employees each in the relatively near future?

The answer to those questions is probably "yes." TCS is already there, with 110,000 employees as of March 2008.[9] Infosys counted 11,000 noses in 2002, and today has something like 91,000 employees in 26 countries.[10] Wipro had 42,000 employees worldwide in 2005; by June 2007, it had something like 72,000 employees in 53 countries.[11] Genpact grew from 19,000 employees in 2005 to 35,500 as of June 2008.[12] Those are astounding growth trajectories.

So absent the kind of bolt from the blue mentioned earlier, the biggest players will keep getting bigger. What we mean by "scale" here, though, is the scale of the projects that are likely to be serviced globally in the coming years. As you've seen in previous chapters, a large offshoring effort—say, 100 jobs' worth—is small by manufacturing standards, which usually involve multiples of that number (and the associated huge capital investments). In the future, the threshold for offshoring a service function will decline precipitously—to as few as a half-dozen jobs. Why? Because suppliers will come up with increasingly specific competencies that will service increasingly specialized market segments.

The homerun-hitting venture capital firm Kleiner Perkins Caufield & Byers saw this trend emerging a decade ago, when it invested heavily in a company called Elance, which proposed to sell professional services on a global scale.[13] In fact, the venture capitalists put almost as much money into Elance as they did into two other online ventures: Google and Amazon. Elance hasn't enjoyed anything like the success of its more visible sister companies—in part because its owners haven't yet taken it public, and in part because many purchasers of, say, legal services are still skeptical about looking offshore for those kinds of services.

But Elance is well positioned to take advantage of changing attitudes in this arena. In 2006, it reached the milestone of $7 billion in "services spend actively managed by Elance customers," and in 2008, its revenues (from subscriptions and sliding-scale transactions fees) rose to $60 million—up 50 percent from 2007. Today it calls itself the "world's leading project-based marketplace and workspace."[14]

Another website, Serebra Connect, runs auctions that bring together individual clients with service providers on a global scale.[15]

Buyers post a potential job on the website, and sellers bid to do the work (with Serebra taking a 15 percent cut as a middleman). Serebra counts 6,500 sellers of services, of whom 4,000 are in developing countries. Typical outsourced/offshored tasks might include translation, website development, PowerPoint preparation, and so on. The company's website explicitly states that one of Serebra's corporate goals is to give people around the world access to the digital economy—and to "provide a platform to provide work to skilled people in developing nations."[16]

This combination of low cost and social responsibility is likely to prove appealing to increasing numbers of individual and corporate clients. According to one estimate, the "person-to-person" offshoring market is likely to reach $2 billion by 2015 (up from something like $250 million in 2005).[17]

Global Sourcing Will Become Increasingly Personal

This is an outgrowth of our previous prediction. We are almost certain to see a dramatic rise in personal services: tutoring, concierge services, schedule management, and so on.

One company founded in 2005 may point the way to this particular future. TutorVista, an online tutoring service, uses instructors in India to tutor American students.[18] The American student (or more likely, his or her parents) signs up for tutoring by the hour (at $19.99 per hour) or unlimited tutoring for $99.99 per month. Tutors are available 24/7, and appointments can be made on 12 hours' notice. Because its tutors work out of their homes, TutorVista is able to engage in a kind of "domestic offshoring," using labor in parts of India that haven't experienced the surging labor rates of places such as Mumbai and Bangalore. "Is the instruction personalized for every student?" the company's website asks rhetorically. The answer turns out to be yes:

Absolutely! TutorVista's tutoring process often begins with the student taking an assessment test that calibrates the student's proficiency in various topics. We then develop a comprehensive learning plan for the student focusing on the topics that need more attention to help the student achieve his or her academic goals. One student per tutor ensures that every student receives 100% attention of the tutor. The student typically uses the same tutor every time thus ensuring continuity.

It's only a short step from subscription tutors to subscription personal assistants. A *New York Times* article from 2007 told the story of a 32-year-old management consultant in New York City who simply doesn't have the time to make travel arrangements, find tech support, call the beauty salon, order Chinese take-out, or buy theater tickets.[19] This "remote concierge" service—offered by a start-up called AskSunday—handles tasks such as these either on a per-request model or on a subscription basis ($29 for 30 requests per month, or $49 for 50 requests per month). Almost all of the staff handling the requests are based in India and are available 24 hours a day. The company's website offers testimonials detailing a broad range of services successfully provided:

> Sunday is a brilliant idea! I had an issue where I was double charged on a past Verizon bill and never got around to looking into it. I emailed Sunday explaining what needed to be corrected and an agent got right after them. He was able to get my bill adjusted—that one request alone was worth the month's membership fee.[20]

We're also likely to see a rise in the offshoring of one-off projects that companies or individuals want to get done inexpensively. *BusinessWeek* recently ran a story about a couple who run four largely offshored businesses—which the magazine dubbed "micro-multinationals"—out of their Dorchester, Massachusetts home.[21] Randy and Nicola Wilbrun paid an Indian artist $300 for the logo for their baby-food company, purchased promotional materials from a London freelancer, and use "virtual assistants" based in Jerusalem to provide transcription and various kinds of technical support. Notably, the Wilbruns use retired brokers in Virginia and Michigan to run the virtual back office of their real estate venture, underscoring the premise presented in earlier chapters that some kinds of services are likely to remain "onshore" indefinitely.

We Will See More Two-Way Travel

One of the earliest phases of outsourcing was the "bodyshopping" phase, in which companies—mainly Indian—deployed skilled workers to remote clients (mostly in the United States) to help those clients perform work more cheaply and efficiently. Gradually, with the improvement of telecommunications and related technologies, Indian workers were able to stay at home and service their clients from a distance.

What does the future hold? Almost certainly, we will see customers traveling to the supplier for some outsourced services.

Take "medical tourism," discussed in Chapter 1, "Globalization of Services: What, Why, and When," in which consumers of health-care services (almost always in the developed world) travel to the developing world to procure health care (usually surgeries) at a more affordable price than it can be procured at home—and, in the process, engage in some local sightseeing. In November 2007, the U.S.-based Medical Tourism Association (MTA) launched *Medical Tourism*, which it calls the "first trade magazine written by professionals in the industry." The first issue of the magazine featured health-care bargains in Costa Rica; subsequent issues focused on Asian and East Asian countries.[22]

In June 2008, MTA announced that it had joined forces with the InterContinental Hotels Group—one of the largest hotel chains in the world—in an initiative to promote medical-related travel to Panama, Costa Rica, Brazil, and Mexico's Monterrey peninsula. The benefits of the program, according to MTA, would include the following:

- Partnerships with some of the top medical insurance companies in the United States

- Special rates and packages provided by IHG hotels, airlines, and doctors in Latin America
- Teaming up with some of the best hospitals in Latin America for a vast array of medical procedures, including plastic surgery, joint replacement, heart bypass surgery, and dental procedures
- Transportation (provided by IHG hotels) to and from the airport as well as to and from the doctor's office pre- and post-operation for check ups

The economics of medical tourism can be compelling, as described in Chapter 1. The knee replacement that might cost $40,000 in the United States costs $18,000 in Singapore and $8,500 in India. With insurance companies (among the prime backers of MTA) and global hotel chains working together to promote medical tourism, the industry is almost certain to grow exponentially—from something like $60 billion in 2006 to $100 billion by 2012, according to McKinsey.[23]

Dental tourism is not far behind. A *USA Today* article told the story of a woman from the Washington, D.C. suburbs who faced a staggering dental bill (something over $11,000) for the eight crowns that she needed. She flew to Vienna, had her teeth fixed at a Hungarian clinic, and spent the bulk of her ten-day visit touring Budapest and Vienna. The dental work cost $2,900, and the total cost of her trip (including air fare of $899 and a hotel room at $45 per night) was just under $4,300. A Philadelphia restaurateur visiting the same clinic paid $6,000 for extractions that would have cost $43,000 back home.[24]

Obviously, the domestic U.S. dental industry is not happy about this particular trend. "The key," said the president-elect of the American Dental Association in 2006, "is educating patients to understand that optimal dental health is not a tour-bus stop, not a one-time visit, but a lifetime of joint effort involving the patient and the dental team."[25] But with so many Americans having little or no dental insurance, dental tourism is also likely to grow enormously in the coming years.

Given the impending retirements of all those Baby Boomers in the United States, we shouldn't overlook the burgeoning field of retirement communities and services. One author who refers to himself as "the guy who invented retirement in Costa Rica" describes the advantages of that country as follows:

> In most areas housing costs less than what it does in the U. S. and hired help is a steal. Utilities—telephone service, electricity, and water—are cheaper than in North America. You never need to heat your home or apartment because of Costa Rica's warm climate. You need not cook with gas, since most stoves are electric. These services cost about 30 percent of what they do at home. Bills for heating in the winter and air conditioning in the summer can cost hundreds of dollars in the States. For those watching their fixed income, retirement dollars, this is an important consideration.[26]

For more adventurous Baby Boomers, there's the Sri Lankan alternative. A website sanctioned by the government of Sri Lanka—an island nation off the southern tip of India—encourages potential immigrants to escape from the high cost of living, "dreary weather," excessive taxation, and other disadvantages of their home countries. Low-cost medical care and "world-class medical facilities" are available for those concerned about health care in their senior years. "This is the place where you can retire early and comfortably," asserts the website. "This is about living well with less money."[27]

Perhaps retirement communities and retirement services stretch the definition of the "services shift" to the breaking point. But to the extent that retirees are buying services offshore—including housing and medical care—those are services that are no longer being provided in the home countries of those retirees. Accordingly, we rule them "in-bounds."

The Services Shift: A Tough Game You May Have to Play

For most companies, making the services shift isn't easy.

Even assuming that infrastructure-related issues don't cause problems for you—and in more and more parts of the world, the technological and physical infrastructure is coming up to world standards—you will almost certainly find that cross-cultural challenges persist. Among 200 U.S. business executives polled in a recent Accenture survey, for example, two-thirds said that their companies had experienced problems offshoring because of cultural differences. The biggest contributing factor (reported by three-quarters of the executives) was incompatible communication styles. Also cited as sources of conflict were different approaches to completing tasks, resolving conflicts, and making key decisions.[28]

A Gartner study of offshored help desks revealed that moving this function offshore saved between 30 and 40 percent—but also led to serious challenges. For example, domestic U.S. turnover on help desks was 14.7 percent, whereas overseas it was 22.1 percent. (Evidently, in places such as the Indian centers of IT outsourcing, job opportunities are plentiful, and people readily switch jobs for even small salary increases.) But the help desk is in many cases the most important customer-facing corporate function, and high turnover inevitably means the help desk is less helpful.[29]

Sometimes difficulties lead to terminations of contracts and retrenchment away from offshoring deals. One survey of IT executives revealed that 21 percent had terminated one or more overseas contracts in the past year. True, some of these terminations reflected consolidations of overseas efforts—but the most common reasons cited were 1) financial difficulties on the part of the provider, and 2) the inability of the provider to deliver the contracted services.[30] And although offshoring failures tend to receive disproportionate publicity in the U.S. media, it's worth noting that some sophisticated players have indeed pulled back from their offshore investments. As noted in Chapter 3, "Making It Real," Conseco brought its customer-service operations back onshore in response to customer complaints. Dell "repatriated" a technical support center (although this reversal represented only a tiny fraction of the jobs that the computer-maker had moved offshore). Lehman Brothers brought home an offshore help desk.

In previous chapters, we've detailed many of the challenges you're likely to face, including figuring out which of your internal tasks and processes lend themselves to offshoring, mapping those tasks or processes, decoding the relevant technology and infrastructure, picking a vendor and a geography, mitigating the risks that are inherent in global sourcing, migrating the selected tasks or processes, and creating an integrated global operation. To that list, we could add *sustaining* an integrated global operation. In looking at global financial services offshoring, Deloitte discovered a phenomenon that it referred to as "offshore fatigue":

> Many companies report a sharp decline in offshore results after the third year. [Deloitte's] GFSI group believes this phenomenon stems from taking offshore benefits for granted, and not replacing top managers with equivalent talent when their tour of duty ends. Companies must stay vigilant, periodically rotating key managers and staff to maintain a constant mix of experience, skills and enthusiasm.[31]

Deloitte concluded that there are four basic ways to combat "offshore fatigue": minimizing and managing complexity, ensuring compliance with local privacy and security laws, creating a culture that brings out the best in both your onshore and offshore workers, and achieving an appropriate balance between cost savings (in the near term) and strategic investments (for the long term).

The Sourcing Landscape Is Becoming More Complex

Again, none of this is easy. And just to complicate matters, there's a rapidly growing cast of characters out there for you to assess and choose among. According to a joint study conducted by Duke University and Booz & Company, the number of knowledge-based outsourcing service providers has almost doubled since 2000.[32]

In addition to more countries and more firms, we're seeing more and more types of firms participating in the global sourcing landscape. The broad-line providers—such as IBM, Accenture, TCS, Genpact, and Infosys—are all rapidly growing their geographic footprint. While adding countries, they are also investing heavily in seamless global delivery, with the goal being one point of contact for the customer and low visibility as to where the work is actually being performed.

We're also seeing hundreds, possibly thousands, of new specialty firms, offering everything from personal concierge services to sophisticated data analysis and research services. These generally small, focused vendors tend to deliver higher-value services, and they account for a growing share of the sector.

A third group is the rapidly proliferating offshore advisory firms. Firms such as EquaTerra, TPI, Diamond Consulting, neoIT, and Everest Group have experienced explosive growth in recent years. These firms prefer to operate below the radar, but are involved in a high percentage of offshoring engagements—particularly those undertaken by Global 500 firms.

Finally, we're seeing more and more "tools" vendors: that is, companies that provide the tools to monitor offshore vendor performance. Broad-line software vendors such as Microsoft and Oracle have moved aggressively into this space. And we're also seeing many start-ups—such as Janeeva, based in Ann Arbor, Michigan—focusing specifically on assurance tools for outsourcing relationships.

A more complex landscape is the natural result of the sector maturing. Think back to the possibilities diagram in Chapter 4, "The

Supply Side." As a customer, you face more and more options to meet your global sourcing needs. Yes, greater complexity creates confusion in the short run, but it also gives you the potential to create and harvest greater value through your operations in the longer term.

A Game You May Have to Play

This is a partial answer to the last question we want to raise in this book: *If the services shift is so difficult, why are companies doing it?*

There are many reasons, but in the end, companies are doing it because they have to. The game of business is never static. Joseph Schumpeter coined the term "creative destruction," and identified it as the essence of capitalism.

The business environment is constantly changing, and forward-looking firms are always searching for and seizing new options. The past decade has seen the sequential removal of various barriers to globalization in the service sector. These include economic liberalization, technological innovation, improvements in education in low-income countries, and the emergence (some might say triumph) of an American-style global business culture.

All of these developments open up new options for sourcing services from abroad. Globalization in the service sector provides a new and compelling opportunity for firms to reduce cost, increase quality, and lower cycle times. You can choose to play offense, exploring these options and using them to establish advantage over your rivals. Or you can wait and play defense, responding to rivals that have used global sourcing to gain an advantage over you.

Some pundits and polemicists would prefer to ignore these new options, and insist that "responsible" firms not pursue them. But this is simply head-in-the-sand logic. Think of the British Army marching in formation (in bright red jackets) during the Revolutionary War, being picked off by the ragtag American colonists. Think of the Polish cavalry facing Nazi tank units in World War II. Those who cling to the past—those who rush into battle with the wrong weapons, or the wrong strategy—will be ground down. Eventually, they will lose the war.

We hope you take the lessons of this book to heart. Offshoring presents a compelling opportunity to improve your competitive position. You may or may not be prepared to seize this opportunity today. You may or may not believe it is ultimately good for your country. But the one thing there can be little doubt about is that offshoring is coming to your sector. If you aren't prepared, you'll be left asking, "What happened?"

We wrote this book so you'll know in advance. We hope you can put our frameworks and experience to good use, as you embrace the services shift.

Endnotes

[1] Cited in "The Outsourcing Revolution," Harvard Business School's *Working Knowledge* (February 2, 2004), http://hbswk.hbs.edu/archive/3885.html.

[2] Interview by the authors, June 2, 2008.

[3] "Outsourcing of knowledge services creating new realm of management challenges," PRWeb press release, July 31, 2008, www.prweb.com/releases/provider/percent/prweb1165654.htm.

[4] Rachael King, "The new economics of outsourcing," *BusinessWeek* (April 7, 2008), www.businessweek.com/technology/content/apr2008/tc2008043_531737.htm.

[5] Heather Timmons, "Cost–cutting in New York, but a boom in India," *New York Times* (Aug 12, 2008).

[6] Heather Timmons, "Cost–cutting in New York, but a boom in India," *New York Times* (Aug 12, 2008).

[7] Susan Dell Orto, "Offshore outsourcing: a problem or a solution?" CENews.com, July 31, 2007, www.cenews.com/article.asp?id=2254.

[8] Harvard Business School, "The Outsourcing Revolution," *Working Knowledge* (Feb 2, 2004), http://hbswk.hbs.edu/archive/3885.html.

[9] www.tcs.com/about/corp_facts/Pages/default.aspx.

[10] Infosys annual report, 2007–08, p. 5.

[11] http://careers.wipro.com/consulting_why_join.asp (accessed August 13, 2008).

[12] http://careers.genpact.com/career/Why_Genpact/why_genpact.jsp (accessed August 13, 2008).

[13] Pete Engardio, "Mom-and-pop multinationals," *BusinessWeek* (July 3, 2008).

[14] www.elance.com/p/corporate/about/history.html.

[15] Claire Cain Miller, "Outsource your chores—and feel good while you're at it," *New York Times* blogs, July 30, 2008, http://bits.blogs.nytimes.com/2008/07/08.

[16] www.serebraconnect.com/index.cfm?fuseaction=static.staticContent&template=csr.

[17] "The outsourcerer," *The Economist* (June 21, 2007).

[18] "The outsourcerer," *The Economist* (June 21, 2007).

[19] Steve Lohr, "Hello, India? I need help with my math," *New York Times* (October 31, 2007), www.nytimes.com/2007/10/31/business/worldbusiness/31butler.html?ex=1351483200&en=d2e32341b1f49699&ei=5090&partner=rssuserland&emc=rss.

[20] www.asksunday.com/testimonials.html.

[21] Pete Engardio, "Mom-and-pop multinationals," *BusinessWeek*, July 3, 2008.

[22] From the Medical Tourism Association's website, www.medicaltourismassociation.com.

[23] Quoted in "Medical Tourism: Global Competition in Health Care," a study published in November 2007 by the National Center for Policy Analysis, www.ncpa.org/pub/st/st304/.

[24] Mary Beth Marklein, "The inciDENTAL tourist," *USA Today*, July 28, 2005, www.usatoday.com/travel/news/2005-07-28-dental-tourism_x.htm.

[25] James Berry, "The phenomenon of 'dental tourism,'" ADA website, August 23, 2006, www.ada.org/prof/resources/pubs/adanews/adanewsarticle.asp?articleid=2064.

[26] From the home page of Costa Rica Books, www.costaricabooks.com.

[27] www.migrationlanka.com/mydreamsrilanka.htm.

[28] Andy McCue, "Offshoring: cultural differences cause offshoring problems," Silicon.com, July 17, 2006, http://services.silicon.com/offshoring/0,3800004877,39160348,00.htm?r=1.

[29] "Gartner says customer satisfaction is key when determining offshore outsourcing options," Gartner press release, May 5, 2008, www.gartner.com/it/page.jsp?id=662211.

[30] Ann Bednarz, "The downside of offshoring," *Network World* (July 5, 2004), www.networkworld.com/supp/2004/offshoring/0705dark.html.

[31] "Global Financial Services Offshoring: Scaling the Heights," Executive Summary, www.deloitte.com/dtt/research/0,1015,cid%253D122164,00.html.

[32] "Outsourcing of knowledge services creating new realm of management challenges," PRWeb press release, July 31, 2008, www.prweb.com/releases/provider/percent/prweb1165654.htm.

Appendixes for Chapter 4

Appendix 4A

Country Attractiveness

Rank	Country	Financial attractiveness	People and skills availability	Business environment	Total score
1	India	3.22	2.34	1.44	7.00
2	China	2.93	2.25	1.38	6.56
3	Malaysia	2.84	1.26	2.02	6.12
4	Thailand	3.19	1.21	1.62	6.02
5	Brazil	2.64	1.78	1.47	5.89
6	Indonesia	3.29	1.47	1.06	5.82
7	Chile	2.65	1.18	1.93	5.76
8	Philippines	3.26	1.23	1.26	5.75
9	Bulgaria	3.16	1.04	1.56	5.75
10	Mexico	2.63	1.49	1.61	5.73
11	Singapore	1.65	1.51	2.53	5.68
12	Slovakia	2.79	1.04	1.79	5.62
13	Egypt	3.22	1.14	1.25	5.61
14	Jordan	3.09	0.98	1.54	5.60
15	Estonia	2.44	0.96	2.20	5.60
16	Czech Republic	2.43	1.10	2.05	5.57
17	Latvia	2.64	0.91	2.00	5.56
18	Poland	2.59	1.17	1.79	5.54
19	Vietnam	3.33	0.99	1.22	5.54
20	United Arab Emirates	2.73	0.86	1.92	5.51
21	United States (tier two)	0.48	2.74	2.29	5.51
22	Uruguay	2.95	0.98	1.54	5.47
23	Argentina	2.91	1.30	1.26	5.47
24	Hungary	2.54	0.95	1.98	5.47
25	Mauritius	2.84	1.04	1.56	5.44
26	Tunisia	3.03	0.90	1.50	5.43
27	Ghana	3.27	0.90	1.25	5.42
28	Lithuania	2.60	0.83	1.98	5.42
29	Sri Lanka	3.18	0.96	1.22	5.36
30	Pakistan	3.23	1.00	1.11	5.34
31	South Africa	2.52	1.18	1.60	5.30
32	Jamaica	2.83	0.96	1.49	5.29
33	Romania	2.88	0.87	1.53	5.28
34	Costa Rica	3.00	0.86	1.36	5.22
35	Canada	0.77	2.09	2.30	5.16
36	Morocco	2.92	0.90	1.33	5.14
37	Russia	2.61	1.38	1.16	5.14
38	Israel	1.97	1.27	1.86	5.10
39	Senegal	3.19	0.82	1.05	5.06
40	Germany (tier two)	0.46	2.19	2.40	5.05
41	Panama	2.88	0.75	1.40	5.02
42	United Kingdom (tier two)	0.50	2.16	2.35	5.01
43	Spain	1.18	1.71	2.06	4.95
44	New Zealand	1.53	1.12	2.25	4.91
45	Australia	0.89	1.69	2.31	4.89
46	Portugal	1.59	1.14	2.11	4.84
47	Ukraine	2.76	0.98	1.09	4.83
48	France (tier two)	0.45	2.07	2.27	4.79
49	Turkey	2.06	1.31	1.41	4.78
50	Ireland	0.40	1.54	2.29	4.18

Source: A.T. Kearney

Appendix 4B

Country Notes

Country	Notes	SWOT Analysis	Outlook
India	Most popular outsourcing location. Well-educated and experienced workforce. Familiarity with global customers. Little cultural risk.	S: Skilled labor pool, cost advantage, government support. W: Poor infrastructure, high attrition rate. O: Shift focus to markets other than U.S. Move up the value chain. T: Emerging low-cost destinations, rising wage levels.	High wage inflation around 14 percent and currency appreciation resulted in lower margin for suppliers. Need to maintain continuous supply of skilled labor.
Philippines	Well-educated labor pool. Good BPO and cultural compatibility with U.S. Political insurgency less likely to affect outsourcing.	S: Cost competitiveness, excellent English proficiency. W: Low maturity and lack of highly skilled resource pool for ITO. O: Leverage existing BPO relations to get into ITO. T: Emerging low-cost destinations especially non-voice BPO.	Good destination for voice-based customer support. Need to develop skilled resource base to be able to become an attractive ITO destination.
China	Software and services outsourcing still to mature. High legal risk and data protection issues. Many western customers outsourcing their manufacturing to China.	S: Cost competitiveness, huge labor pool, strong government support. W: Low service maturity. O: Further penetration to Japanese market, non-voice BPO. T: Increasing wage level.	Huge domestic market and large resource base makes China a potential competitor for India. Need to develop domain expertise and project management skills.

Country	Notes	SWOT Analysis	Outlook
Brazil	Huge labor pool and decent infrastructure. Major players including IBM and several Indian players investing in Brazil. Potential to become a major player.	S: Vibrant domestic market and proximity with target markets. W: Limited English language skills, scalability of qualified resources. O: Utilize government partnership with private sector to develop IT. T: Other emerging Latin American countries.	Brazil can use its domestic market expertise in value-added services to take IT to the international level. Need to develop and promote Brazil IT as a brand.
South Africa	Still a small outsourcing market. Excellent language compatibility. Sound infrastructure and legal system. Competitive but rising wage level.	S: English language skills, compatible time zone for Western Europe. W: Low service maturity, high wage levels. O: Penetrate further into U.K. market. T: High cost structure and other emerging destinations.	Likely to develop as one of the key destinations in near future. Need to focus on improving education, IT skills, and project management skills.
Mexico	Stronger near-shore destination for IT projects and BPO. Primarily serves Spanish-speaking U.S. customers. Strong competition with Latin American nations.	S: Proximity with U.S., labor pool, Spanish language proficiency. W: Low service maturity, not very cost competitive, English skills. O: Near-shore advantage to penetrate other Spanish-speaking nations. T: Other emerging Latin American destinations.	A natural choice for Spanish-speaking call centers, albeit the cost is comparatively higher. Need to enhance service maturity and English proficiency.

Country	Notes	SWOT Analysis	Outlook
Russia	IT services market is growing with focus on niche. Highly skilled and creative workforce. Poor government support. Poor enforcement of IP protection regulations.	S: Skilled resources for ITO, ability to carry out complex projects. W: Lacks large-scale project management expertise. O: High-end niche jobs, technical non-voice BPO. T: Brain drain, government apathy.	Low-cost destination for high-quality R&D and scientific work. Need to maintain niche and high-end activities and seek policy support.
Canada	Excellent supplier capabilities. Technically skilled labor pool. Excellent regional destination for Asian companies competing for business in U.S.	S: Geographic proximity to U.S., excellent business environment. W: High wage levels. O: Penetrate U.S. market further, high-end jobs. T: Increasing service capabilities and maturities of low-cost nations.	Continue to be competitive player with specialized high-level services with competitive R&D and BPO. Need to maintain cost attractiveness as nearshore location for U.S.
Ireland	Excellent infrastructure and cultural compatibility. Significant government incentives for software. Low turnover of skilled professionals.	S: Highly skilled labor pool, high service maturity. W: High labor cost, labor demand supply gap. O: High-end and niche jobs. T: Low-cost destinations in the region.	Big potential to mature itself as key destination based on past experience. Need to position for high-end niche jobs and improve labor situation.

Country	Notes	SWOT Analysis	Outlook
Czech Republic	Language and cultural compatibility with Europe. Cost is low now but will go up rapidly. Rising wage level and property prices.	S: Proximity to Western Europe, cost competitiveness. W: Low level of service maturity. O: Further penetration into Europe. T: Other emerging Central and Eastern European nations.	Decent infrastructure, English language skills. Need to build labor pool and enhance service maturity.
Romania	IT workers particularly strong in specialized software development. Cost level and cultural risks are comparatively lower.	S: Cost competitiveness. W: Low service maturity and very small labor pool. O: Likely membership into EU. T: Neighboring countries already have a head start.	Lower investment into Romania because of corruption rumors and uncertain legal systems. Need to focus on improving education, IT skills and customer management skills among locals.
Poland	Strong in near-shoring from continental Europe. Recently included as EU member country. Popular choice for Western defense contractors. Educated IT workforce, R&D skills, and good infrastructure.	S: Proximity to Western Europe, compatible time zone. W: Lack of service maturity, relatively smaller labor pool. O: Lucrative Western European market. T: Other emerging Central and Eastern European nations.	Labor cost is expected to rise and cost advantage is diminishing. Need to build up size and competency of labor pool.

Country	Notes	SWOT Analysis	Outlook
Malaysia	An emerging destination for BPO. Good investment in infrastructure. Attractive business environment.	S: Low costs, investment in infrastructure, stable government. W: Relatively small labor pool. O: Further penetrate U.S. BPO market. T: China's growing capabilities (mainly due to proximity).	Continues to remain a good destination for English-based smaller BPO operations.
Singapore	Excellent infrastructure. Major regional hub for Southeast Asian operations. High cost of living.	S: Stable government, financial hub, good quality of living. W: High costs and growing further. O: High-end work in specialized fields such as R&D and biotech. T: Growing emergence of China as a regional hub.	No longer suitable for volume-based work. Focus on high-end specialized work.
Vietnam	Growing as an IT base. One of the lowest wage costs. Strong local economy.	S: Low cost, skilled labor pool, low attrition, young workforce. W: English language skills, IT and telecom infrastructure, IPR. O: Further penetrate IT services market. T: Other low-cost destinations in the region.	Big potential to mature as an IT services destination. Needs to make significant investments in IT and telecom infrastructure.

Country	Notes	SWOT Analysis	Outlook
Hungary	Highly skilled technical labor pool. Cultural affinity to Western Europe. Costs are low but rising fast.	S: Skilled labor pool, stable government, good infrastructure. W: Rising costs. O: Further penetrate Western European market. T: Other low-cost destinations in the region.	Will continue to develop as a leading near-shore destination for Western Europe.
Bulgaria	Highly skilled IT labor pool, with advanced coding skills. Excellent university system for science and technology.	S: Highly skilled employees, cultural affinity to Western Europe. W: Costs likely to increase further post recent accession to EU. O: Further penetrate European IT market, move up the value chain. T: Other low-cost destinations in the region.	A strong near-shore destination for highly technical skills.
Ukraine	Second largest population in Eastern Europe after Russia, has good availability of skilled IT labor pool. Weak rule of law, poor enforcement of IP protection regulations.	S: Highly skilled labor pool, good education system. W: Uncertain political environment, IP protection an issue. O: Potential to further penetrate the Western European market. T: Other low-cost destinations in the region.	Political stability and stronger rule of law will go a long way in strengthening Ukraine's position as a near-shore hub.

Country	Notes	SWOT Analysis	Outlook
Thailand	An emerging destination for BPO and low-complexity IT activities. Low costs of operation. Seen by IT companies as a convenient additional location for Southeast Asian clients.	**S:** Low cost, good availability of labor. **W:** Political instability. **O:** Outsourcing hub to serve Southeast Asian clients. **T:** Growth of Vietnam as a Southeast Asian outsourcing hub.	Potential to emerge as a suitable location for low-complexity IT and BPO services.
Israel	Excellent infrastructure. Highly qualified graduates but limited labor pool. High cost of labor.	**S:** IT and telecom infrastructure, skilled resources. **W:** Regional unrest, small pool of resources, high cost. **O:** High-end IT market. **T:** Emergence of high-end IT capabilities in low-cost India.	Will continue to remain a base for specialized, skill-intensive R&D activities.
Ghana	Similar time zone and proximity to Western Europe. Low wages and cost of living. Best infrastructure in West Africa.	**S:** Low-cost English-speaking labor pool, low attrition. **W:** Limited vendor presence. **O:** Low-end IT outsourcing, technical support. **T:** Emergence of Tunisia and Morocco as rival locations.	Unsuitable for high-end IT activities. Suitable as a near-shore location for U.S./U.K. call center services.

Country	Notes	SWOT Analysis	Outlook
Costa Rica	Low-cost Central American destination. Similar time zone as Central U.S. Availability of skilled labor pool. Low wages and tax breaks.	S: Cultural and physical proximity to U.S., low cost. W: Relatively small labor pool. O: English and Spanish language call centers. T: Emergence of other Latin American countries such as Chile.	Promising location for U.S. call centers.
Argentina	Abundant availability of highly qualified IT workforce. Good quality infrastructure. Similar time zone to U.S.	S: IT infrastructure, low cost, cultural affinity with EU and U.S. W: Arbitrage may not last, due to potential appreciation of peso. O: Hub for open-source software development. T: Emergence of Brazil and Chile as competing locations.	Potential to become a near-shore IT hub for U.S. and EU companies. Government needs to push for the development of the IT outsourcing industry in Argentina.
Egypt	Largest talent base among Middle Eastern countries. Proximity to Europe, and a multicultural atmosphere.	S: High availability of manpower, low cost. W: Inadequate government push for offshore services. O: Low-complexity IT activities and call-center services. T: Emergence of Dubai as an outsourcing destination, with its excellent government sponsorship.	Potential to become an attractive BPO destination.

Source: EquaTerra Analysis

Appendix 4C

Country Profiles

Philippines

Macroeconomic Snapshot

GDP Growth	2005: 5.0 percent
	2006: 5.4 percent
	2007/2011: 5.1–5.3 percent
Education	Literacy rate: 92.6 percent
Higher Education	Philippines has about 1,600 higher-education institutions with over 2.3 million students. About 10 percent are technical graduates as of 2005.
Labor	Hiring is not easy in the Philippines, due to rigid regulations. There are many restrictions on contracting and expanding the number of working hours as well. It is relatively easier to dismiss a worker as compared to Vietnam and China.
Telephony	The deregulation of the telecommunications sector in 1993 has improved the telecom infrastructure in the Philippines. Mobile communication is expanding at a rapid pace. In 2005, the country had more than 3.4 million fixed-line subscribers and over 34.4 million mobile subscribers; resulting in penetration of 38 and 391 users, respectively, per 1,000 people.
Internet backbone	In 2005, the country had over 4 million Internet users and over 0.2 million broadband connections, resulting in penetration of 47 and 3 users, respectively, per 1,000 people.

Macroeconomic Snapshot

Transport infrastructure	The Philippines has inadequate transport infrastructure, due to underinvestment. The system is essentially bimodal, with roads carrying 60 percent of freight and 80 percent of passenger traffic and the balance by water transport. The air transport is oriented toward carrying passengers on journeys between islands. The rail network is minimal. The total road network is 200,000 kilometers, and only 10 percent of the road network is paved. There are seven major ports—namely Cagayan de Oro, Cebu, Davao, Iligan, Iloilo, Manila, and Surigao—and over 50 airports.
Salaries	Despite a relatively high unemployment rate of about 8 percent, the ITO and BPO firms in the Philippines find it difficult to recruit English-speaking employees. An entry-level call-center employee earns an average of US$5,457 (yearly), whereas an employee with a higher expertise level, such as a team lead, earns an average of US$9,153 (yearly), which is 80 percent lower than the U.S. salary level. But, salary levels in the Philippines are still competitive with other Asia Pacific countries, though slightly higher than China and India.

The Industry Takes Shape

Philippines has attracted companies and FDI for quite some time. IBM Philippines, which started distributing products in 1925, was officially registered as Watson Business Machines in 1937. Setting up of Accenture operations in Philippines in 1992 led to the growth of the business process outsourcing industry. Even the domestic companies have been around for some time. For example, SPi started with low-end data-entry operations in 1983, but expanded into higher-value offerings from the late 1990s.

The industry started to grow in the late 1990s, with companies such as eTelecare global solutions and PeopleSupport getting established in call-center services. Widespread English language skills, an education system that produces employable and trainable professionals, a strong Western-oriented work ethic, and an entrepreneurial culture helped the industry take root and grow. Pioneers such as Accenture (in software and Business Process Outsourcing/Offshoring [BPO]) and PeopleSupport (for call-center work) helped manifest the country's potential. The industry is still very young, but has promising potential.

The Industry

The Philippines is emerging as a leading destination for business process and IT services. Growing at the rate of 50 percent over the past three years, the industry exported services worth $4.9 billion in 2007 and employed approximately 400,000. The sector is projected to grow to $12.2 billion and employ nearly a million by 2010.

The industry consists of a healthy mix of multinationals, such as Accenture and IBM, and domestic third-party players, such as SPI and eTelecare. There were 108 contact centers and 62 business process service providers in early 2006 in the country. Manila and Cebu were the leading cities—they together accounted for approximately 90 percent of the services.

Revenue (in Millions)

	2004	**2005**	**2006**	**2007**	**2008**	**2009**	**2010**
Customer Care	1,024	1,792	2,688	3,488	4,192	4,816	5,926
Back Office	120	180	288	488	880	1,496	2,392
Transcription	46	76	135	251	496	980	1,744
Software	222	278	383	559	876	1,350	2,034
Others	63	94	133	206	326	489	734
Total	1,474	2,419	3,627	4,992	6,769	9,130	12,199

Workforce

	2004	**2005**	**2006**	**2007**	**2008**	**2009**	**2010**
Customer Care	64,000	112,000	168,000	218,000	262,000	301,000	331,000
Back Office	15,000	22,500	36,000	61,000	110,000	187,000	299,000
Transcription	3,300	5,450	9,675	18,013	35,519	70,126	124,764
Software	12,800	16,000	22,000	32,000	50,000	77,000	116,000
Others	4,200	6,300	9,000	14,000	22,000	33,000	50,000
Total	99,300	162,250	244,675	343,013	479,519	668,126	920,764

Specialties

Philippine industry is very strong in voice-based contact centers as well as medical and legal transcription services. In fact, contact center services contributed more than 70 percent of the industry's export earnings of $4.9 billion in 2007. Of late, the industry is diversifying into other sectors, such as back office, animation, software development, and engineering design.

Growth Rate of Business Functions (Past Three Year Average)

Function	**Growth Rate**
Engineering Services	55
Contact Center	52
Back Office	46
Animation	38
Software	35
Transcription	24

Key Players

Several leading multinationals service business processes out of the Philippines. These include the big service providers such as Accenture, IBM and HP, as well as those headquartered in emerging economies, such as Infosys and Satyam. Sykes, a leading provider of customer contact management solutions, established a presence in the Philippines through an acquisition of 19 seats in 1997, and has since grown to more than 8,000 employees in 2006. PeopleSupport, a provider of outsourced customer management and other back-office services, also has a substantial presence in the Philippines, with eight delivery centers and over 8,000 employees. Several global corporations carry out their captive and shared service center operations out of the Philippines. For example, Nestle has located its shared service center for financial and employee services in the country. Through its global resourcing group, HSBC delivers end-to-end offshore banking and financial services solutions out of the Philippines. Others include Shell, Citibank, Chevron-Texaco, AIG, and Safeway.

Domestic provider companies have scaled up their operations substantially over the past few years and are now providing higher-value services. SPi, which started operations providing low-end data-entry solutions in 1983, has of late emerged as a leading BPO provider—it has expanded rapidly into higher-value offerings such as content editorial and production, electronic data discovery, and transaction processing for health care, legal, and publishing.

Some of the leading companies are Accenture, Amdatex (American Data Exchange), HP, and SPi (now part of PLDT) in BPO, and Accenture, Headstrong, Logica, Software Ventures Intl (SVI) in software.

Egypt

Macroeconomic Snapshot

GDP Growth	2004: 4.4 percent
	2005: 6.4 percent
	2007/2011: 6.9 percent
Education	Literacy rate: 71 percent
Higher Education	Egypt has 12 state universities, 8,674 private universities, and 125 technical institutes. Egypt's Ministry of Education estimates that the number of students enrolled in higher education rose from 1.4 million in 2001 to 1.76 million in 2005.
Labor	In Egypt, hiring of workers is easier than most Organisation for Economic Co-operation and Development (OECD) countries and countries in that region. There are no restrictions on night or weekly holiday work. However, Egypt has a higher level of firing costs as compared to other countries in the region or OECD.
Telephony	In 2007, Egypt had about 10.9 million fixed lines and 20.3 million mobile subscribers. Egypt's teledensity (mainlines per 1,000 people) in 2005 was 142, which was lower than the MENA region, which had a teledensity of 159.
Internet backbone	Egypt's Internet user base has increased more than four times since 2000. In 2000, there were about 535,000 Internet users, and this number rose to 6.78 million in May 2007. The Egyptians formed about 20 percent of all Internet users in the MENA region in 2005. In 2005, the country's penetration rate per 1,000 people was 67.5.

Macroeconomic Snapshot

Transport infrastructure	Egypt's railway system is the oldest in the region. On average, the network carries about 1.2 million passengers a day and about 11 tons of goods per year. With a modernization and expansion program since the 1980s, Egypt had 78,641 kilometers of road as of 2005. One of the greatest sources of foreign exchange for Egypt is the Suez Canal, with about 18,664 vessels passing through it in 2006, an increase from 18,193 vessels in 2005. Traffic has also been boosted because of efforts by the Egyptian government to deepen the canal by 2012 to enable bigger tankers to pass through.
Salaries	Salaries prevailing in the IT and ITES sectors are around US$38,000 per annum. The nominal wage prevailing in the country is around US$17.8 per hour and has been growing at two to four percent annually. The average salary at the project manager level is around 45 percent lower than that in the United States. An expected shortage of IT graduates may move the salaries upward in the near future.

The Industry Takes Shape

The government of Egypt's investments in infrastructure and human capital, the availability of an educated workforce and European language skills, and close proximity to Europe contributed to the rise of the industry. It started around 2003, mainly with voice-based call-center services. Improvements in the nation's copper and fiber-optic networks—including the nationwide rollout of ADSL and universal dial-up Internet access—enabled remote delivery from the country. To incentivize the growth of the sector, the government initiated a training program for young graduates interested in working in the call-center industry, focusing on computer literacy, language skills, and the fundamentals of the industry.

The Industry

Offshore services revenues in Egypt were estimated to be $250 million in 2005. The industry employed 138,000 agents in 2004. As shown next, the sector is composed of a vast number of activities—including IT services and products, tech support, and contact centers.

Total Offshore Services Revenue

	2005	**2010**
Total	250,000,000	1,085,000,000

The industry was projected to grow to $1.085 billion by 2010. The number of agent positions was projected to increase to 241,000 agent positions in 2007.

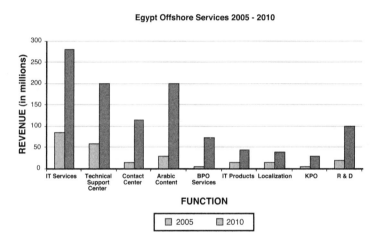

Egypt Offshore Services 2005 - 2010

Specialties

IT services and tech support services account for almost 60 percent of the industry. Besides these are a number of other sectors, including generic services such as BPO and call centers, as well as niche areas such as Arab content services—a sector that is projected to grow substantially in the near future.

Key Players

Increasing numbers of corporations—both domestic and multinationals—now offer services from Egypt.

Several multinationals—including IBM, Mentor Graphics, Intel, Microsoft, Cisco, Oracle, Orange, and Alcatel Lucent—are present in Egypt. Multinationals from emerging economies such as Satyam (a leading Indian IT services provider) and Huawei (a Chinese telecom company) have also set up operations in the country. Microsoft's Innovation Center in Egypt focuses on Applied Research and Incubation as well as collaboration with local research interests in the Middle East and Africa. Huawei opened a state-of-the-art regional Technical Assistance Center with over 50 technical support engineers and a network extending across the whole region.

Companies such as Allied Soft, EGO, MNS, and Teletech offer business and knowledge process outsourcing services whereas Xceed, Raya contact center, and ECC deliver contact center solutions. ACT, Cairo IT & Eng, Egypt Soft Commerce, Econnect, CITE, and IT Worx are some of the leading IT outsourcing vendors. Glory Egypt, Infomateks, IT Soft, and SYSDSoft are leading software development providers. These companies are increasing their portfolio of services and also providing increasingly more sophisticated offerings. For example, AlliedSoft provides network solutions and security, project management, advanced IT training, software development, hospital management system, offshore development, and call center services.

Romania

Macroeconomic Snapshot

GDP Growth	2006: 7.7 percent
	2007: 6.1 percent
	2008: 5.4 percent
Education	Literacy rate: 98.4 percent
Higher Education	There are 122 higher education institutes and institutions. Romania produces about 62,078 engineering, science, and mathematics graduates each year.

Macroeconomic Snapshot

Labor	Hiring of workers is a relatively tougher task as compared to countries such as Poland, Hungary, and Slovakia. Romania scores lower than these countries in terms of flexibility in the work environment. The country has rigid regulations on dismissals, role of trade unions, and re-employment and replacement rules.
Telephony	In 2005, the country had more than 4.4 million fixed-line subscribers and over 13.3 million mobile phone users. The teledensity is 204 subscribers and 618 users per 1,000 for fixed lines and mobile phone users, respectively, as compared to the respective regional average of 298 and 858. The leading mobile phone maker, Nokia, has signed a preliminary agreement to invest approximately US$81 million to set up a research and production center in Cluj. Nokia and its suppliers expect to create 15,000 jobs by 2008.
Internet backbone	In 2005, the country had more than 4.7 million Internet users and more than 0.075 million broadband connections; with a penetration of 217 users and 35 connections per 1,000 for Internet users and broadband connections, respectively. The penetration figure is lower than the respective regional average of 324 and 42.
Transport infrastructure	Romania is poor in terms of transport infrastructure as compared to five other countries in the region. It has 60,043 kilometers of road network, which connects to 25.3 percent of the country's area. The railways reach out to 12 percent of the country, with a rail density of around 0.05 km/km. The country has four major ports: Braila, Constanta, Galati, and Tulcea. In 2005, the passenger traffic at major airports of the country was around 3.05 million.
Salaries	Salaries prevailing in IT and ITES sectors in Romania are the lowest in comparison to countries such as Poland, Czech Republic, Hungary, and Slovakia. The salaries are over 40 percent lower than the average salaries in the IT/ITES sectors in Poland. In comparison to India, the average Romania salary is about 40 percent more expensive and the difference in salary rises with seniority. The nominal wage prevailing in the country is around US$7.30 per hour and it has been growing at approximately 17 percent.

The Industry Takes Shape

Romania, which became a democracy in 1989, has made substantial progress in recent years. After the recessionary economy of the 1990s, it has experienced considerable growth in recent years. The country, a member of NATO, joined the European Union in early 2007 and is the second largest of the 12 new member states.

A large, multilingual and cost-effective labor force, attractive price-versus-performance proposition, and a close cultural fit with the West are some of the attractions. Government support has been important to the establishing of the industry. It provides 100-percent income tax exemption for IT workers, and has launched a program promoting construction of IT-oriented technology parks—special zones that have an established infrastructure and enjoy a favorable tax and customs regime. Another factor stimulating the IT sector growth in Romania is the presence of global technology corporations such as Intel, Motorola, Sun Microsystems, Boeing, Nokia and others, which have intensified their software development activities and opened their R&D centers in Romania.

The Industry

In 2007, business and software services exports from Romania were valued at Euros 450 million (about USD 695 million). The market, which was estimated to be about $250–$280 million in 2005 by the Romanian Association for Electronic and Software Industries, has grown rapidly in the past few years. In 2005, the IT export industry employed about 17,000.

Romania Total Offshore Services

	2005	2007
Total	250–280 million	695 million

Specialties

Romania is a growing center of software and services expertise. Software products from Romania, such as BitDefender (antivirus), have gained international recognition and popularity. Multinational vendors have made acquisitions/investments in Romanian products and companies. Microsoft purchased the RAV antivirus product from Gecad (2003), TechTeam acquired offshore vendor Akela Informatique, and Adobe acquired InterAKT (2006). Romanian IT services companies can deliver business-critical, technically complex projects.

Key Players

Several multinationals—such as Siemens, Amazon, Adobe, Alcatel, Motorola, Oracle, Intel, Sun Microsystems, Boeing, and Nokia—have set up operations in the country. Amazon Development Center in Romania is developing new and innovative website features to help Amazon's customers find and discover anything they want to buy online. Adobe's office in Romania serves as a Research and Development center and focuses on improving Adobe products such as Dreamweaver, Flex, and Apollo and researching related web technologies.

Some of the leading Romanian service providers include Arobs, Bis, BitDefender, IT Six global services, iQuest, SIVECO Romania, The Red Point, and TotalSoft. BitDefender provides security solutions to over 41 million home and corporate users in more than 280 countries. It has captured over 1 percent of the global antivirus market (estimated to be around $5 billion in 2006). SIVECO Romania earned approximately 35 percent of its $42 million revenue in 2006 by delivering services from offshore.

China

Macroeconomic Snapshot

GDP Growth	2006: 10.7 percent 2007/2011: > 8 percent
Education	Literacy rate: 91 percent
Higher Education	China has about 15.6 million students enrolled in higher education institutions. About 5.5 million of these students study engineering.
Labor	The hiring conditions are easier in China compared to other nations in the Asia Pacific region. However, the labor laws are more rigid in China when it comes to the firing of workers. In addition to this, the cost of firing an employee is higher than other nations in the Asia Pacific region.
Telephony	PRC continues to develop its telecommunications infrastructure and is partnering with foreign providers to expand its global reach. Mobile cellular subscribers have increased rapidly in the last few years. In 2005, the country had more than 350 million fixed-line subscribers and over 393 million mobile subscribers, resulting in penetration of 268 and 301 users, respectively, per 1,000 people.
Internet backbone	In 2005, the country had over 111 million Internet users and over 37.5 million broadband connections, resulting in penetration of 85 and 29 users, respectively, per 1,000 people.
Transport infrastructure	China is connected internally with a fairly strong transportation network. The country is connected internally by 1,870,661 kilometers of roadways, 74,408 kilometers of rail transport, 123,964 kilometers of water transport.
Salaries	The average IT salaries in China are around US$10,000 per annum, and the average BPO salary is around US$7,634 per annum. The salaries are close to the Indian average salary of US$9,867 and US$7,779 per annum in the IT and BPO sectors, respectively. A relatively small supply of IT professionals with English language proficiency allows these employees to command higher salaries. The rapid growth in China's IT industry has pushed the salary levels above other industries in PRC.

The Industry Takes Shape

The outsourcing industry took hold in China in the late 1990s and has grown rapidly over the last few years, emerging as the sourcing destination of greatest interest after India. Low-cost abundant talent pool, excellent infrastructure, and government support is making it attractive. Some constraints remain in the availability of English language skills, midlevel management talent, and quality maturity. The industry is fragmented, but the vendor ecosystem is developing rapidly.

Several factors contributed to the growth of IT and business process offshoring to China. Following the opening up of the economy, domestic industry began to take hold in the 1990s. The dot-com burst left behind substantial industry capabilities in systems thinking and development methodology. The presence of large multinationals—such as GE, Microsoft, Dell, SAP, and HP—in the country and their setting up of R&D centers, a push by Japanese companies to move software development work to China, and government support and promotion, all helped the industry scale up during the last few years.

The Industry

The Chinese Information Industry Ministry estimated that the country's software outsourcing industry revenues grew by over 40 percent year-on-year to reach US$1.4 billion in 2006. The ministry also expected the Chinese software and information services market to reach about US$131.32 billion (CNY 1 trillion) by 2010.

The Chinese ITO industry is expected to generate revenues worth US$18 billion by 2010 and US$56 billion by 2015. The industry is also expected to create job opportunities for about 4 million professionals by 2015.[1]

China Software Industry and Exports (in Millions USD)

	Revenue of Software Industry	**Software Exports**
1999	6,392	304
2000	8,586	478
2001	11,525	869
2002	15,926	1,795
2003	23,166	2,389
2004	33,301	3,113
2005	43,436	4,792

Source: NASSCOM, IDC, AT Kearney.

Value of IT Software and Services Exports from China (in Billions USD)

	ITO	**BPO**
2000	0.3	0.0
2005	1.4	0.4
2010F	6.1	0.9

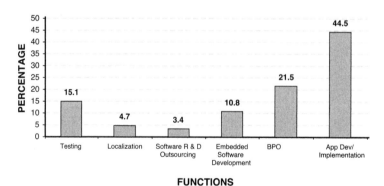

**Composition of IT Software and Services
Exports from China (2006)**

Specialties

A lot of outsourcing work carried out in China is relatively low end—basic applications, software testing, and some R&D (mostly for multinational companies' Chinese operations). However, firms are beginning to move up the value chain. Many have established good relationships with software and high-tech companies, doing a lot of the product development and testing required for releases of software packages. Some are beginning to move up to services such as package implementation and infrastructure management. The geographic breakdown of offshore customers is heavily concentrated in Japan, and to a lesser extent Korea, with these markets accounting for nearly 60 percent of the Chinese offshore business.

Key Players

Within the services sector, the country has attracted several leading multinational corporations, such as IBM, Motorola, SAP, Microsoft, NEC, BEA, Accenture, BearingPoint, and GE. Several have set up R&D centers. The GE China Technology Center (CTC), located at the Zhangjiang Hi-Tech Park, Shanghai, is a multidisciplinary research center conducting leading-edge research, engineering development, and sourcing for GE's diverse businesses across the world. In 2007, General Motors entered into a partnership with the Chinese government and one of the country's leading universities to build a state-of-the-art $250 million research center focusing on alternative energy and the environment. Besides the multinationals from the West, China has also attracted leading offshore vendors such as TCS, Infosys, Satyam, and Wipro.

Domestic Chinese companies have also grown and matured over time. Neusoft Group Ltd., the largest software company in China (founded in 1991), has established overseas branches in Japan and the United States, as well as service-center offices in the Middle East, Europe, and South Asia. Other leading domestic companies include Bleum, Longtop, and VanceInfo.

Russia

Macroeconomic Snapshot

GDP Growth	2005: 6.8 percent
	2006: 7.3 percent
	2007/2011: 6.6 percent
Education	Literacy rate: 99.44 percent
Higher Education	Russia has mandatory but free education for all children up to 17 years of age. In 2006, there were 7.3 million students enrolled in higher education. There were about 1,100 higher education institutions in 2006.
Hiring and Firing	In Russia, the rigidity in hiring workers is greater than most Organisation for Economic Co-operation and Development (OECD) countries and countries in that region. Although in general there is less difficulty in hiring workers in Russia than in the region or other OECD countries, it's considerably more difficult to fire workers in Russia. However, Russia has a much lower level of firing costs as compared to other countries in the region or OECD.
Telephony	In 2006, Russia had less than 30 fixed lines per 100 people. In 2005, Russia had about 40.1 million fixed lines and three times more mobile subscribers, totaling 120 million. Russia's teledensity (mainlines per 1,000 people) in 2005 was 280, which was lower than in countries such as Poland and Belarus.
Internet backbone	Russia's Internet usage rate has been slow to take off but appears to be gaining ground. Internet usage is estimated to have grown from around 4 million in 2000 to over 25 million in 2006. Despite rapid growth in recent years, this still amounts to less than 18 per 100 people, far lower than that of comparable countries. In 2005, there were a total of 21.8 million Internet users.
Transport infrastructure	Russia's road transport system, which consisted of around 870,000 kilometers of roads in 2005 (of which 738,000 kilometers were paved), remains below Western standards. In addition, slightly more than half of the railway system, which consists of 87,000 kilometers of track, is electrified. Although Russia has 43 sea ports, it is currently under pressure to cope with oil exports and the expansion of the Baltic pipeline system.

Macroeconomic Snapshot

Salaries	Salaries prevailing in the IT and ITES sectors are around US$17,882 per annum. The prevailing wage is forecasted to rise to $25,316 in the country by 2010. The average salary of an entry-level IT professional in Russia was around 74 percent lower than that in the United States in 2005. By 2010, the average salary in Russia's IT/BPO industry will rise to be about 70 percent lower than that in the United States.

The Industry Takes Shape

The outsourcing industry in Russia has grown rapidly in the last few years. The Soviet Union was always regarded as a super power in terms of science and technology—some members of the Russian industry even started their careers in Soviet scientific institutions. A strong educational system with a focus on science and math, strong programming skills, and low attrition rate have enabled Russia to emerge as an attractive destination for high-end IT work—product engineering, embedded systems design, and critical application development.

Though the industry in the country has strong growth potential, it is still highly fragmented. With its vast oil, gas, and mineral resources, the country did not probably have the same critical need to focus on its human resource as it emerged as an independent country. However, of late, the government as well as organizations such as RUSSOFT have made efforts to promote Russia as an outsourcing destination. A separate government ministry is responsible for the development of the IT industry; high-tech parks have been set up, tax benefits are provided, and anticorruption laws are enforced. RUSSOFT acts as a forum and intermediary between the government and the industry.

The Industry

The country's software exports grew by 54 percent in 2006 and accounted for approximately US$1.5 billion.

Russian Software Exports

Year	Exports
2002	352
2003	546
2004	760
2005	972
2006	1,495
2007	2,100*

*Forecast

Russian industry has seen some consolidation over the past couple years. Large companies have grown faster and contributed more to the software export.

Russian Software Industry Composition

Type	Percentage of Exports (2005)	Percentage of Exports (2006)
Large companies°	49	55
Small and mid-size companies	19	18
International development centers	21	19
Research institutes	7	5

° Employing more than 120

Specialties

Application services are the key focus of the Russian outsourcing industry; BPO and infrastructure management are very limited. A special mixture of science, mathematics, and software engineering will become increasingly attractive to potential client companies as those companies begin to outsource innovation and research.

Key Players

The Russian IT industry has a number of local players. Luxoft, EPAM, Reksoft, and Exigent Services are some of the leading ones. Local companies have gone more global and grown rapidly of late—for example, Luxoft has grown from $8 million in revenue in 2002 to $105 million in 2007. It has development centers in Russia, Ukraine, and Canada, and offices in several cities in the United States and Europe.

Several leading multinationals, such as Siemens, Boeing, Dell, IBM, Intel, and Motorola, have also set up development centers in Russia. Many of them carry out high-end R&D functions.

◆◆◆

South Africa

Macroeconomic Snapshot

GDP Growth	2004: 4.4 percent
	2005: 4.8 percent
	2007/2011: 4.6 percent
Education	Literacy rate: 82.4 percent
Higher Education	South Africa currently has 21 universities and 15 "technikons" in the tertiary sector. According to a 2001 census, about 8.4 percent of the population have received higher education. However, the country is struggling to reform its university system and battling the problems in bridging the gap in enrollment by whites and the non-whites.
Hiring and Firing	The level of difficulty in hiring workers is higher than the other countries in the region as well as OECD countries, although it is much easier to fire workers as compared to these countries. The cost of firing is also about the level of other OECD countries, which is at a level that is very much lower than that of other countries in the region.
Telephony	With a costly fixed-line telephony, there were only about 280 fixed mainlines per 1,000 people in 2005. Contrastingly, there were about seven times more mobile subscribers in South Africa in 2005, with about 724 mobile subscribers per 1,000 people.

Macroeconomic Snapshot

Internet backbone	The South African telecommunications and technology markets are well-developed for an African country. There were about 5.1 million Internet users in 2005, or about 105 users per 1,000 people.
Transport infrastructure	South Africa's transport infrastructure is certainly the best in the Africa continent, with about 20,000 kilometers of rail lines (total routes) and about 364,131 kilometers total network roads. Lacking a public transport system, urban South Africans rely heavily on the informal taxi system.
Salaries	ITO salaries in South Africa are significantly higher than other emerging countries in the Europe, Middle East, and Africa region. In 2005, the average IT/BPO salary was $31,957 annually. This is about 54 percent lower than that in the United States. The average salary is expected to rise to $38,881 by 2010, as compared to that of $83,464 in the United States.

The Industry Takes Shape

South African industry primarily exports BPO and call-center services to clients in Europe and the United States. The first contact centers in Cape Town were developed in the mid 1980s to service companies with a high customer contact requirement, mostly in the financial services industry. Until quite recently, the industry consisted exclusively of captive corporate contact centers owned and operated by companies such as Telkom, Woolworths, Sanlam, and Old Mutual. The industry remained largely stable in the 1980s and 1990s, growing in employment and seats by about 10 percent.

From 2003 onward, there has been substantial growth in the number of new contact centers offering outsourced customer contact services and telesales to domestic as well as international markets.

The Industry

South African Contact Centers: An Overview

Year	Agents	Seats	Staff
2004	8,141	9,784	10,014
2005	11,312	13,362	14,345
2006	15,899	18,976	22,156

Specialties

South African industry largely consists of call centers and back-office work. Telecommunications, retail, and financial services are the key sectors being serviced out of the country.

Key Players

Several multinationals have set up operations in South Africa. These include IBM, Fujitsu, Lufthansa, Virgin Mobile, Sykes, Admital, Finnair, ASDA (Wal-Mart), CSC, Budget, Sitel, Avis, Barclays, and JPMorgan Chase. Global Telesales, a fully owned subsidiary of Lufthansa, was set up in 1996 and employs over 360 staff members. It leverages its travel and tourism industry expertise and delivers a variety of services such as flight reservations, direct sales and ticketing, and customer loyalty program management. It is also the first Lufthansa call center to host a global load control center outside Germany. Weight and balance calculations for aircraft load sheets are prepared at the load control center.

Domestic corporations such as Dialogue and DRG Outsourcing also deliver services globally. DRG Outsourcing provides human resource management solutions such as payroll processing and employee benefits administration.

Poland

Macroeconomic Snapshot

GDP Growth	2005: 3.5 percent
	2006: 5.8 percent
	2011: 4.5 percent
Education	Literacy rate: 99.8 percent
Higher Education	More than 400 higher education institutes and institutions. Over 380,000 graduate from these institutions annually. Poland produces more than 65,000 engineering, science, and mathematics graduates each year.
Labor	For the hiring of workers, Poland provides the highest flexibility in the region. However, the country has extremely rigid regulations in terms of the firing of workers and the flexibility of working hours concerning working during the weekend and/or at night.
Telephony	Poland has the highest number of telephone and mobile subscribers. However, due to its large population base, its average rating in the penetration level is lower than the Czech Republic and Hungary. In 2005, the country had more than 13 million fixed-line subscribers and more than 29.2 million mobile phone users. It has a teledensity of 342 subscribers and 766 users per 1,000 for fixed lines and mobile phone users, respectively, against the respective regional average of 298 and 856.
Internet backbone	The Internet connectivity in Poland ranks lower than the Czech Republic and Hungary. The country, however, has better penetration of broadband in the region after Hungary. In 2005, the country had more than 11.8 million Internet users and more than 1.8 million broadband connections, with a penetration of 309 users and 47 connections per 1,000 for Internet users and broadband connections, respectively, against the respective regional average of 324 and 42.

Macroeconomic Snapshot

Transport infrastructure	Poland has 423,997 kilometers of road network, which connects to 95 percent of the country's area. The railways reach out to 7.4 percent of the country, with a rail density of around 0.07 km/km². The regional average (excluding Romania) is around 79 percent and 8.8 percent for roads and railways paving, respectively. Poland has four major airports: Gdansk, Gdynia, Swinoujscie, and Szczecin. In 2006, the passenger traffic at major airports doubled to 8.1 million passengers, from 4 million passengers in 1999.
Salaries	In terms of salaries, Poland is the costliest location in the region. Salaries in the IT and ITES sectors are 15 to 25 percent higher compared to the Czech Republic and Hungary. In comparison to India, Poland is three times costlier, and the difference in salary rises with seniority.

The Industry Takes Shape

Liberalization of the economy in the early 1990s attracted multinational corporations such as Procter and Gamble (P&G) and EDS to set operations focused on the domestic market in the country. For example, EDS provided IT solutions to domestic customers. Other leading technology companies—such as SAP, IBM, and Oracle—followed. The growth of domestic IT and business services industries led to the development of new capabilities and skills in the country. This, along with increasing globalization of information technology (IT) and business services, led to the interest in Poland as an offshore hub.

Poland's accession to the European Union (EU) in 2004 further accelerated investments by foreign companies. Between 2004 and 2005, at least 12 large and well-known multinational companies started operations in the country while existing IT and BPO operations grew in scale and several companies moved their regional centers to Poland. A number of third-party service providers—many of them from India—also entered the country. These included Accenture, EDS, Genpact, and TCS. As corporations began embracing a global delivery model, Poland emerged as an important hub in the network. For example, Poland is now a part of EDS's "best shore" strategy for IT services as well as payroll and financial operations services—services delivered to clients are rotated around its development centers around the world so that the outsourced function is available at all times of the day.

The Industry

Poland's services exports totaled approximately 3 billion dollars in 2006 and are projected to grow to approximately 5.5 billion dollars by 2010.

Specialties

R&D constitutes a large part of services being exported from Poland, while F&A is the biggest business function being serviced out of the country. Wide availability of Western European language skills has enabled the growth of call-center industry catering to those regions.

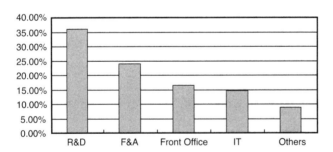

Activity breakdown by function

Source: WDI Research, PAIZ.

Key Players

The Polish industry consists of several multinationals as well as domestic players carrying out a variety of activities. Established in 1998, Motorola's center in Krakow was one of the first to be involved in offshoring activities; its focus was on business processes and software R&D for mobile networks. Siemens, which focused on mobile technology networks, set up an R&D center in Wroclaw while Delphi set up an automotive R&D center in Warsaw in 2000. Offshoring of business processes followed R&D; TNT Express and Lufthansa set up call centers in Warsaw and Krakow, while Transcom established a presence in Olsztyn.

Local companies have also grown and started exporting their services. For example, Call Center Poland—the first Polish company to provide outsourcing services in Poland—was set up in 1997 and has expanded to about 1,600 employees, with estimated revenues of US$20 million as of 2007. The company provides contact solutions through a variety of channels, including phone, email, and SMS.

Company Profiles

IBM: IBM acquired a facility set up in 1996 by Pricewaterhouse-Coopers. In 2002, the MCS division of PwC became part of IBM. The operations have experienced rapid growth in the past few years. The focus of its business service activities is on F&A—a group that has grown aggressively, from 1,100 in 2003 to 1,990 by the end of 2007. It is projected to grow to about 1,400 by the end of 2008. In addition, IBM also has a software laboratory in Krakow where it employs about 200 people. IBM Poland works in collaboration with IBM's India facility—back-office work is primarily carried out in India while Krakow focuses on the front-office leveraging of strong language skills in Poland.

Capgemini: Opened in 2007, Capgemini's technology center in Poland is primarily an operation for development and integration of customized IT solutions. Capgemini is spending about $3.1 million to open the center, which will initially house about 135 workers. The center, located in the Katowice Special Economic Zone, will ultimately expand to more than 400 specialists. Among other services to be offered at the center will be help-desk support, infrastructure management, and IT systems monitoring.[2]

Motorola: Motorola established its Polish presence in 1992, when it opened an office in Warsaw with ten employees. Six years later, Motorola opened its Krakow office with 12 employees. Today, Motorola employs 280 people in Poland, including both the Warsaw and Krakow locations. The Motorola Polska Software Center launched in 1998 is one of the 19 centers within Motorola's Global Software Group. The center, located in the Krakow Technological Park, develops software for Motorola's wireless devices, telecommunications and public safety systems, web networks, and software engineering tools. Motorola presently employs over 230 persons in Krakow and expects eventually to employ up to 500 software engineers.[3]

◆ ◆ ◆

Brazil

Macroeconomic Snapshot

GDP Growth	2005: 2.9 percent
	2006: 3.7 percent
	2007/2011: 3.6 percent
Education	Literacy rate: 86.4 percent
Higher Education	Brazil produces about 55,000 engineering and science graduates each year, with a total of 420,000 graduates each year.
Labor	Due to the rigid regulatory system in Brazil, the hiring of workers is the most difficult in the region. However, the firing of workers is much easier than in other Latin American countries because there is little interference from trade unions. The unemployment rate has remained stable over the years and stands at 9 percent, but the labor force keeps rising year-on-year by 1.3 percent.
Telephony	Mobile telephony dominates the landscape with the growing subscriber base over fixed-line services. Voice over Internet Protocol (VoIP) is also growing rapidly and is offered by a large number of service providers, including foreign companies. In 2006, the number of mobile subscribers was estimated to surpass the 100-million mark, whereas fixed line will shrink to 35.4 million users. The penetration per 1,000 people stands at 541 and 190 for mobile and fixed-line users, respectively.

Macroeconomic Snapshot

Internet backbone	Brazil is the largest market for Internet services in Latin America in terms of the number of users. In 2006, it was estimated that Internet subscribers would be over 30 million people and the country would have about 5 million broadband connections. The penetration per 1,000 people stands at 160 and 27 for Internet and broadband users, respectively.
Transport infrastructure	Brazil has the largest road network in Latin America, of which 60 percent of freight is transported by road. At present, only 20 percent of the country is connected through roads, of which 72 percent of the roads are in poor state. The rail network, which covers 30,000 kilometers, is in a very poor condition. However, it is getting a facelift from private contractors.
	Brazil enjoys a relatively advanced port system to facilitate international trade, and one of the world's mightiest rivers, the Amazon, which provides access to many remote areas of the country.
Salaries	Salaries of IT and ITES professionals in Brazil are second lowest in the region, with a CAGR of 5.6 percent. In comparison to India, salaries in Brazil are 50 percent higher for IT and ITES processionals.

The Industry Takes Shape

Geographic and cultural proximity with the United States has attracted attention as a "near-shore" destination for delivery of IT and business processing services. Similar time zones and a closer geographic proximity to North American companies allows for more effective interactions and communication. The United States also shares more cultural similarities with Brazil than other outsourcing countries in Asia. This, along with emerging capabilities in IT and BPO, have led to the offshore industry taking shape in the country.

The Industry

Brazilian software and IT services are a USD 7.7 billion industry, or 1.6 percent of the country's GDP (mainly domestic—$7.3 B).[4]

According to Brazil-IT, software development offshore revenue was estimated to be USD 205.3 million. BPO services accounted for USD 76.5 million. In 2007, Brazil hopes to tally $800 million in outsourcing revenue, compared with $600 million in 2006. The sector employs 892,000 IT professionals.

The country's software and service exports are estimated to grow at a CAGR of 35 percent from 2007 to 2010.[5] The country aims to raise exports to beyond $5 billion by 2010.[6]

Specialties

A big part of the industry is focused on IT services, although the BPO sector is emerging and growing.

Key Players

Brazil has attracted several MNCs, such as Whirlpool Corp. and Gap Inc., as outsourcing clients for business tasks ranging from IT services to back-office work. Service providers such as IBM, Accenture, and Electronic Data Systems are expanding and hiring more employees in Brazil to accommodate projected growth. Other leading MNCs who have set up operations in Brazil include HP, Siemens, HSBC, Microsoft, Unisys, Dell, Goodyear, Xerox, Google, and Fujitsu. Emerging economy multinationals such as Satyam and TCS have also set up a presence in the country. Some of them are even carrying out high-end work. For example, Google's Research and Development Center in Belo Horizonte, Brazil is one of the company's latest full-fledged engineering facilities outside the United States. The Google Belo Horizonte R&D Center is a full peer of its other engineering facilities in California, New York, Washington, India, London, Zurich, and Tokyo. Fujitsu has also set up an R&D center in the country.

Domestic firms are also growing in scale. Politec, with 2006 revenues of $1.5 billion, is the largest IT services provider in Brazil involved mainly in the development and maintenance of enterprise solutions. Others include CPM (2006 revenue of $180 million), G&P (2006 revenue of $39 million), and Serpro—a public IT services provider company to the government.

◆◆◆

Chile

Macroeconomic Snapshot

GDP Growth	2004: 6.2 percent
	2005: 6.3 percent
	2006: 4.2 percent
	2007/2011: 5.5 percent
Education	Literacy rate: 96.2 percent
Higher Education	Chile has about 65,000 students graduate from higher education institutions each year. About 11,600 of these students study engineering and science.
Hiring and Firing	The hiring of workers is relatively easier than in the other Latin American countries. However, the firing of workers is a relatively tougher task as compared to Brazil, but more flexible than Mexico. Chile is very attractive in terms of flexible working hours, its extension of the workday to 12 hours, and night working regulations.
Telephony	The telecommunication costs are higher in Chile in comparison to the LATAM average. In terms of connectivity, it is above the LATAM average with an estimated 3.4 million fixed lines and 12.1 million mobile subscribers in 2006, resulting in penetration of 209 fixed telephone lines and 737 mobile phone subscribers per 1,000 of the population.
Internet backbone	Internet connectivity is the best in the region. Chile ranks thirty-fourth in the EIU e-readiness survey conducted among 68 countries. In 2006, the country had more than 5.6 million Internet users and over 1 million broadband connections. The PC penetration is 160 PCs per 1,000 of population.

Macroeconomic Snapshot

Transport infrastructure	Chile has a good transport infrastructure built through privatization of construction and maintenance of commercially viable roads. The motorway network between the La Serena and Puerto Montt areas, where over 90 percent of Chileans reside, has been well developed. It aims to increase the network of paved roads to 25,000 kilometers by 2010. In 1999, operations of four larger ports were privatized, resulting in efficiency and reduction in port tariff rates by 30 percent.
Salaries	Chile has the highest salaries prevailing in the IT and ITES sectors among LATAM countries, but less than Mexico. In comparison to India, the salary level is almost double, and the difference in salary rises with seniority. However, the expected salary rise will be at 4.7 percent annually, marginally lower than other LATAM countries.

The Industry Takes Shape

Chile has attracted considerable attention from foreign companies as an offshoring destination. An attractive regulatory environment, low infrastructure costs, good quality of life, and time zone proximity with United States have contributed to this attraction. The government is actively promoting investments in R&D (from mining taxes) and the growth of the high-technology sector in the country.

The Industry

Chile's IT and BPO market in 2005 was estimated to be $500 million.[7]

Specialties

The industry consists of call centers, back office, and IT services. Higher-value R&D and knowledge services are also beginning to be delivered globally from Chile.

Key Players

The country has attracted several multinationals. Several U.S. and European companies have located service operations in Chile's major cities, primarily to serve Latin American customers. These include Delta Air Lines and Air France reservations operations as well as customer service units run by Citigroup, JPMorgan Chase, Unilever, and Zurich Financial Services.

Synopsys, a California-based provider of semiconductor design, has opened its first design center in Latin America in Santiago. Yahoo! has established an Internet Research Lab where the PhDs it has hired develop mathematical algorithms that will facilitate Internet searching. General Electric's International Center of Excellence in Chile has hired many software developers. Software AG, a German company with a large presence in the United States, develops enterprise software for government and businesses from its operation in Chile.

Indian firms have also set up operations in the country to leverage its time zone proximity to the United States. In 2005, Tata Consultancy Services acquired Comicrom, market leader in the banking and pensions BPO business in Chile, for USD 23 million. Global knowledge process outsourcing (KPO) firm Evalueserve opened a Latin American operations center in Valparaiso, Chile on June 7, 2007.

Several domestic companies—such as ATCOM, Prego, and DTS—also deliver IT and BPO solutions.

Vietnam

Macroeconomic Snapshot

GDP Growth	2005: 8.4 percent 2006: 8.2 percent 2007/2011: 7.9 percent
Education	Literacy rate: 90 percent
Higher Education	Vietnam had about 797,086 students enrolled in higher education institutions in 2003, with approximately 125,000 annual graduates. 15 percent of these students receive an engineering degree.
Hiring and Firing	Vietnam offers the most flexibility for hiring people with respect to term contracts, which can be used for any task, duration, and minimum wages. There seems to be rigid regulations on dismissals, re-employment, and replacement, and a lot of interference from trade unions makes it difficult to fire people.
Telephony	In 2005, the country had around 5.6 million landline users and around 8.4 million mobile phone users, leading to penetration of 68 and 100 users for landline and mobile, respectively, per 1,000 people.
Internet backbone	In 2005, the country had around 6.5 million Internet users and 0.2 million broadband subscribers, resulting in penetration of 78 and three subscribers for Internet and broadband, respectively, per 1,000 people.
Transport infrastructure	The country has 329,560 kilometers of road network, which connects to all the major cities. In the aviation industry, the state-owned company has the maximum market share of around 80 percent.
Salaries	Salaries of information technology professionals in Vietnam are the lowest in the Asia Pacific region. It is around 40 percent lower than China and India and about 86 percent lower than Singapore. An expected shortage of qualified software engineers indicates a hike in the average salaries in the future.

The Industry Takes Shape

Over the past few years, Vietnam has attracted attention for its potential as a base for global business services. A big talent pool of young professionals, lower costs compared to established sourcing hubs such as India, a good education system, and government support have contributed to this increased attention. It is a young country—60 percent of its 84 million population is under 30 years of age—and it graduates more than 10,000 IT professionals every year. The government has invested in technology parks and offers preferential tax treatment at personal and company levels.

Microsoft discovered Glass Egg Digital—a small outfit in Ho Chi Minh City—and Vietnam as it went searching offshore for the design of 3-D racing cars in its *Forza Motorsport* game. On a visit to the country in 2006, Bill Gates expressed optimism about its potential as a services hub. The country has since attracted the attention of several foreign corporations such as Intel, which announced plans for a billion-dollar investment in the country.

The Industry

The country's software industry, estimated at $350 million, has grown at around 40 percent in the past five years. With exports of $110 million in 2007, the country was ranked in the top 20 software-exporting countries. There are 750 software firms in Vietnam, employing around 35,000 workers. Around 150 companies are involved in software outsourcing, with an average of 100 to 150 workers. The software industry aims to maintain a growth rate of 35 to 40 percent per year from now until 2010, with exports of $800 million to $1 billion.[8]

Japan is emerging as a key market for software exports; corporations such as Hitachi, NEC, Sanyo, Nissan, and NTT have procured services from Vietnam.

Specialties

The industry in Vietnam consists largely of software exports. Services include application development and maintenance, ERP implementation, testing and validation, and system migration. Some firms specialize in graphics and components of gaming software.

Key Players

Several multinational software corporations—such as Microsoft, Nortel, Alcatel-Lucent, IBM, Oracle, Hitachi, and NEC—have outsourced to Vietnam.

With its acquisition of FCG, CSC also obtained operations capacity in Vietnam. As a part of CSC's network, CSC Vietnam will build up the local software development market and deliver information technology (IT) services around the globe. The branch, which targets clients operating in the finance, banking, and insurance sectors, will deliver services including outsourcing, enterprise resource planning (ERP), IT infrastructure, and other IT applications.

Domestic firms are also scaling up their range of offerings and exports operations. FPT is the largest domestic information and communication technology provider in the country. In 2006, it received a total investment of USD 36.5 million from Texas Pacific Group venture fund and Intel Capital. The company provides a range of services catering to both the domestic and exports market. In the first quarter of 2008, FPT Corporation signed three contracts with foreign partners in software processing and export worth nearly US$6 million. A US$3.5 million contract between FPT and Agilis Solutions was among the biggest software export contract ever signed between Vietnam and the United States. TMA Solutions provides a full range of software services, from testing and maintenance to full application development and product ownership. Growing at an average rate of 60 percent annually, it serves premier customers such as Nortel, Alcatel-Lucent, Juniper Networks, Flextronics, Oracle, IBM, DBS, KPMG, UPS, and TCS.

India

Macroeconomic Snapshot

GDP Growth	2005: 9.7%
	2006: 9.9%
	2011: 7.9%
Education	Literacy Rate: 61%
Higher Education	More than 8,400 universities in India, both public and privately owned. In 2004, the United States graduated 137,437 engineers versus 112,000 from India and 351,537 from China (including information technology and related majors).[9]
Hiring and Firing	Although there is a lot of flexibility in the hiring of workers in India, the level of difficulty in firing them is much higher than countries in the region. In addition, the cost of firing workers is more than double that of OECD countries but its non-wage labor cost is about 85% that of OECD countries. India also has no restriction on night work.
Telephony	India had one of the world's lowest levels of basic telephone penetration (teledensity) in 2007, with just 5.7 main lines per 1,000 people. Since the telecoms industry's liberalization in 1994, India's telecoms industry has seen exponential growth since 2000. In 2007, mobile subscribers outnumbered fixed mainline telephony subscribers by 3 to 1. In 2005, there were 49.75 million fixed mainline subscribers compared to 90 million mobile subscribers.
Internet backbone	In Internet connectivity, India has about 41.8 million Internet users and a low level of Internet penetration rate of just about 3.8 users per 100 people.
Transport infrastructure	India had about 3.8 million kilometers of total networked roads in 2002. About 47% of these roads are paved. In addition, India had 63,465 kilometers of total route railways in 2005. Indian Railways employs 1.4m staff and is the world's largest non-military employer. Roads carry about 70% of total freight and 85% of India's passenger traffic. India has about 12 major sea ports that are poorly run by the Port Trust of India.

Macroeconomic Snapshot

Salaries	The average IT/BPO salary in India was about US$8,485 per annum in 2005 and it's expected to raise to about $12,877 by 2010. Although India still offers a wage difference of about 85% in salaries to the United States and other onshore countries, rapidly rising wage level is eroding this advantage.

The Industry Takes Shape

The roots of Indian IT industry can be traced back to 1951 when IBM opened its subsidiary. In 1968, the Tata Group, an industrial conglomerate, established Tata Consultancy Services as a software services unit with six employees and one computer; this became India's first non-government domestic IT firm. When IBM quit the country in 1977 in protest of new anti-business nationalization regulations, it left a significant number of skilled IT professionals jobless; that provided significant stimulus for growth of domestically owned IT industry.

NASSCOM—the Indian IT association born in 1988—worked with the government on several policy measures such as Software Technology Parks Scheme (STP) to stimulate growth of the sector. A breakfast meeting between Jack Welch, then chairman of General Electric (GE), and the chief technology adviser to the Indian Prime Minister led to GE's technology partnership with India in the early 1990s.

Telecom reforms heralded the golden era for the ITES and BPO industry and ushered in a large cohort of inbound and outbound call centers and data processing units. Basic processes, such as medical transcription, were some of the first to get serviced from India. Business processes like data processing, billing, and customer support were being serviced from India by the end of the 1990s. The IT remote delivery platform that had been perfected over the past several years formed the basis for growth of newer business services.

While Indian domestic companies—like TCS, Infosys, and Wipro—led the growth of Indian IT services industry, subsidiaries of the multinationals such as American Express, British Airways, and GE that catered to BPO requirements of their parent companies were largely responsible for establishing the BPO sector.

The Industry

The Indian IT and BPO sector was expected to reach USD 64 billion and employ nearly 2 million by the end of 2008. This sector's contribution to Indian economy grew substantially over the past few years—from 1.2% of GDP in FY 1998 to an estimated 5.5% in FY 2008. Exports have been the mainstay; they were expected to cross USD 40 billion and employ 1.6 million professionals in FY 2008.

The United States and the United Kingdom were the largest markets for the industry, accounting for about 61 percent and 18 percent, respectively, in 2007.

Growth of Indian IT-BPO Industry

	2004	**2005**	**2006**	**2007**	**2008 (E)**
IT Services (Exports)	7.3	10.0	13.3	18.0	23.1
IT Services (Domestic)	3.1	3.5	4.5	5.5	7.9
IT Services (Total)	10.4	13.5	17.8	23.5	31.0
BPO (Exports)	3.1	4.6	6.3	8.4	10.9
BPO (Domestic)	0.3	0.6	0.9	1.1	1.6
BPO (Total)	3.4	5.2	7.2	9.5	12.5

(continues)

Growth of Indian IT-BPO Industry

	2004	2005	2006	2007	2008 (E)
Engineering, R&D, and Product Services (Exports)	2.5	3.1	4.0	4.9	6.3
Engineering, R&D, and Product Services (Domestic)	0.4	0.7	1.3	1.6	2.2
Engineering, R&D, and Product Services (Total)	2.9	3.8	5.3	6.5	8.5
Total (Exports)	12.9	17.7	23.6	31.3	40.3
Total	16.7	22.5	30.3	39.5	52.0

Source: Nasscom Indian IT-BPO Industry Factsheet (2008)

Growth of Employment in Indian IT-BPO Sector (in thousands)

	2000-2001	2001-2002	2002-2003	2003-2004	2004-2005	2005-2006	2006-2007	2007-2008(E)
IT Services Exports	162	170	205	296	390	513	690	865
BPO Exports	70	106	180	216	316	415	553	704
Domestic Market	198,114	246,250	285	318	352	365	378	427
Total	430,114	522,250	670	830	1,058	1,293	1,621	1,996

Source: Nasscom Indian IT-BPO Industry Factsheet (2008)

Specialties

The industry has experienced broad-based growth across its various segments—IT services, business process services, product development, engineering and R&D services. IT services contributed 57% to the total exports, remained the dominant segment, and was expected to cross USD 23 billion in 2008. Indian firms, as well as the MNCS, have been scaling steadily with headcount estimated to be growing by about 30 percent. A range of IT services are being offered from India now. These include application development and maintenance services, architecture services, testing services, information management services, infrastructure services, packaged application services, and systems integration services.

BPO services constitute the fastest growing segment that is increasing scale as well as scope of offerings. It started with basic data entry tasks, but then moved into voice-based services and a range of back-office activities. Over the last few years, increasingly complex processes that involve judgment and rule-based decision making are being serviced from India. BPO services out of India largely fall into Finance and Accounting (F&A), Customer Interaction Services (CIS), Human Resource Administration (HRA), and other vertical-specific and niche services. F&A is the largest segment accounting for approximately 40–45 percent of Indian BPO activities. These include activities such as general accounting, accounts receivables and payables management, corporate finance, compliance management, and statutory reporting. CIS includes all forms of IT-enabled customer contact; inbound or outbound, voice or non-voice based support used to provide customer services, sales and marketing, technical support, and help desk services. The HR administration services include payroll and benefits administration, travel and expense processing, talent acquisition and talent management services, employee and manager self-service delivery services, employee communication design, and administration.

As the IT-enabled services industry has moved up the value chain, new segments like product development and engineering services have also emerged. These high value services were expected to contribute USD 6.3 billion in FY 2008.

BFSI (Banking, Financial Services and Insurance), Telecom, and Hi-tech are the leading verticals to which these services are being delivered.

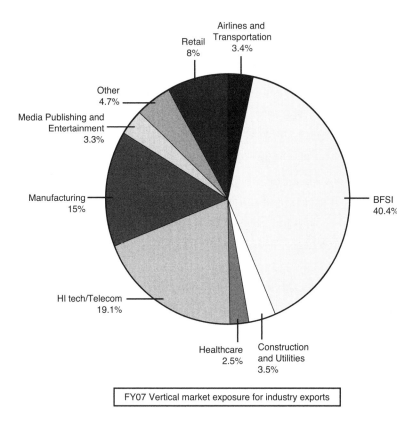

FY07 Vertical market exposure for industry exports

Key Players

Indian IT and BPO sector consists of a variety of firms: large scale generalist service providers as well as smaller ones that are focused on a particular market niche, domestic companies, and subsidiaries of MNCs. NASSCOM, the industry organization, had a membership of 1,200 companies of which 250 were global companies from across the United States, United Kingdom, European Union, and Asia Pacific.

NASSCOM ranks IT and BPO companies based on their revenues. Leading companies follow.

Rank	Company
	NASSCOM Top 20 IT Software and Service Exporters FY07-08
1.	Tata Consultancy Services Ltd.
2.	Infosys Technologies Ltd.
3.	Wipro Technologies Ltd.
4.	Satyam Computer Services Ltd.
5.	HCL Technologies Ltd.
6.	Tech Mahindra Ltd.
7.	Patni Computer Systems Ltd.
8.	I-flex Solutions Ltd.
9.	Mphasis an EDS company
10.	Larsen & Toubro Infotech Ltd.
11.	CSC in India
12.	Aricent
13.	Syntel Inc.
14.	Prithvi Information Solutions Ltd.
15.	Hexaware Technologies Ltd.
16.	Polaris Software Lab Ltd.
17.	NIIT Technologies Ltd.
18.	Sonata Software Ltd.
19.	Mastek Ltd.
20.	Genpact India

Source : NASSCOM

This list does not include some companies whose corporate headquarters are located outside India, but have significant India-centric delivery capabilities and have not shared their India-centric revenue figures. Had they been ranked based on their India revenues, companies such as Accenture, Cognizant, HP, and IBM would have also appeared in this ranking.

NASSCOM Top 15 BPO rankings for FY07-08	
Rank	**Company**
1.	Genpact India
2.	WNS Global Services Ltd.
3.	IBM-Daksh Business Process Services Pvt. Ltd.
4.	Aditya Birla Minacs Worldwide Ltd
5.	Tata Consultancy Services BPO
6.	Wipro BPO
7.	Firstsource Solutions Ltd.
8.	Infosys BPO
9.	HCL BPO
10.	EXL Service Holdings, Inc.
11.	Citigroup Global Services Ltd.
12.	HTMT Global Solutions Ltd.
13.	Aegis BPO Services Ltd.
14.	Intelenet Global Services
15.	Mphasis an EDS Company

Source : NASSCOM

This list does not include some companies whose corporate headquarters are located outside India, but have significant India-based delivery capabilities, and have not shared their India-based revenue figures. Had they been ranked based on their India revenues, companies such as Convergys and Sutherland Global Services would have also appeared in this list. Since several companies are privately held, in order to maintain uniformity, revenue figures for the ranked companies are not being shared.

Endnotes

[1] EDS, "Building a World-Class IT Services Outsourcing Industry in China."

[2] Source: *Informationweek*, www.informationweek.com/news/management/ showArticle.jhtml?articleID=199000339

[3] Source: AmCham Poland, http://poland.ic2.org/success/motorola_01.pdf

[4] A.T. Kearney and BRASSCOM. "Developing a Strategic Agenda for the 'IT Offshore Outsourcing' Sector" (2006).

[5] www.reuters.com/article/pressRelease/idUS141683+03-Dec-2007+BW20071203

[6] www.24-7pressrelease.com/press-release/after-football-now-its-outsourcing-for-brazil-39826.php

[7] "How **Chile can win** from offshoring," *The McKinsey Quarterly* (March 2007).

[8] Saigon Hi-Tech Park website, www.shtp.hochiminhcity.gov.vn/webshtp/news/content.aspx?cat_id=540&news_id=640

[9] http://blogs.zdnet.com/Burnette/?p=125

INDEX

FINANCIAL TIMES

In an increasingly competitive world, it is quality
of thinking that gives an edge—an idea that opens new
doors, a technique that solves a problem, or an insight
that simply helps make sense of it all.

We work with leading authors in the various arenas
of business and finance to bring cutting-edge thinking
and best-learning practices to a global market.

It is our goal to create world-class print publications
and electronic products that give readers
knowledge and understanding that can then be
applied, whether studying or at work.

To find out more about our business
products, you can visit us at www.ftpress.com.